ULTIMATE COMICS
SPIDER-MAN

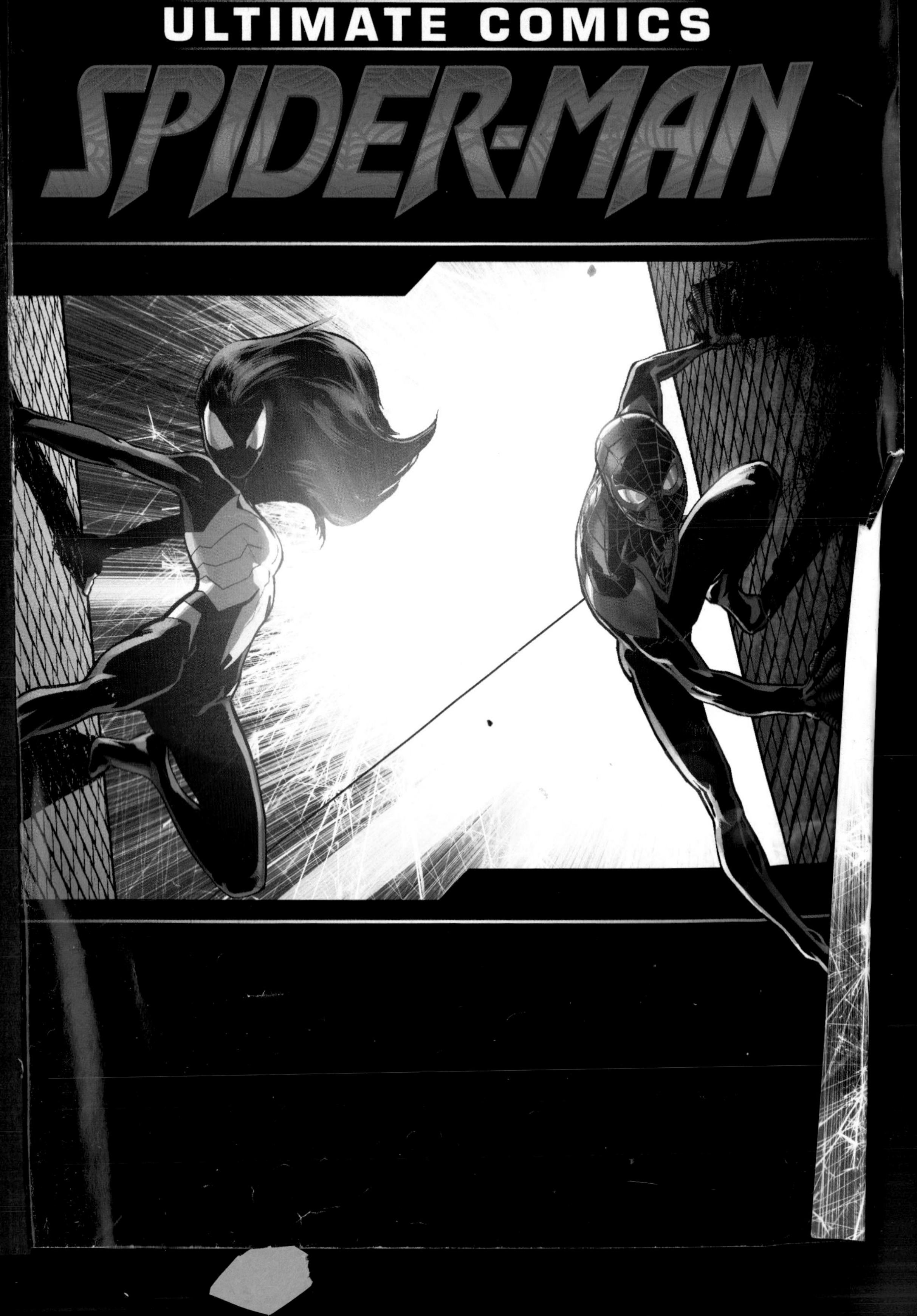
ULTIMATE COMICS
SPIDER-MAN

WRITER: **BRIAN MICHAEL BENDIS**

ARTIST: **DAVID MARQUEZ**

COLOR ARTIST: **JUSTIN PONSOR** WITH **PAUL MOUNTS** (#28)

LETTERER: **VC'S CORY PETIT**

COVER ART: **DAVID MARQUEZ** WITH **JUSTIN PONSOR** (#23 & #26-27) & **RAINIER BEREDO** (#24-25 & #28)

ASSISTANT EDITORS: **EMILY SHAW** & **JON MOISAN**

EDITOR: **MARK PANICCIA**

....

COLLECTION EDITOR: **JENNIFER GRÜNWALD**

ASSISTANT EDITORS: **ALEX STARBUCK & NELSON RIBEIRO**

EDITOR, SPECIAL PROJECTS: **MARK D. BEAZLEY**

SENIOR EDITOR, SPECIAL PROJECTS: **JEFF YOUNGQUIST**

SVP OF PRINT & DIGITAL PUBLISHING SALES: **DAVID GABRIEL**

....

EDITOR IN CHIEF: **AXEL ALONSO**

CHIEF CREATIVE OFFICER: **JOE QUESADA**

PUBLISHER: **DAN BUCKLEY**

EXECUTIVE PRODUCER: **ALAN FINE**

SPIDER-MAN BY BRIAN MICHAEL BENDIS VOL. 5. Contains material originally published in magazine form as ULTIMATE COMICS SPIDER-MAN #23-28. First printing 2014. ISBN# 978-0-7851-
MARVEL WORLDWIDE, INC., a subsidiary of MARVEL ENTERTAINMENT, LLC. OFFICE OF PUBLICATION: 135 West 50th Street, New York, NY 10020. Copyright © 2013 and 2014 Marvel Characters,
d. All characters featured in this issue and the distinctive names and likenesses thereof, and all related indicia are trademarks of Marvel Characters, Inc. No similarity between any of the names,
and/or institutions in this magazine with those of any living or dead person or institution is intended, and any such similarity which may exist is purely coincidental. **Printed in the U.S.A.** ALAN
the President, Marvel Worldwide, Inc. and EVP & CMO Marvel Characters B.V.; DAN BUCKLEY, Publisher & President - Print, Animation & Digital Divisions; JOE QUESADA, Chief Creative Officer;
of Publishing; DAVID BOGART, SVP of Operations & Procurement, Publishing; C.B. CEBULSKI, SVP of Creator & Content Development; DAVID GABRIEL, SVP of Print & Digital Publishing Sales; JIM
ations & Logistics; DAN CARR, Executive Director of Publishing Technology; SUSAN CRESPI, Editorial Operations Manager; ALEX MORALES, Publishing Operations Manager; STAN LEE, Chairman
ation regarding advertising in Marvel Comics or on Marvel.com, please contact Niza Disla, Director of Marvel Partnerships, at ndisla@marvel.com. For Marvel subscription inquiries, please call
ufactured between 12/6/2013 and 1/13/2014 by WORZALLA PUBLISHING CO., STEVENS POINT, WI, USA.

PREVIOUSLY:

Months before Peter Parker was shot and killed, grade-schooler Miles Morales was about to start a new chapter in his life at a new school — when he was suddenly bitten by a stolen, genetically altered spider that gave him incredible arachnid-like powers. News he has shared only with his best friend Ganke.

But after a disastrous battle with Venom that killed his mother and left his father in the hospital, Miles Morales gave up being Spider-Man.

SPIDER-MAN NO MORE

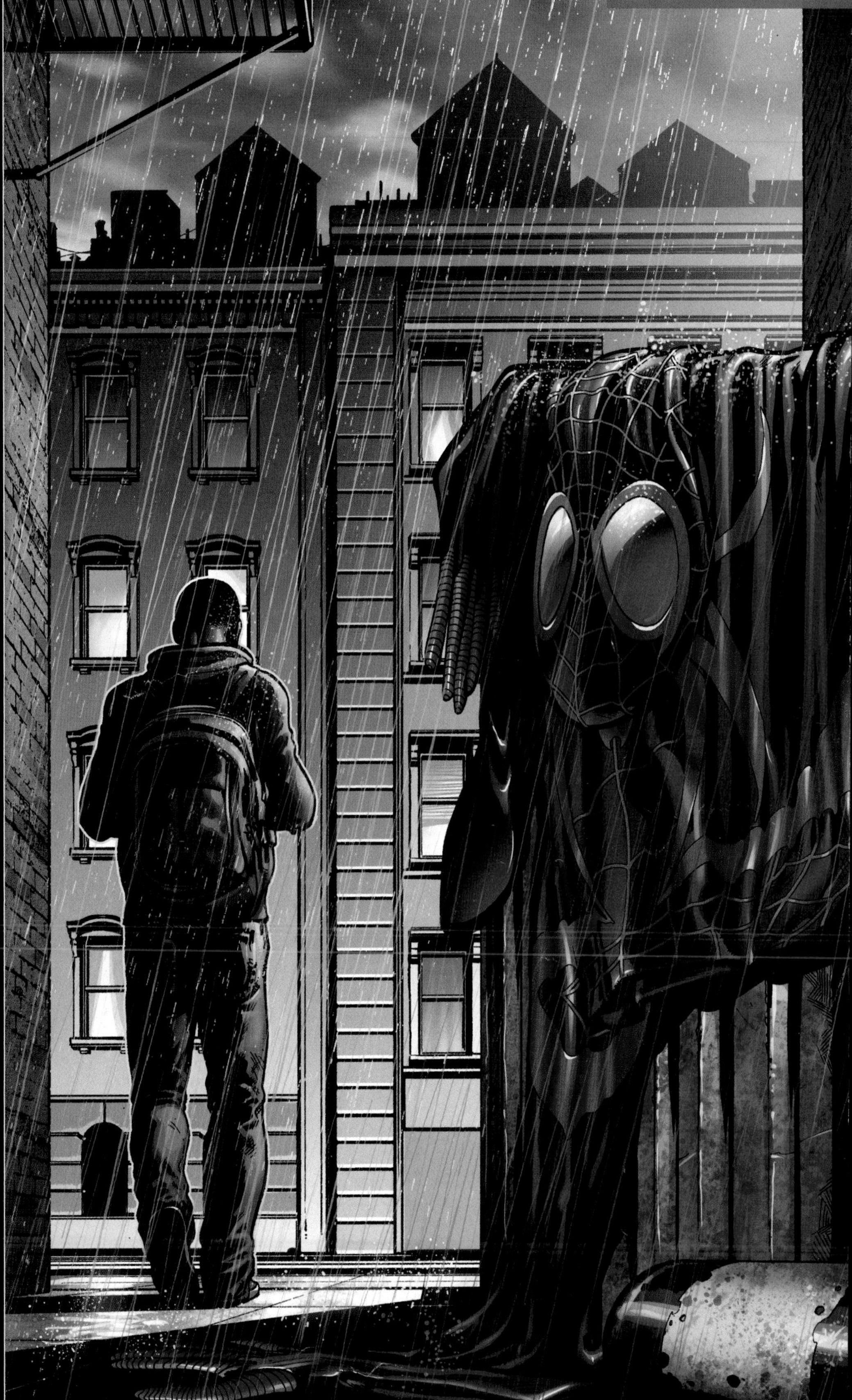

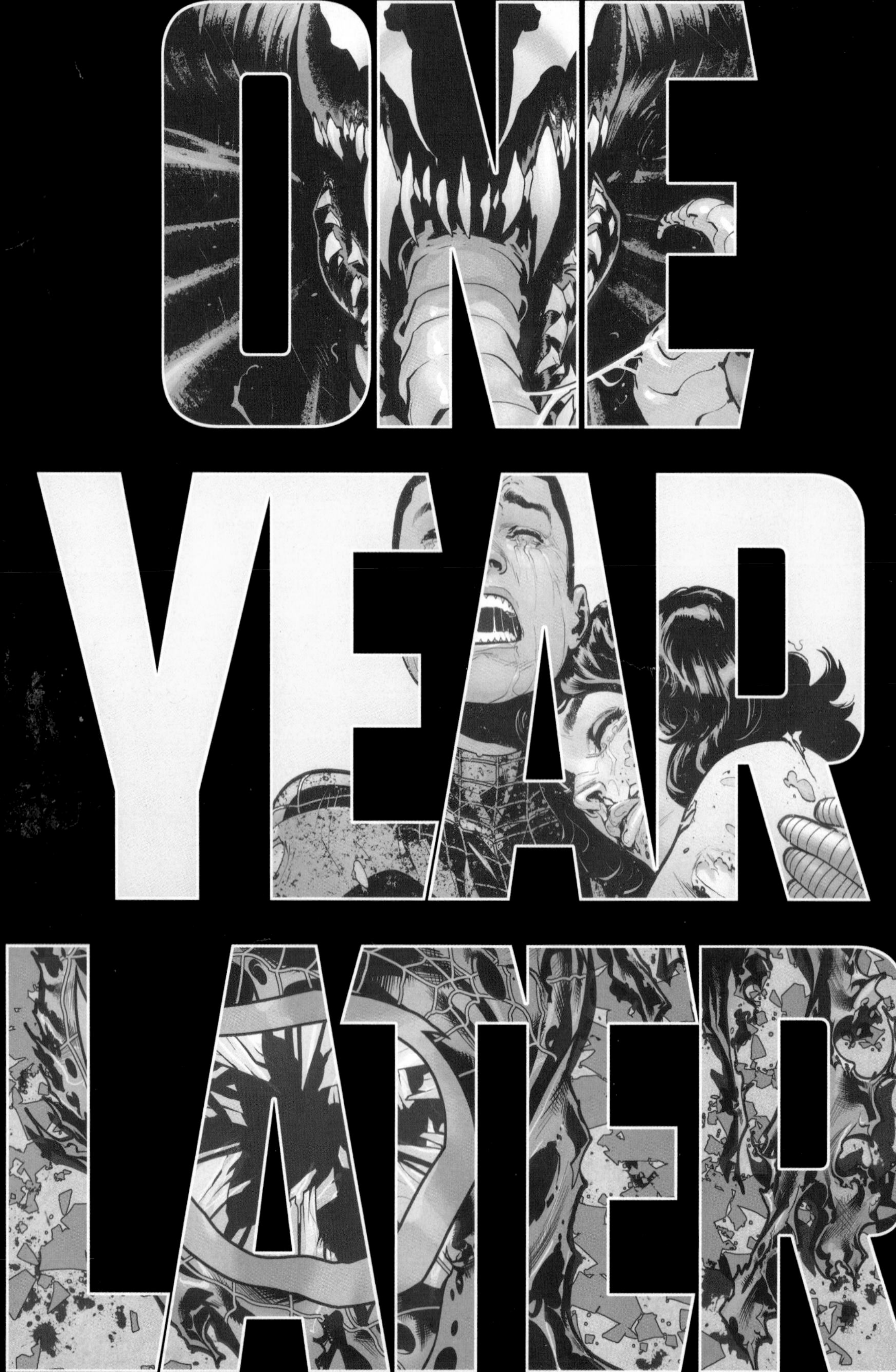
ONE
YEAR
LATER

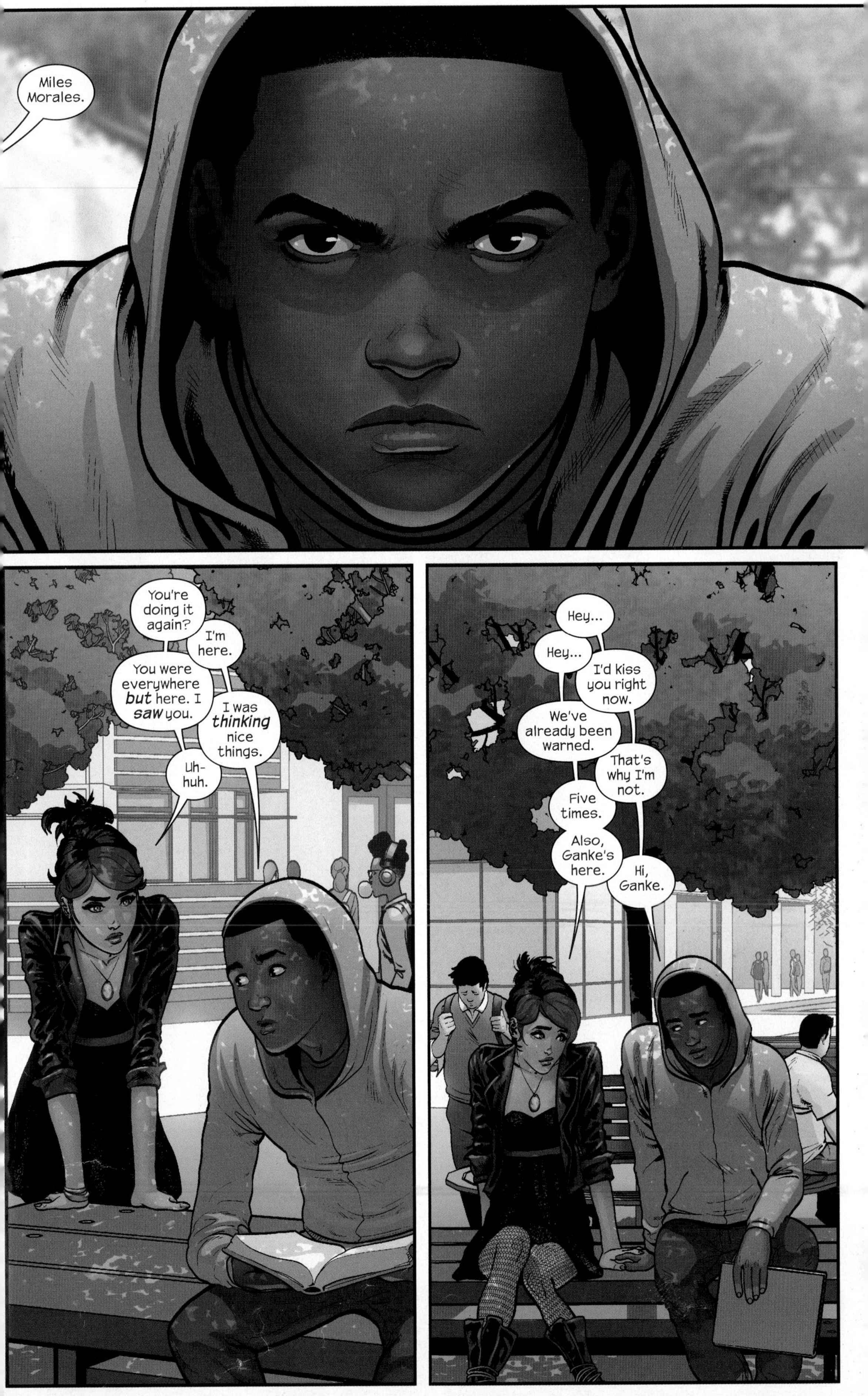
Miles Morales.
You're doing it again?
I'm here.
You were everywhere *but* here. I *saw* you.
I was *thinking* nice things.
Uh-huh.
Hey...
Hey...
I'd kiss you right now.
We've already been warned.
That's why I'm not.
Five times.
Also, Ganke's here.
Hi, Ganke.

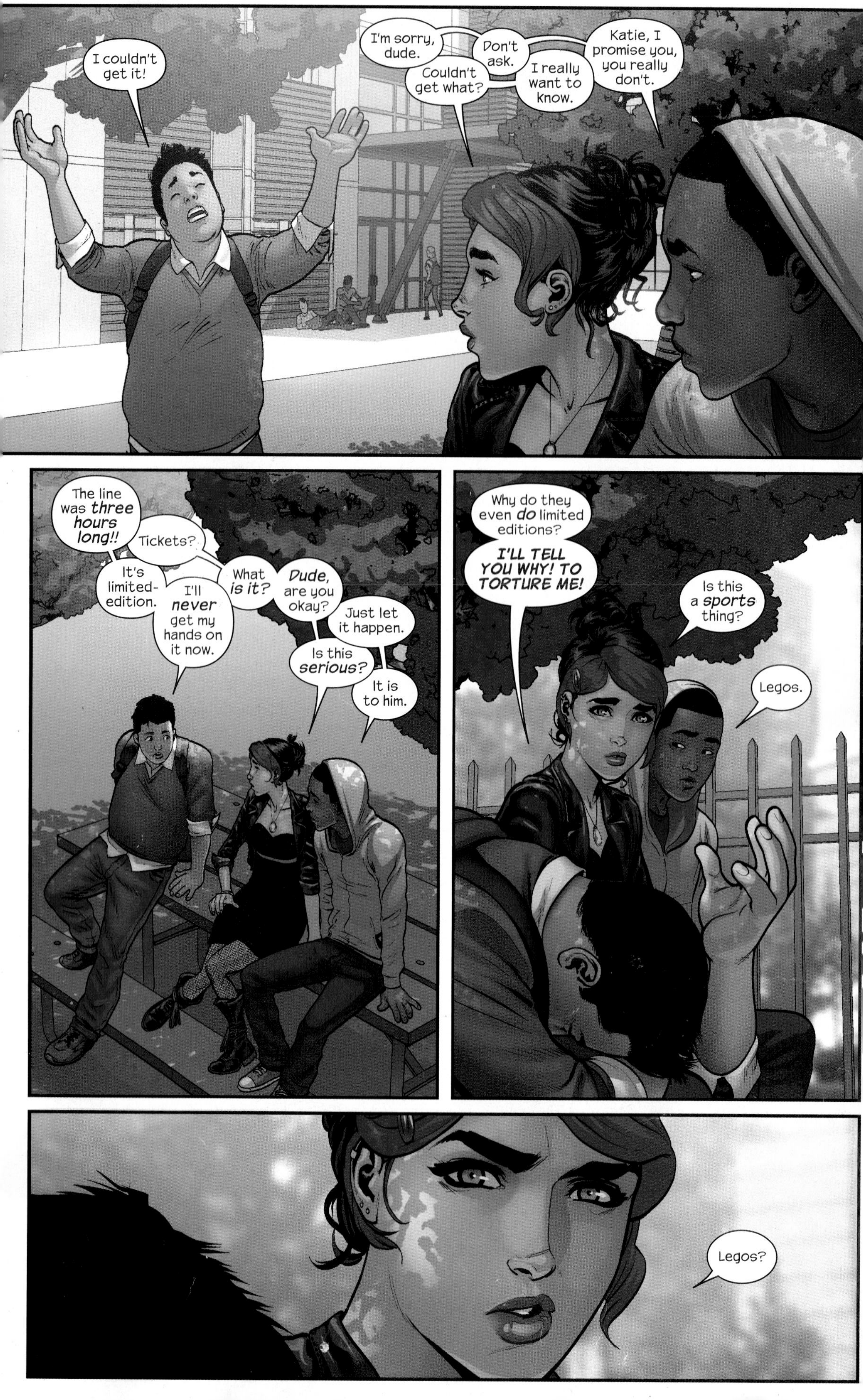
I couldn't get it!
I'm sorry, dude.
Couldn't get what?
Don't ask.
I really want to know.
Katie, I promise you, you really don't.
The line was *three hours long!!*
Tickets?
It's limited-edition.
What *is it?*
I'll *never* get my hands on it now.
Dude, are you okay?
Just let it happen.
Is this *serious?*
It is to him.
Why do they even *do* limited editions?
I'LL TELL YOU WHY! TO TORTURE ME!
Is this a *sports* thing?
Legos.
Legos?

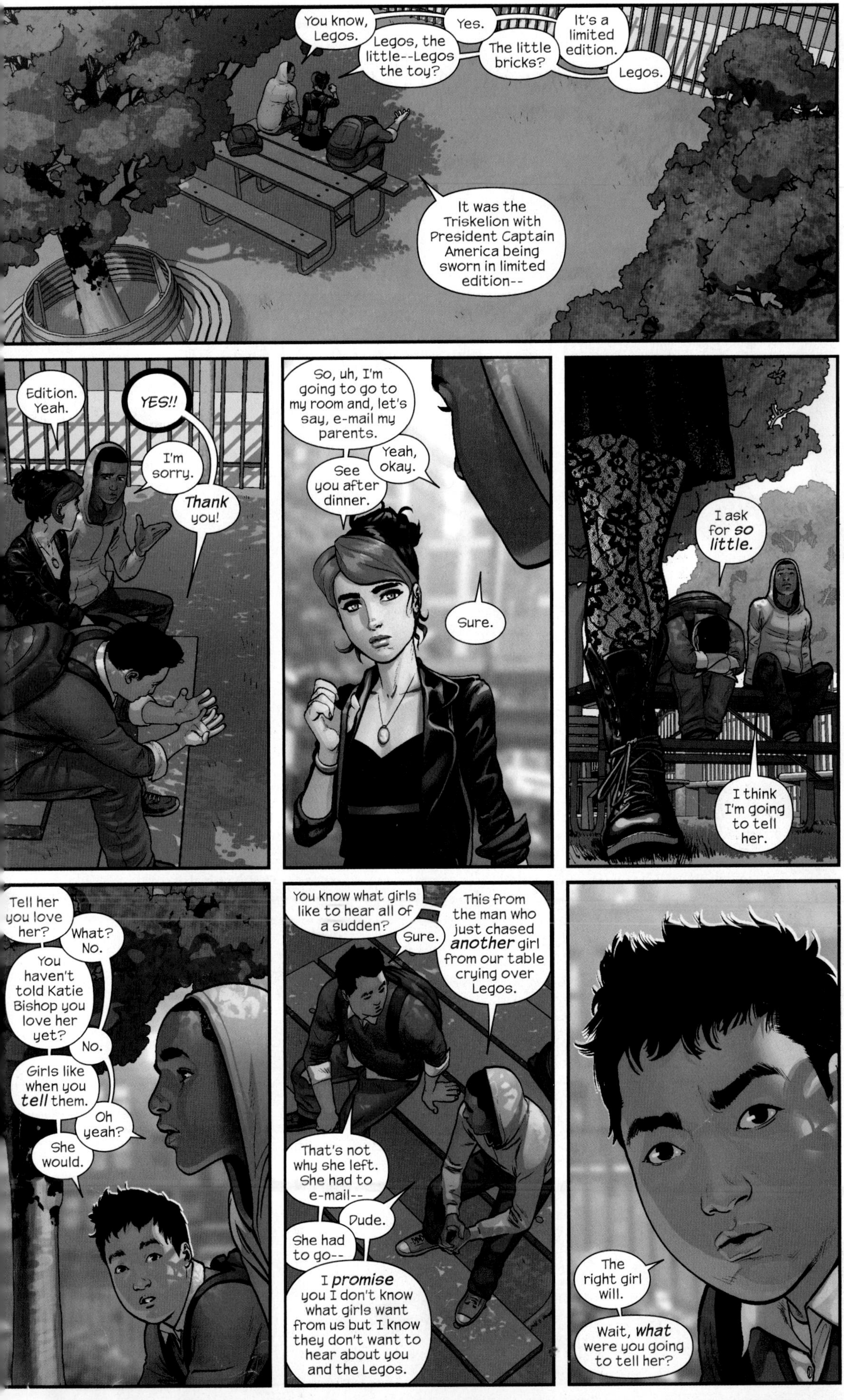
You know, Legos.
Legos, the little--Legos the toy?
Yes.
The little bricks?
It's a limited edition.
Legos.
It was the Triskelion with President Captain America being sworn in limited edition--
Edition. Yeah.
YES!!
I'm sorry.
Thank you!
So, uh, I'm going to go to my room and, let's say, e-mail my parents.
Yeah, okay.
See you after dinner.
Sure.
I ask for so little.
I think I'm going to tell her.
Tell her you love her?
What? No.
You haven't told Katie Bishop you love her yet?
No.
Girls like when you tell them.
Oh yeah?
She would.
You know what girls like to hear all of a sudden?
Sure.
This from the man who just chased another girl from our table crying over Legos.
That's not why she left. She had to e-mail--
Dude.
She had to go--
I promise you I don't know what girls want from us but I know they don't want to hear about you and the Legos.
The right girl will.
Wait, what were you going to tell her?

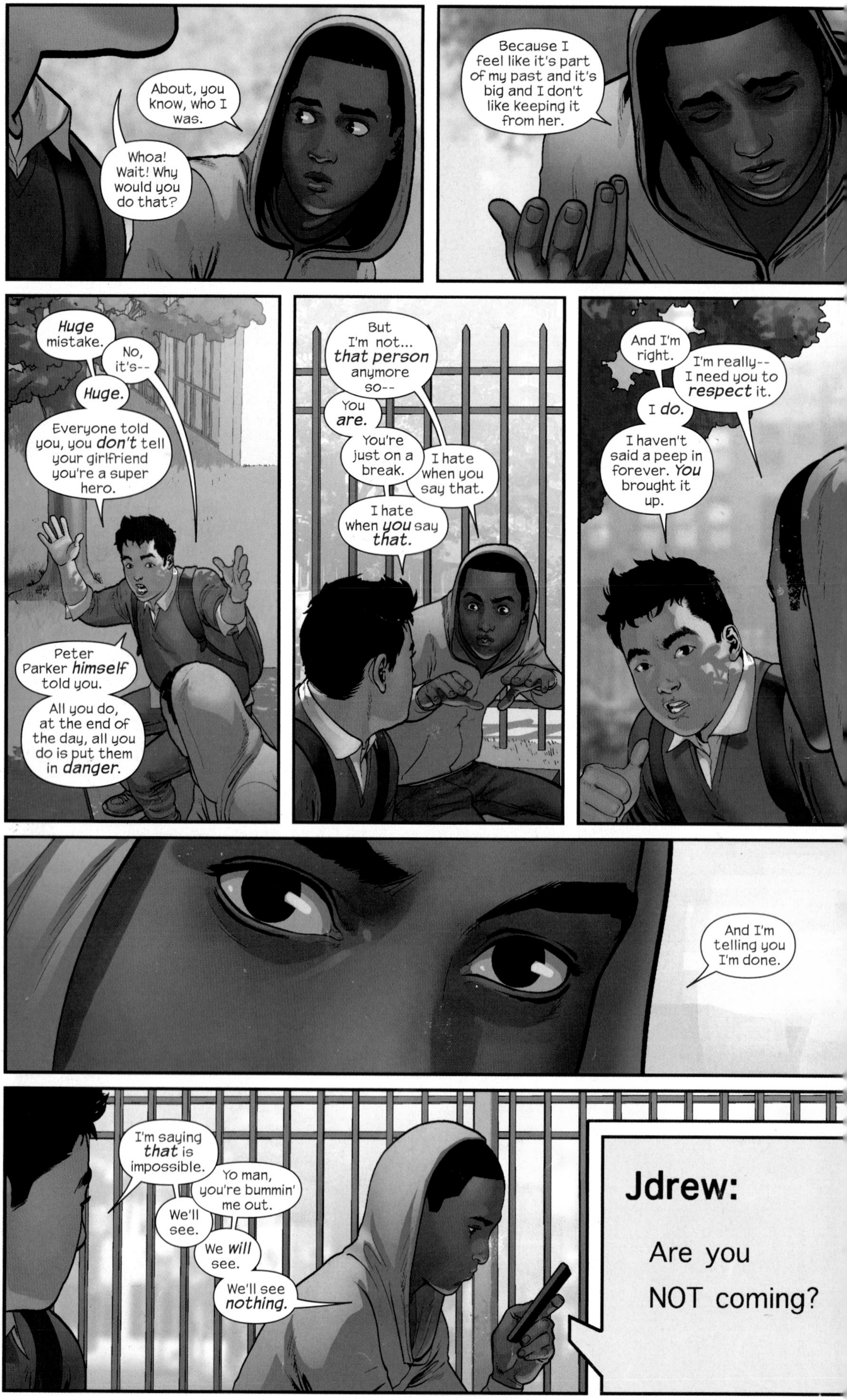
About, you know, who I was.
Whoa! Wait! Why would you do that?
Because I feel like it's part of my past and it's big and I don't like keeping it from her.
Huge mistake.
No, it's--
Huge.
Everyone told you, you don't tell your girlfriend you're a super hero.
Peter Parker himself told you.
All you do, at the end of the day, all you do is put them in danger.
But I'm not... that person anymore so--
You are.
You're just on a break.
I hate when you say that.
I hate when you say that.
And I'm right.
I'm really-- I need you to respect it.
I do.
I haven't said a peep in forever. You brought it up.
And I'm telling you I'm done.
I'm saying that is impossible.
We'll see.
Yo man, you're bummin' me out.
We will see.
We'll see nothing.
Jdrew:
Are you NOT coming?

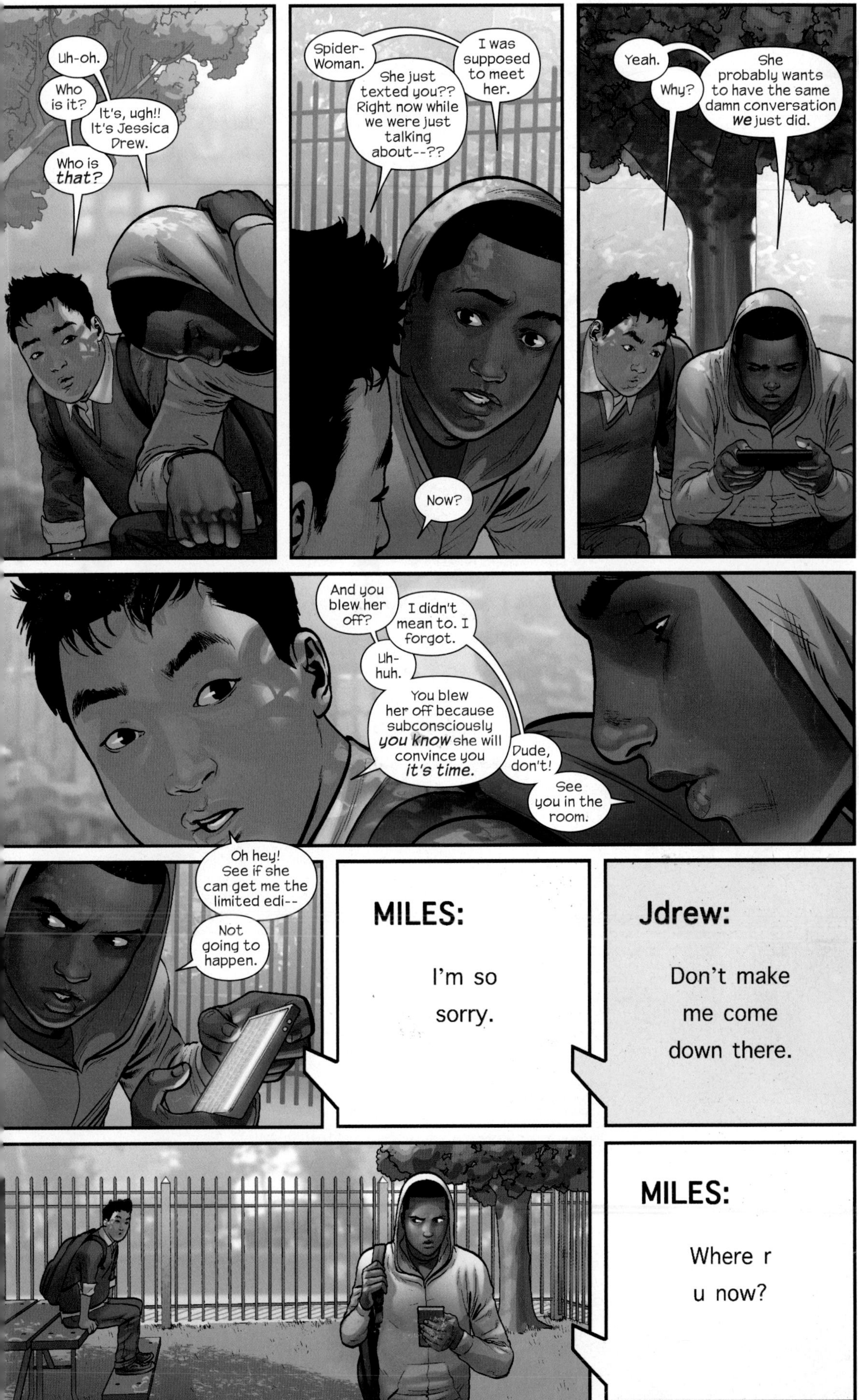
Uh-oh.
Who is it?
It's, ugh!! It's Jessica Drew.
Who is *that?*
Spider-Woman.
I was supposed to meet her.
She just texted you?? Right now while we were just talking about--??
Now?
Yeah.
Why?
She probably wants to have the same damn conversation *we* just did.
And you blew her off?
I didn't mean to. I forgot.
Uh-huh.
You blew her off because subconsciously *you know* she will convince you *it's time.*
Dude, don't!
See you in the room.
Oh hey! See if she can get me the limited edi--
Not going to happen.
MILES:
I'm so sorry.
Jdrew:
Don't make me come down there.
MILES:
Where r u now?

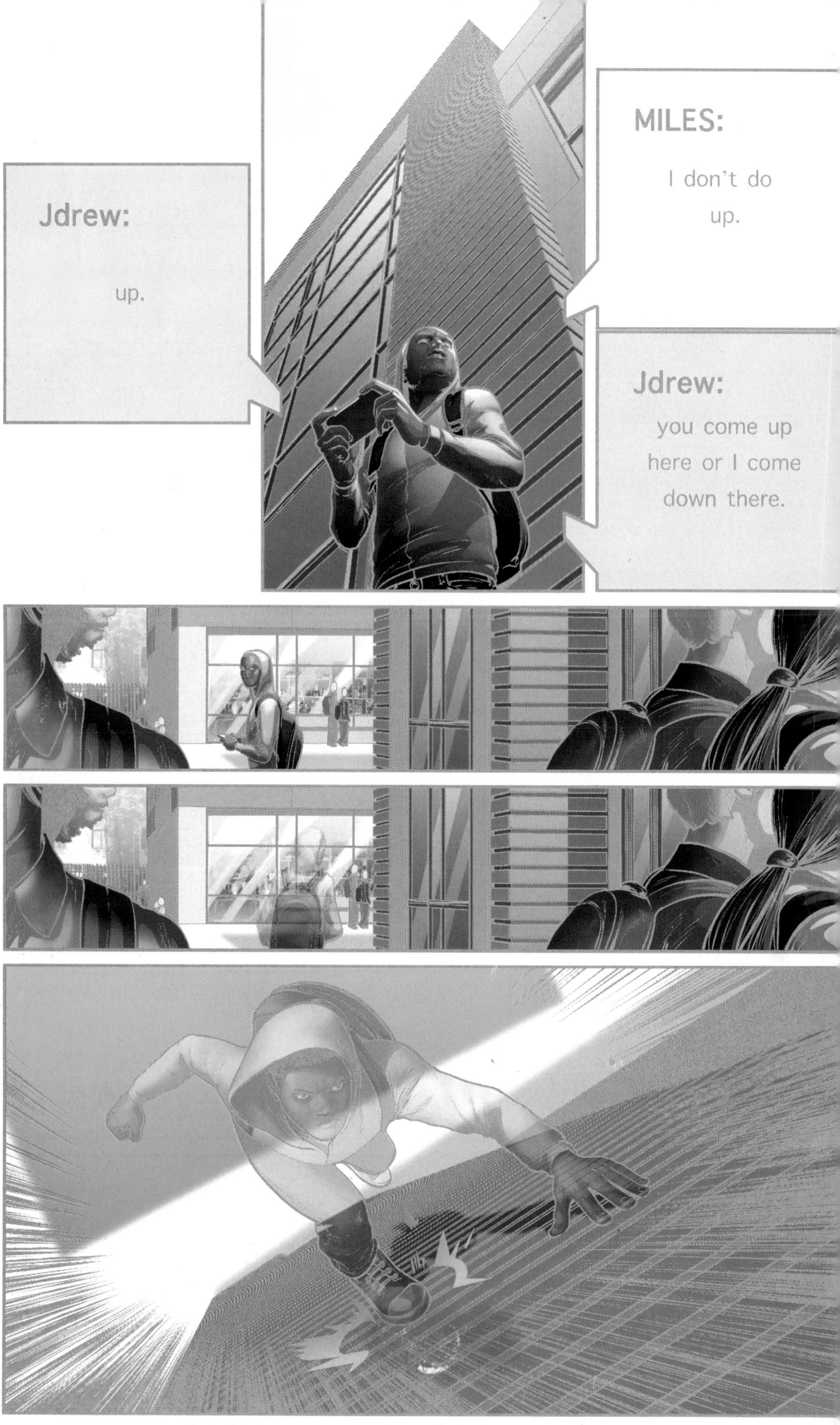
Jdrew:
up.
MILES:
I don't do up.
Jdrew:
you come up here or I come down there.

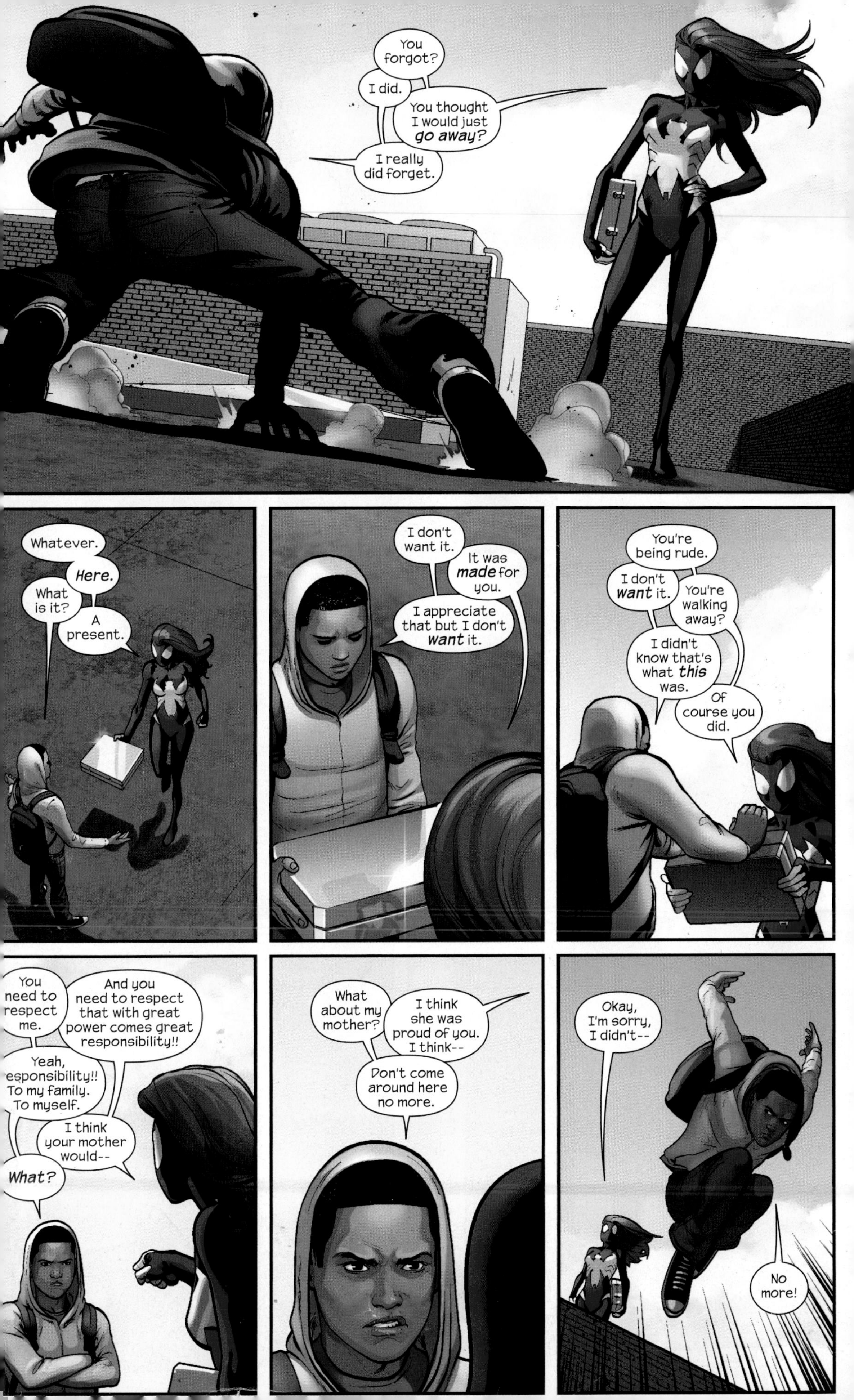
You forgot?
I did.
You thought I would just *go away?*
I really did forget.
Whatever.
Here.
What is it?
A present.
I don't want it.
It was *made* for you.
I appreciate that but I don't *want* it.
You're being rude.
I don't *want* it.
You're walking away?
I didn't know that's what *this* was.
Of course you did.
You need to respect me.
And you need to respect that with great power comes great responsibility!!
Yeah, esponsibility!! To my family. To myself.
I think your mother would--
What?
What about my mother?
I think she was proud of you. I think--
Don't come around here no more.
Okay, I'm sorry, I didn't--
No more!

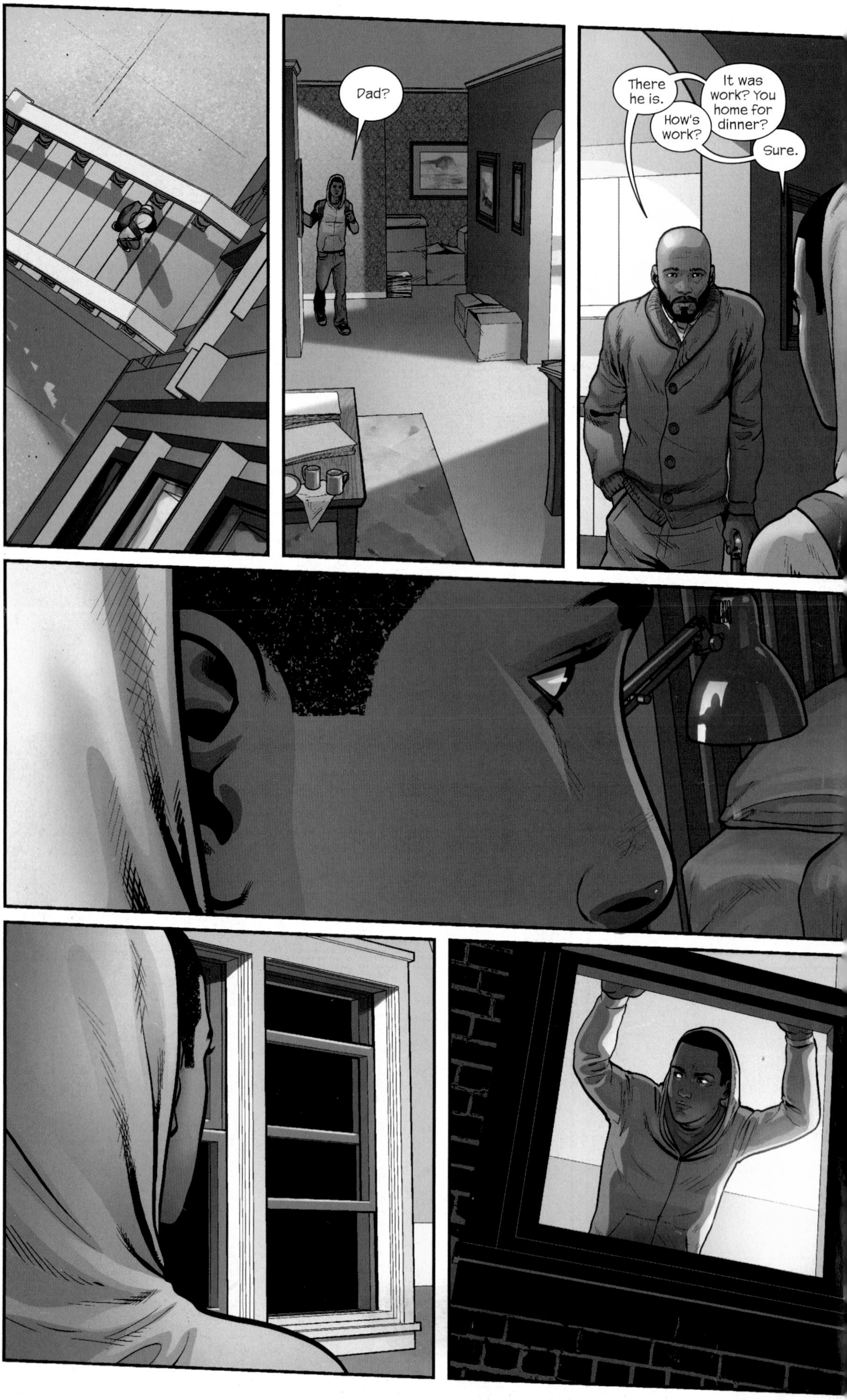
Dad?
There he is.
How's work?
It was work? You home for dinner?
Sure.

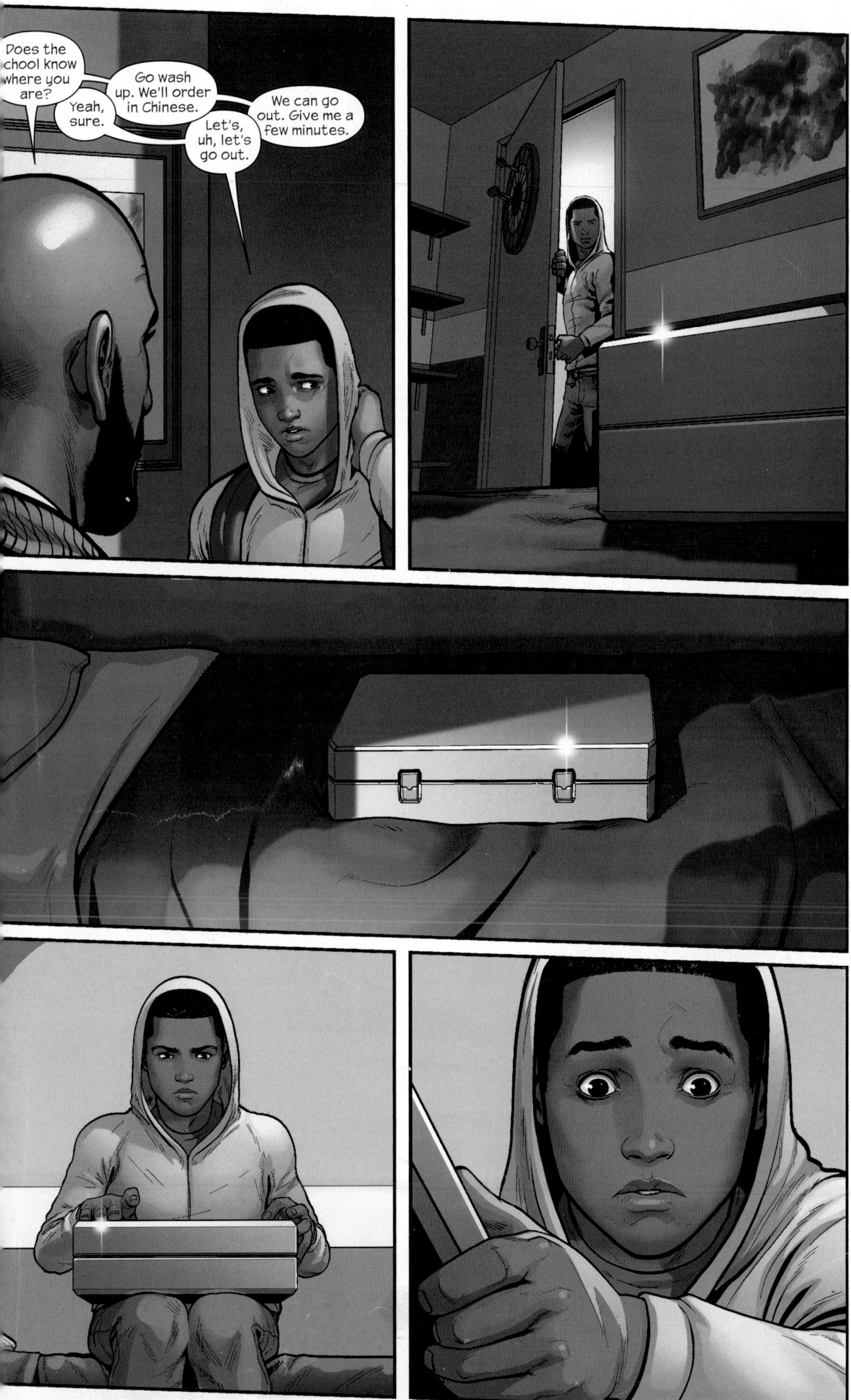
Does the
chool know
where you
are?
Yeah,
sure.
Go wash
up. We'll order
in Chinese.
Let's,
uh, let's
go out.
We can go
out. Give me a
few minutes.

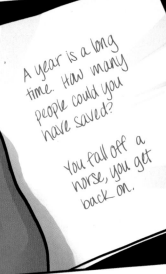

A year is a long time. How many people could you have saved?

You fall off a horse, you get back on.

You ready?

Almost.

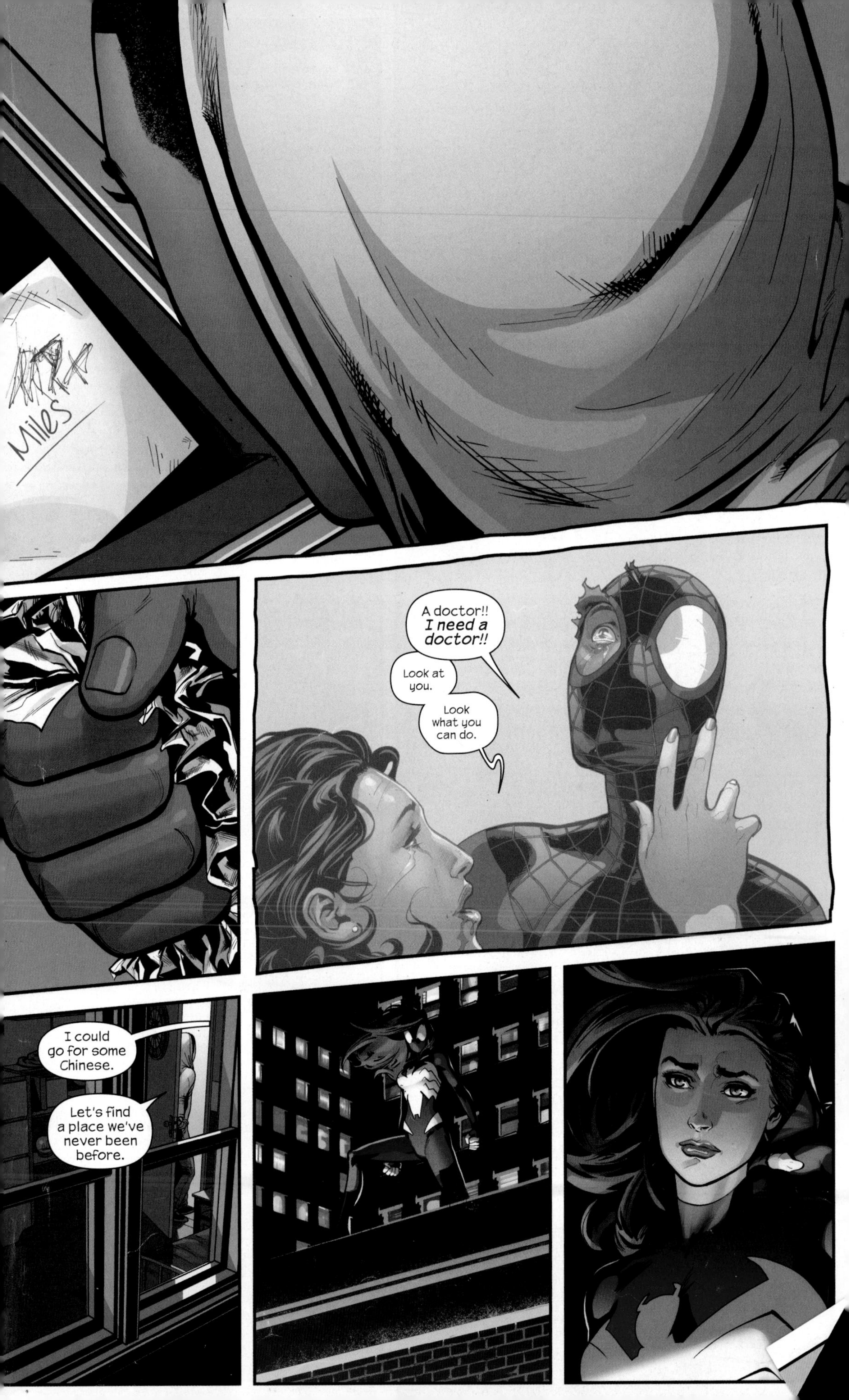
Miles
A doctor!! *I need a doctor!!*
Look at you.
Look what you can do.
I could go for some Chinese.
Let's find a place we've never been before.

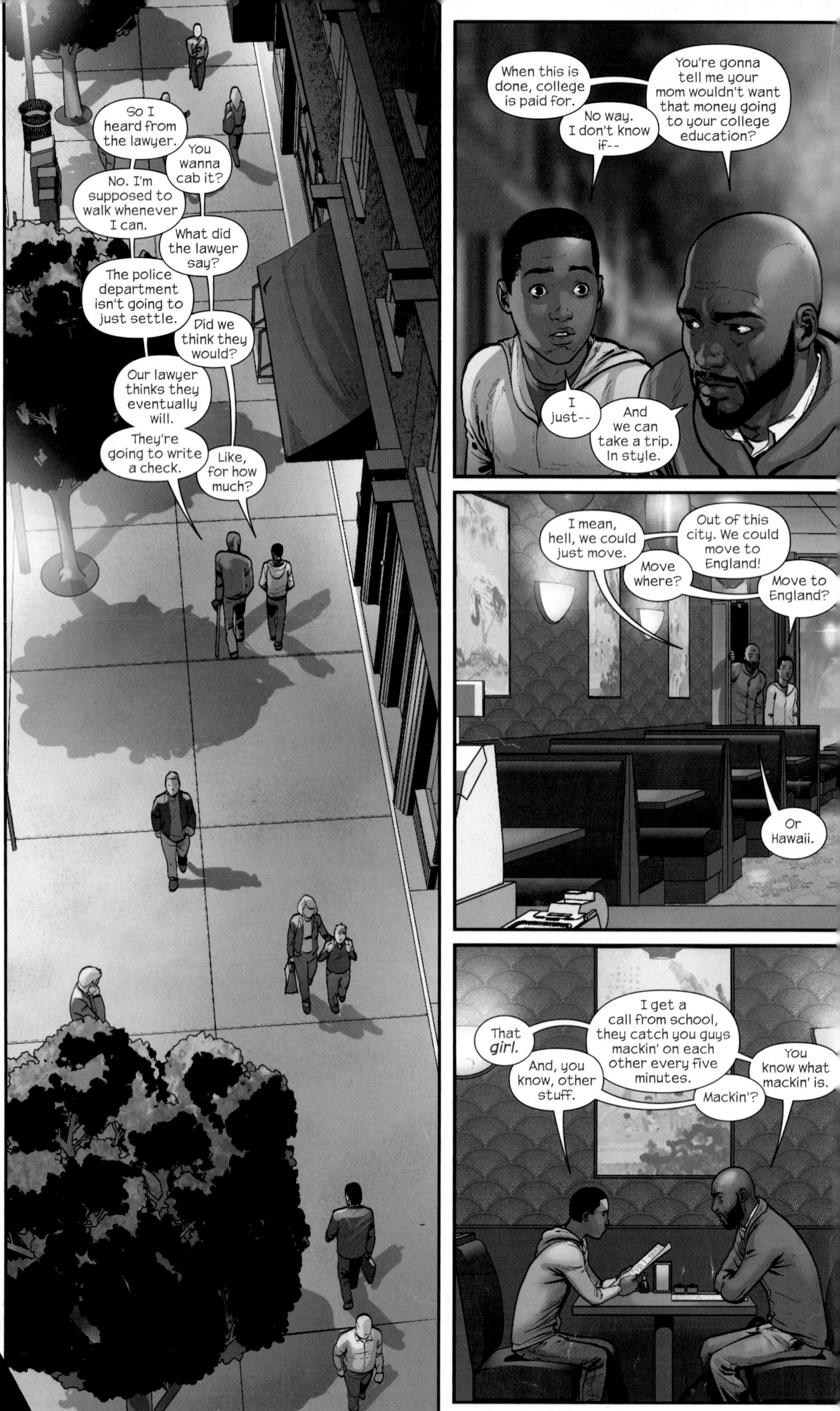
So I heard from the lawyer.
You wanna cab it?
No. I'm supposed to walk whenever I can.
What did the lawyer say?
The police department isn't going to just settle.
Did we think they would?
Our lawyer thinks they eventually will.
They're going to write a check.
Like, for how much?
When this is done, college is paid for.
No way. I don't know if--
You're gonna tell me your mom wouldn't want that money going to your college education?
I just--
And we can take a trip. In style.
I mean, hell, we could just move.
Out of this city. We could move to England!
Move where?
Move to England?
Or Hawaii.
That *girl.*
I get a call from school, they catch you guys mackin' on each other every five minutes.
And, you know, other stuff.
Mackin'?
You know what mackin' is.

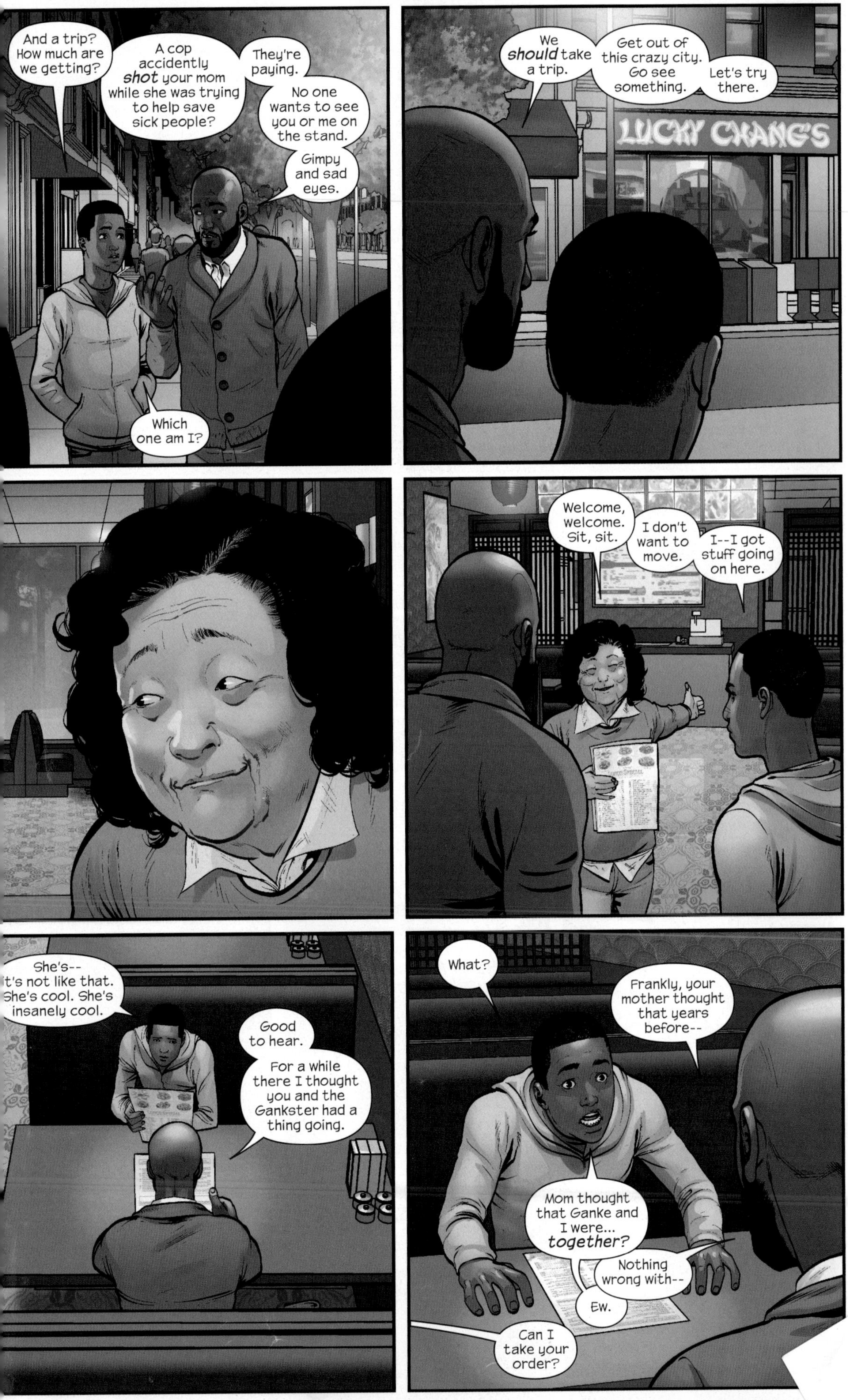

And a trip? How much are we getting?
A cop accidently *shot* your mom while she was trying to help save sick people?
They're paying.
No one wants to see you or me on the stand.
Gimpy and sad eyes.
Which one am I?
We *should* take a trip.
Get out of this crazy city. Go see something.
Let's try there.
LUCKY CHANG'S
Welcome, welcome. Sit, sit.
I don't want to move.
I--I got stuff going on here.
She's--
it's not like that. She's cool. She's insanely cool.
Good to hear.
For a while there I thought you and the Gankster had a thing going.
What?
Frankly, your mother thought that years before--
Mom thought that Ganke and I were... *together?*
Nothing wrong with--
Ew.
Can I take your order?

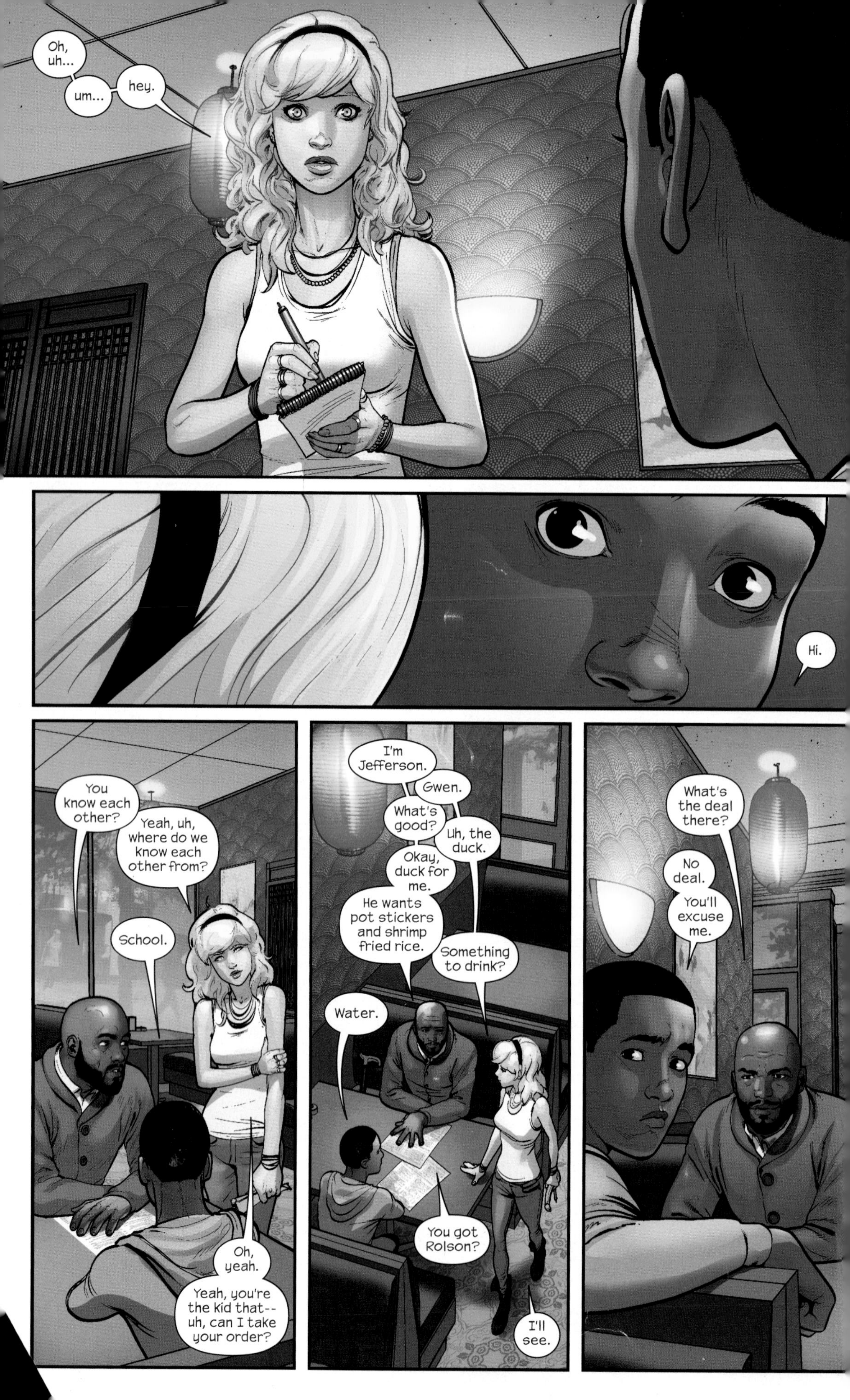

Oh, uh...
um...
hey.
Hi.
You know each other?
Yeah, uh, where do we know each other from?
School.
Oh, yeah.
Yeah, you're the kid that--uh, can I take your order?
I'm Jefferson.
Gwen.
What's good?
Uh, the duck.
Okay, duck for me.
He wants pot stickers and shrimp fried rice.
Something to drink?
Water.
You got Rolson?
I'll see.
What's the deal there?
No deal.
You'll excuse me.

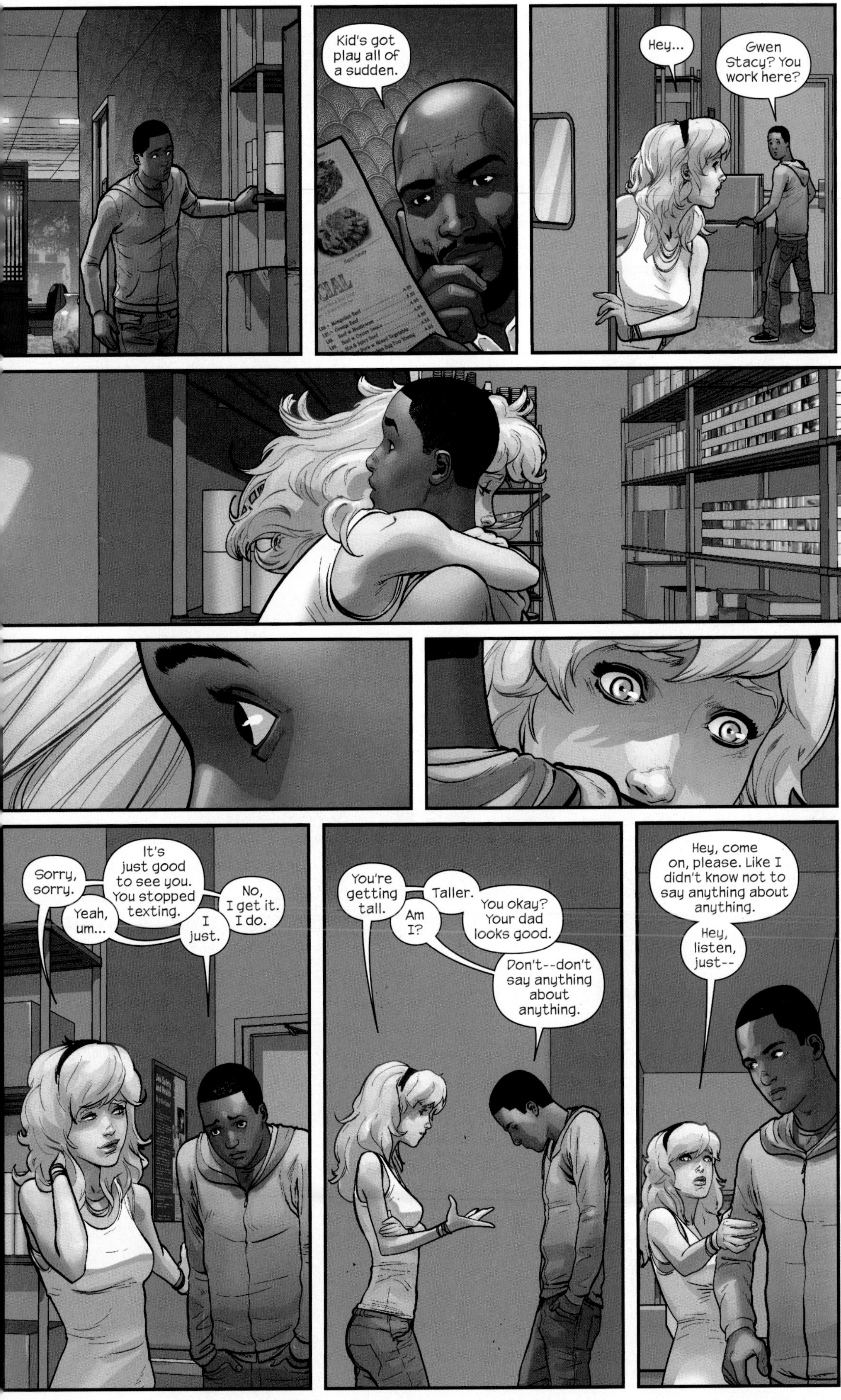

Kid's got play all of a sudden.
Hey...
Gwen Stacy? You work here?
Sorry, sorry.
It's just good to see you. You stopped texting.
Yeah, um...
I just.
No, I get it. I do.
You're getting tall.
Am I?
Taller.
You okay? Your dad looks good.
Don't--don't say anything about anything.
Hey, come on, please. Like I didn't know not to say anything about anything.
Hey, listen, just--

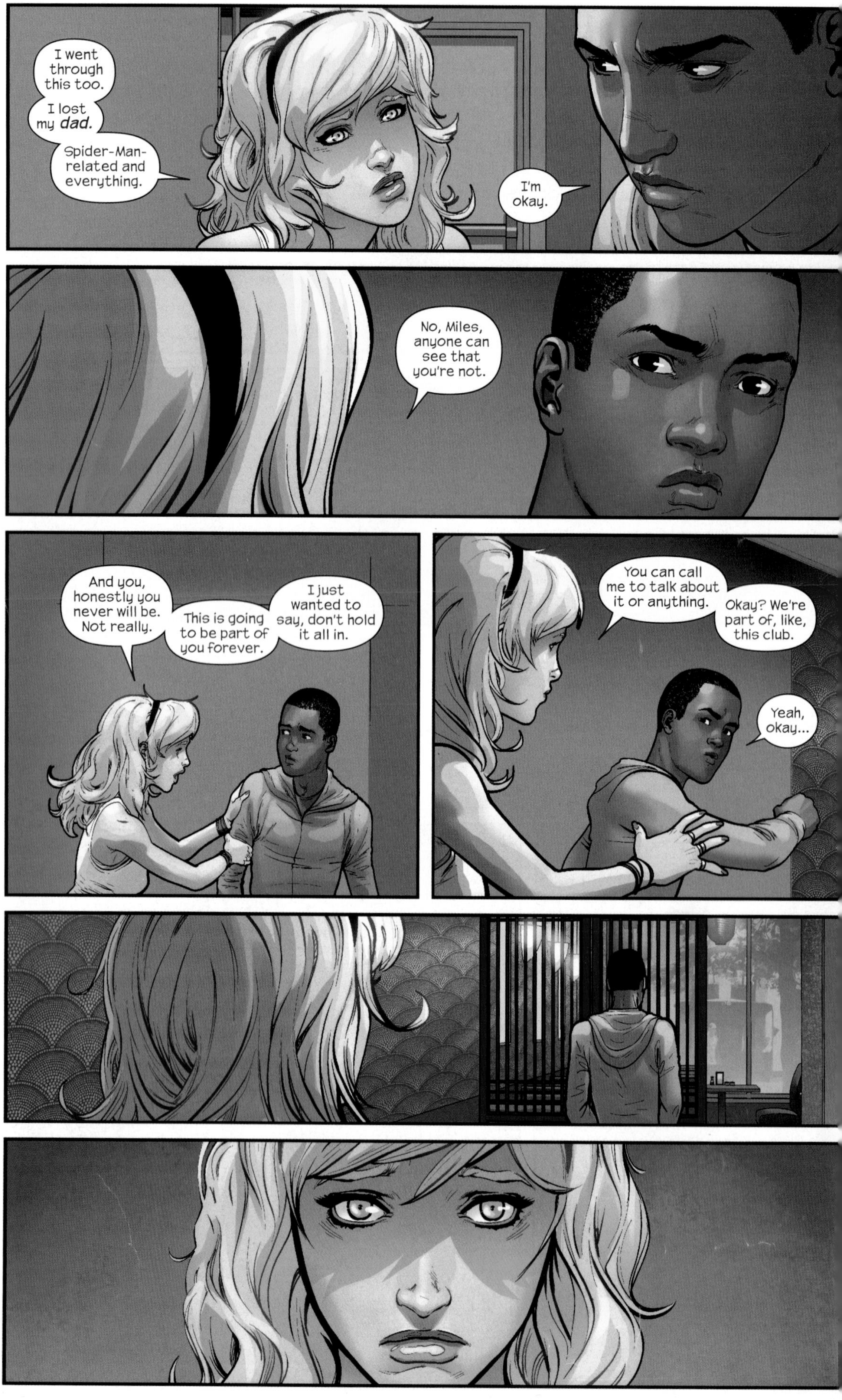
I went through this too.
I lost my *dad.*
Spider-Man-related and everything.
I'm okay.
No, Miles, anyone can see that you're not.
And you, honestly you never will be. Not really.
This is going to be part of you forever.
I just wanted to say, don't hold it all in.
You can call me to talk about it or anything.
Okay? We're part of, like, this club.
Yeah, okay...

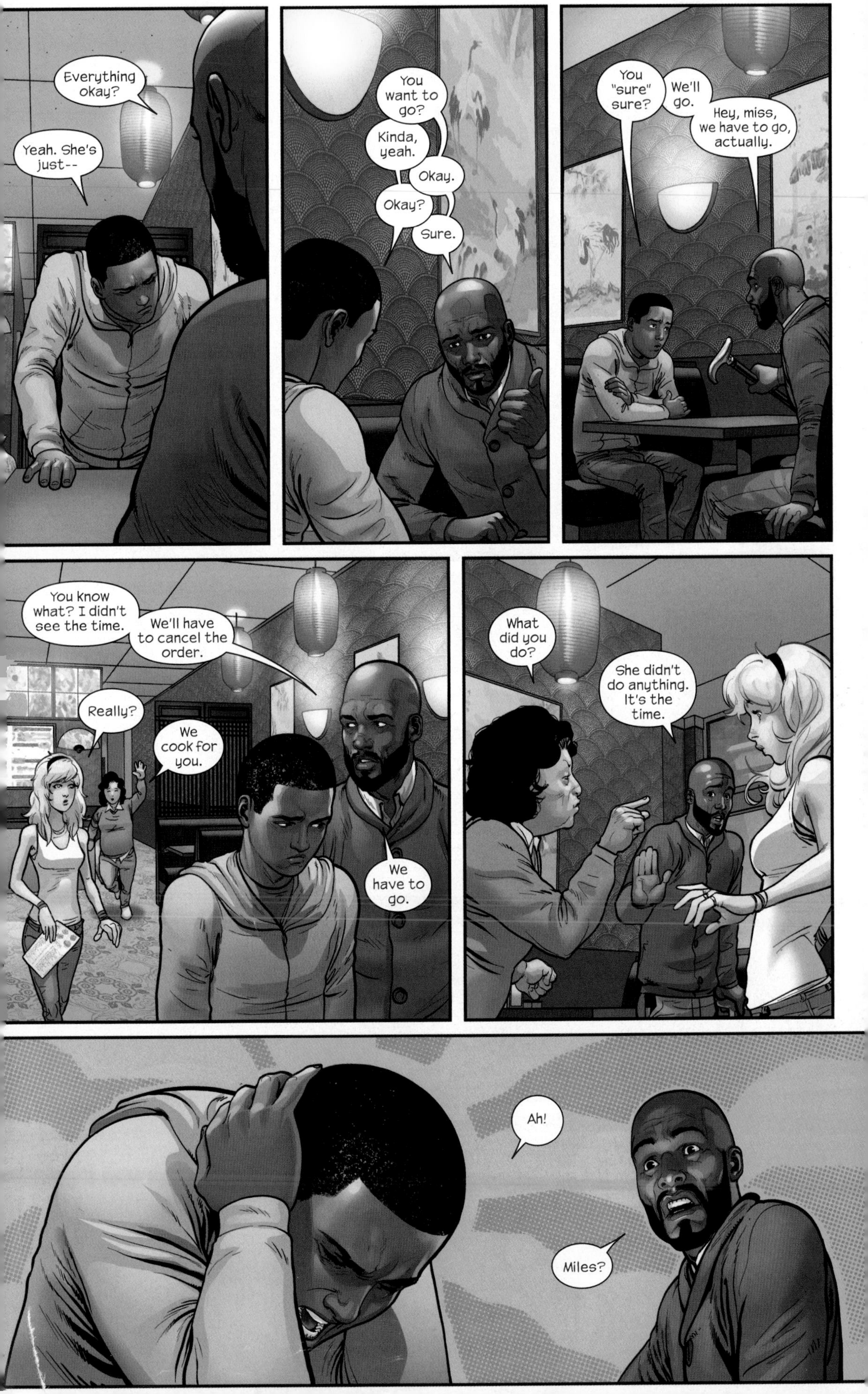
Everything okay?
Yeah. She's just--
You want to go?
Kinda, yeah.
Okay.
Okay?
Sure.
You "sure" sure?
We'll go.
Hey, miss, we have to go, actually.
You know what? I didn't see the time.
We'll have to cancel the order.
Really?
We cook for you.
We have to go.
What did you do?
She didn't do anything. It's the time.
Ah!
Miles?

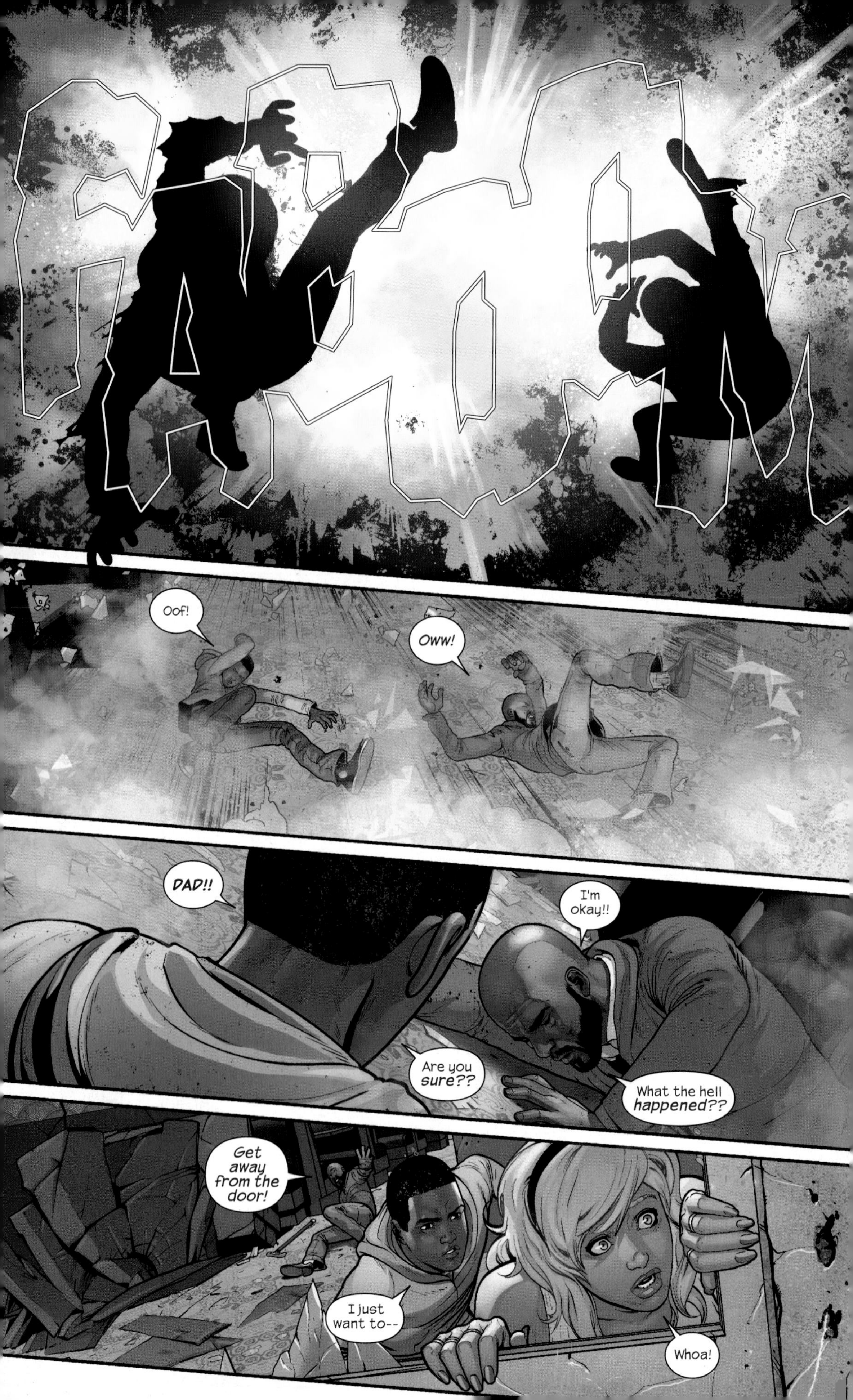
Oof!
OWW!
DAD!!
I'm okay!!
Are you sure??
What the hell happened??
Get away from the door!
I just want to--
Whoa!

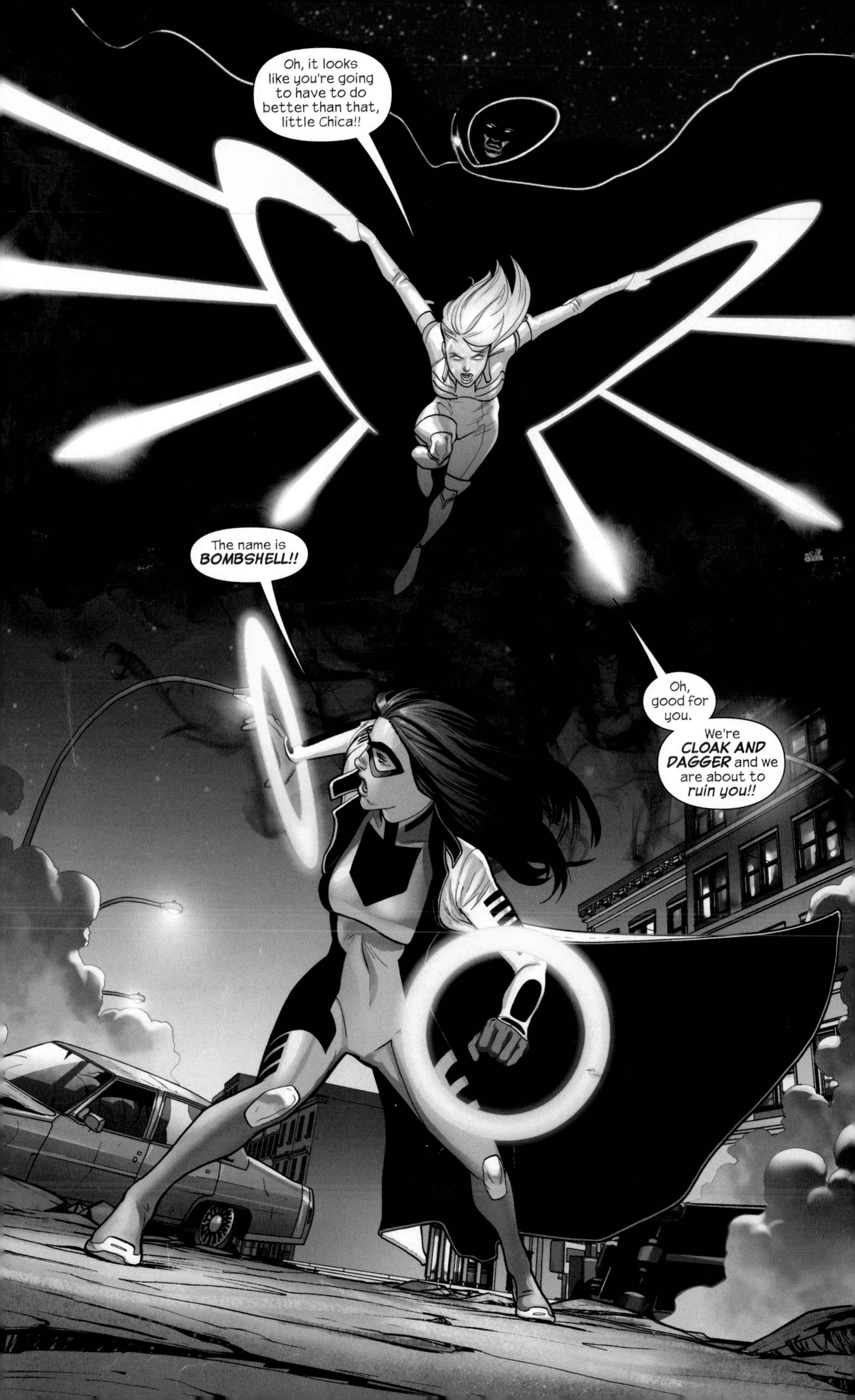
Oh, it looks like you're going to have to do better than that, little Chica!!
The name is **BOMBSHELL!!**
Oh, good for you.
We're **CLOAK AND DAGGER** and we are about to *ruin you!!*

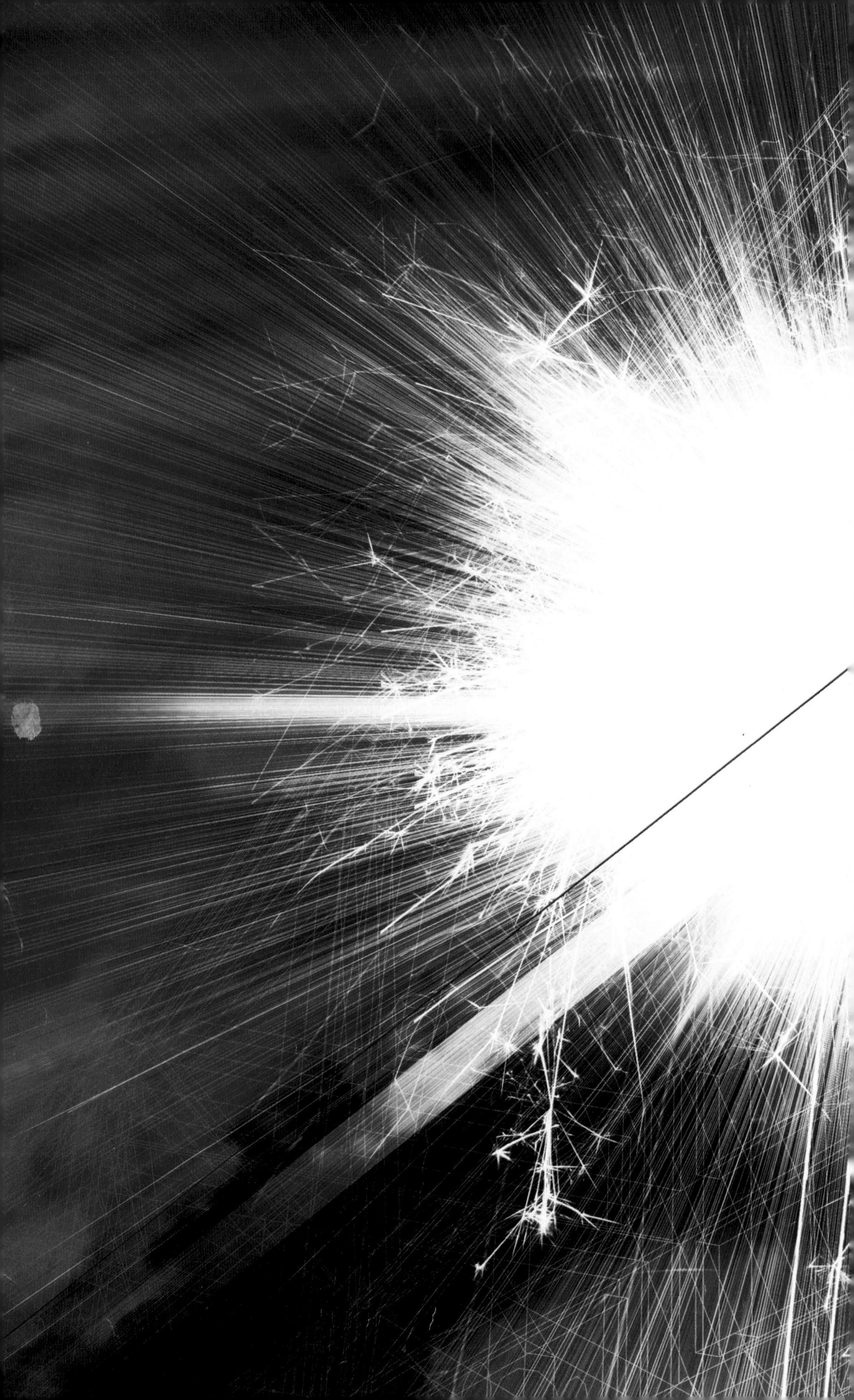

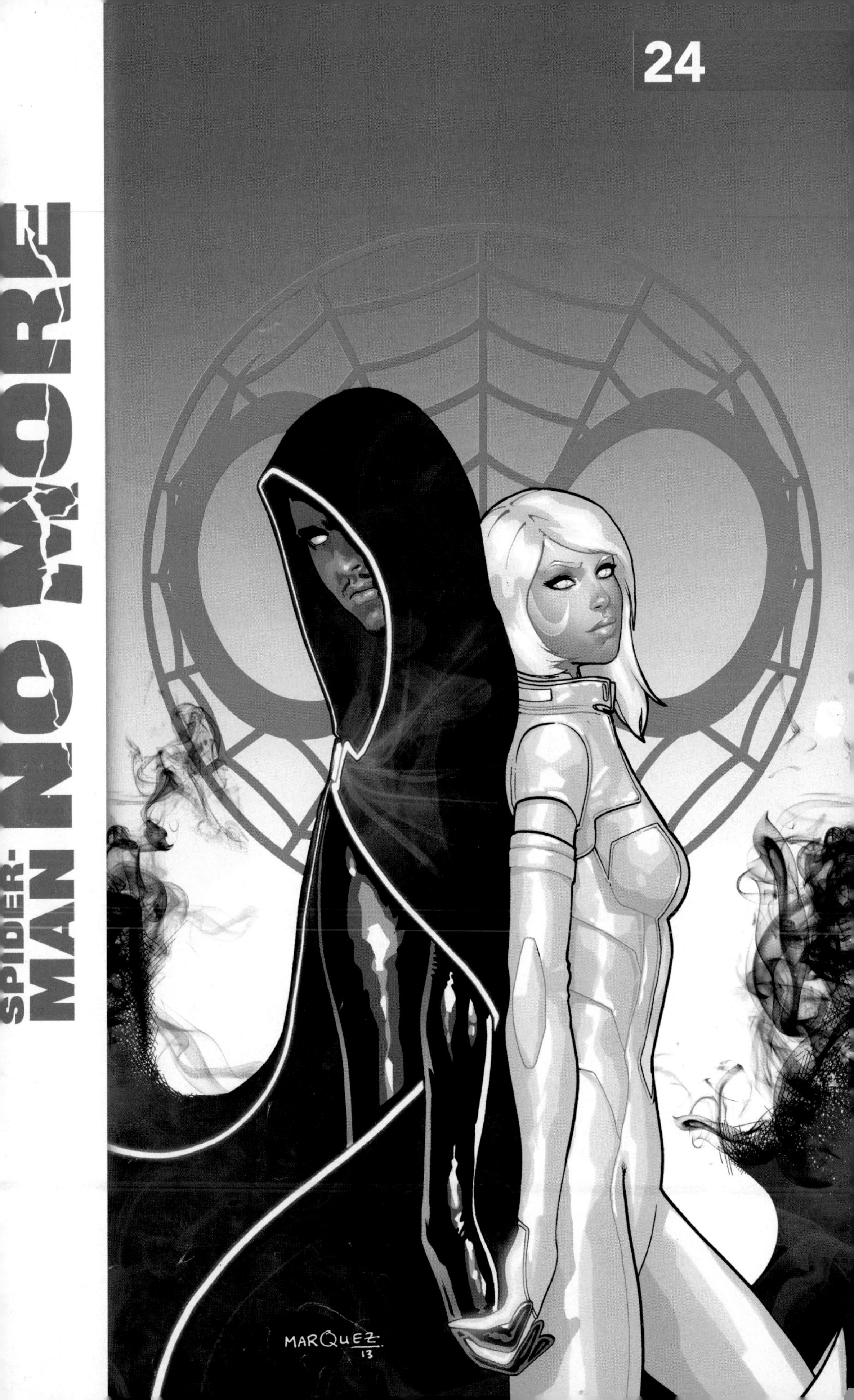
24
SPIDER-MAN NO MORE
MARQUEZ 13

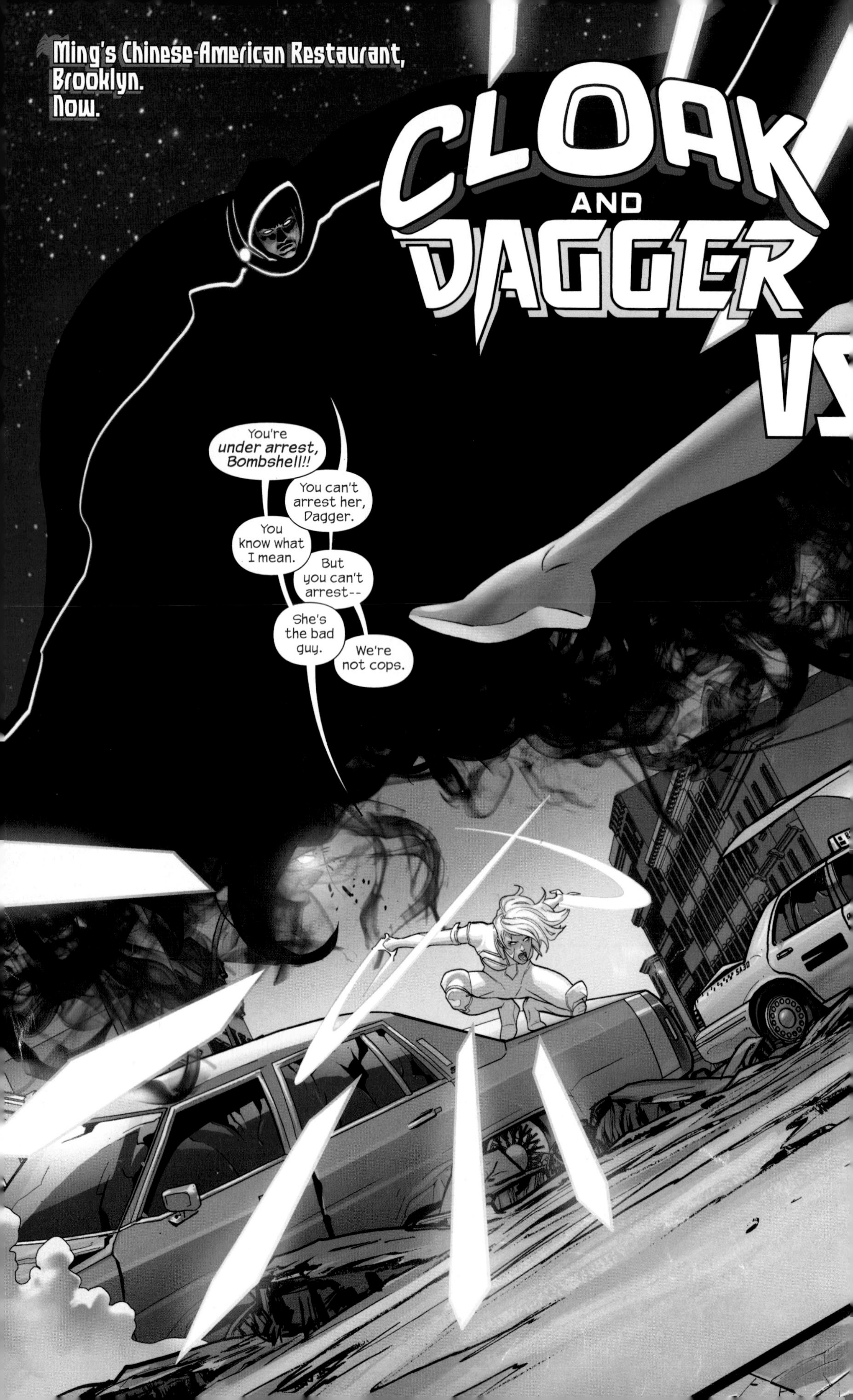
Ming's Chinese-American Restaurant, Brooklyn. Now.
CLOAK AND DAGGER VS
You're under arrest, Bombshell!!
You can't arrest her, Dagger.
You know what I mean.
But you can't arrest--
She's the bad guy.
We're not cops.

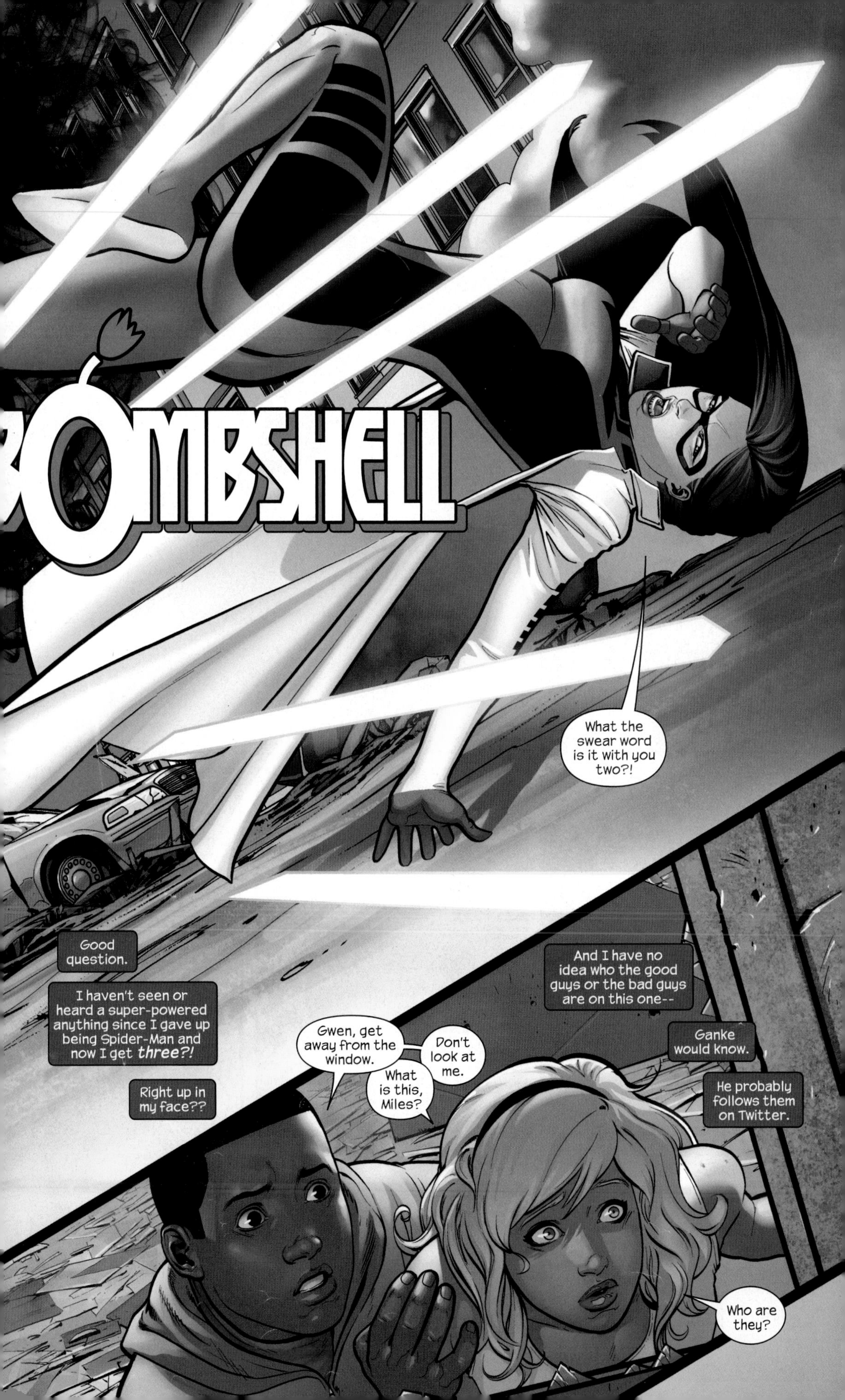
BOMBSHELL
What the swear word is it with you two?!
Good question.
I haven't seen or heard a super-powered anything since I gave up being Spider-Man and now I get *three?!*
Right up in my face??
And I have no idea who the good guys or the bad guys are on this one--
Ganke would know.
He probably follows them on Twitter.
Gwen, get away from the window.
What is this, Miles?
Don't look at me.
Who are they?

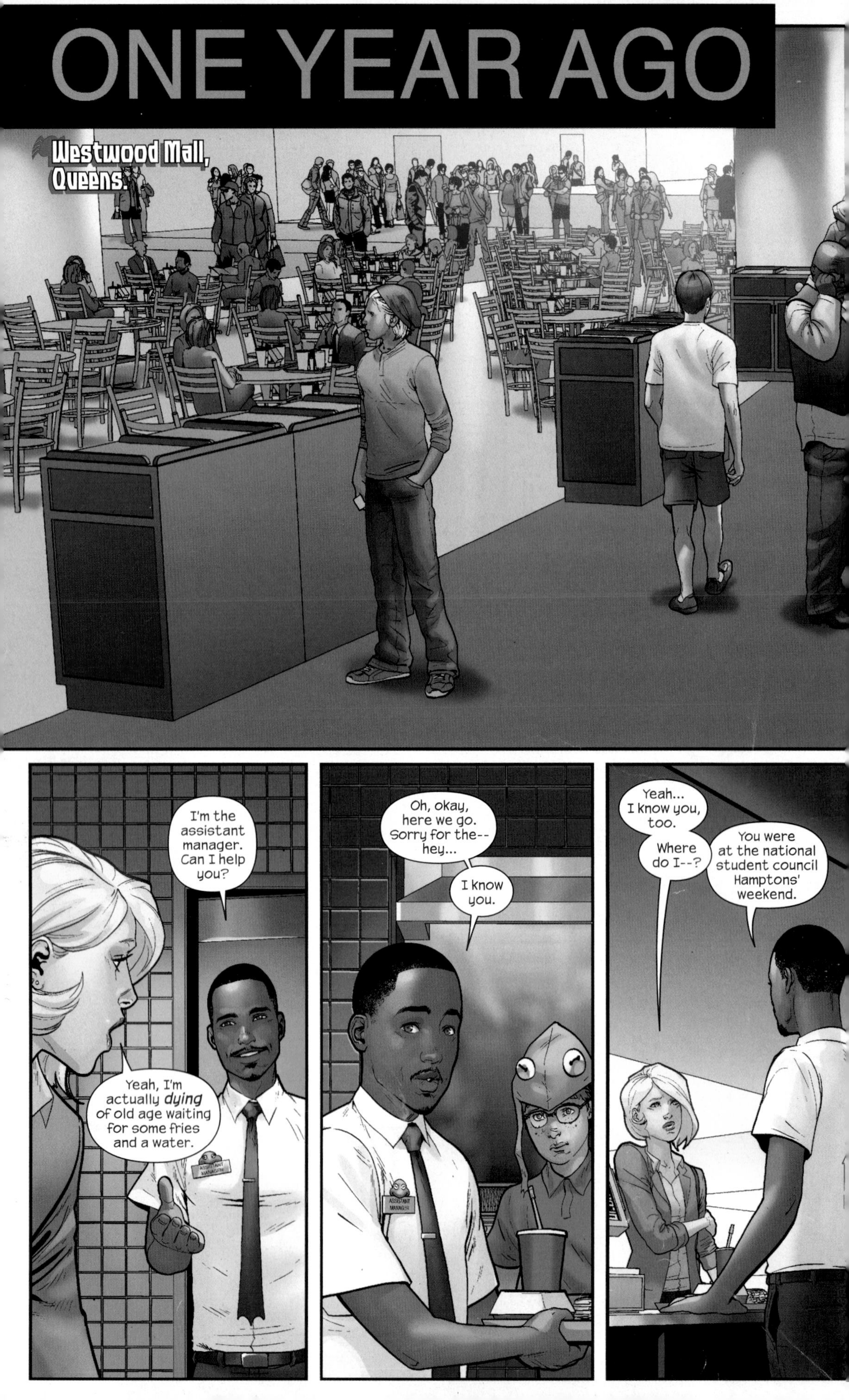
ONE YEAR AGO
Westwood Mall, Queens.
I'm the assistant manager. Can I help you?
Yeah, I'm actually dying of old age waiting for some fries and a water.
ASSISTANT MANAGER
Oh, okay, here we go. Sorry for the-- hey...
I know you.
ASSISTANT MANAGER
Yeah... I know you, too.
Where do I--?
You were at the national student council Hamptons' weekend.

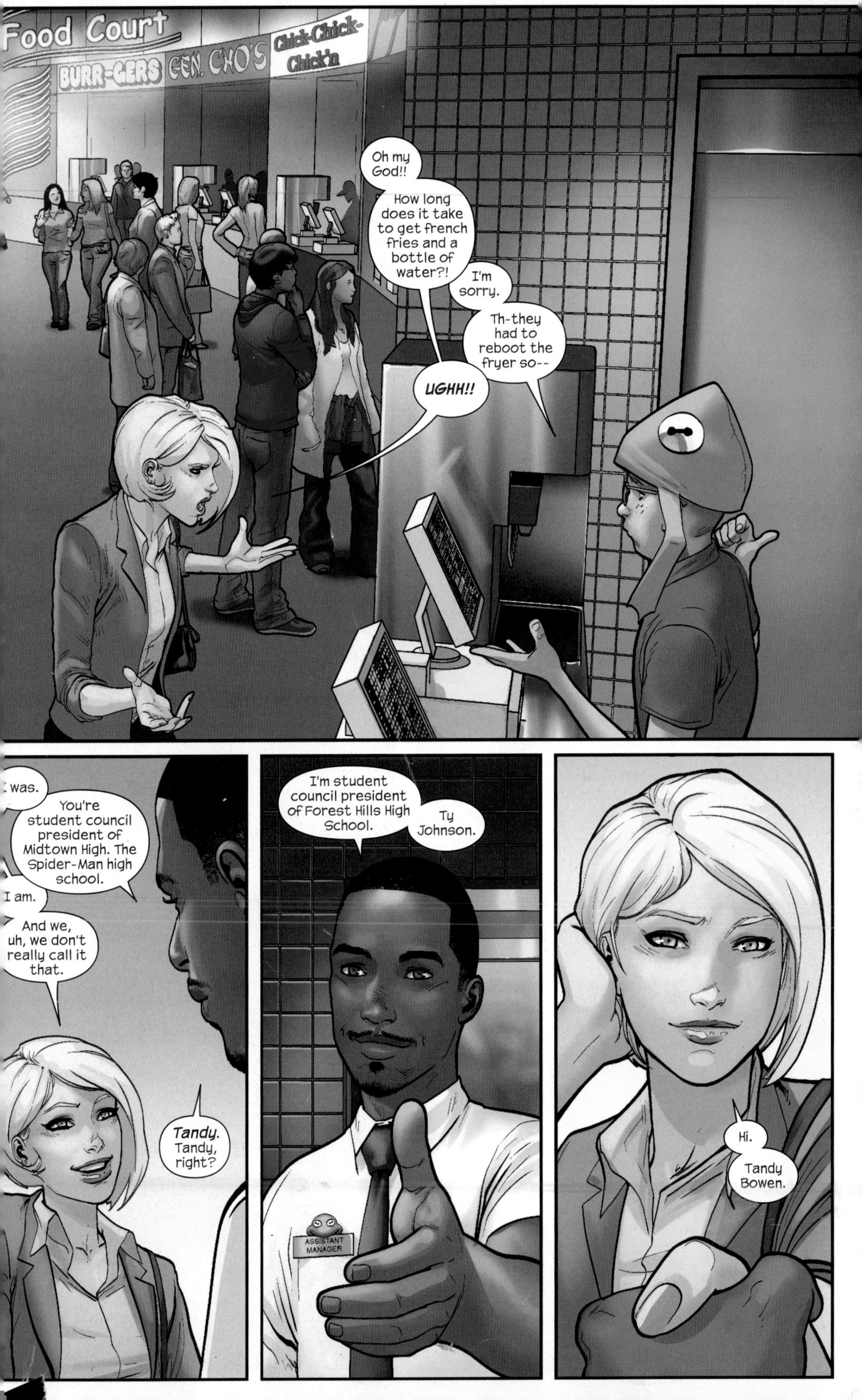

Food Court
BURR-GERS
GEN. CHO'S
Chick-Chick-Chick'n
Oh my God!!
How long does it take to get french fries and a bottle of water?!
I'm sorry.
Th-they had to reboot the fryer so--
UGHH!!
was.
You're student council president of Midtown High. The Spider-Man high school.
I am.
And we, uh, we don't really call it that.
Tandy. Tandy, right?
I'm student council president of Forest Hills High School.
Ty Johnson.
ASSISTANT MANAGER
Hi.
Tandy Bowen.

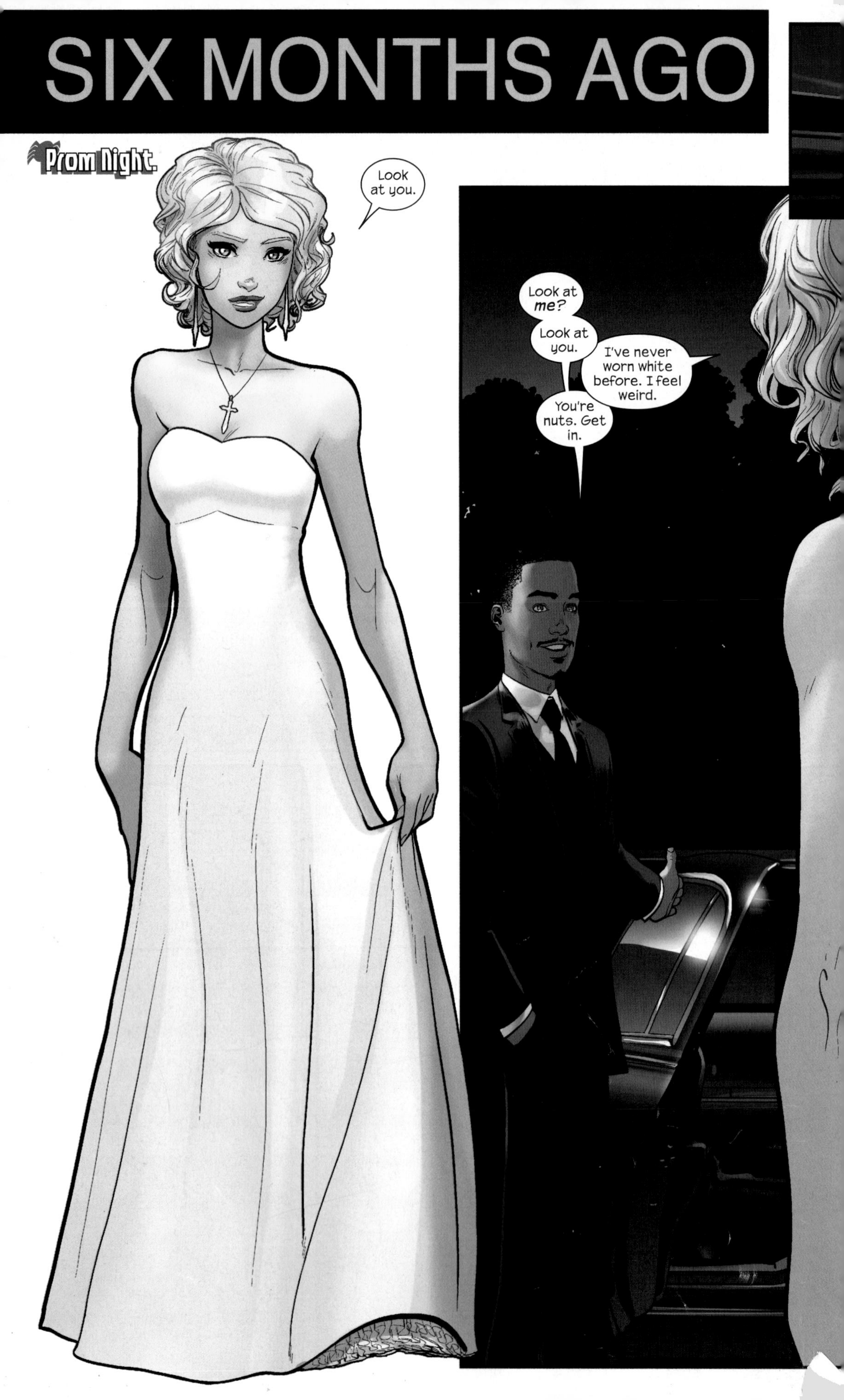
SIX MONTHS AGO
Prom Night.
Look at you.
Look at me?
Look at you.
I've never worn white before. I feel weird.
You're nuts. Get in.

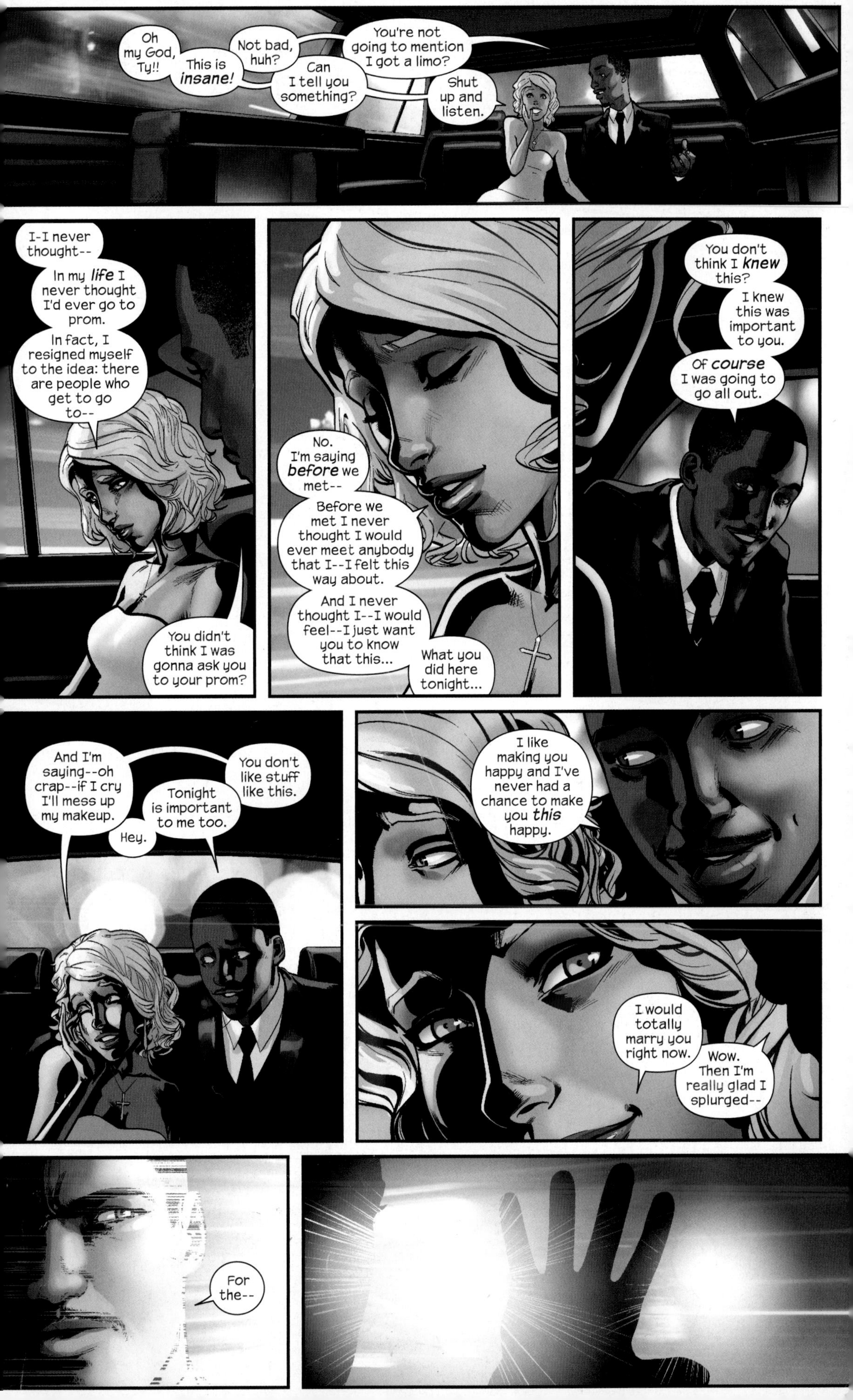
Oh my God, Ty!!
This is insane!
Not bad, huh?
You're not going to mention I got a limo?
Can I tell you something?
Shut up and listen.
I-I never thought--
In my life I never thought I'd ever go to prom.
In fact, I resigned myself to the idea: there are people who get to go to--
You didn't think I was gonna ask you to your prom?
No. I'm saying before we met--
Before we met I never thought I would ever meet anybody that I--I felt this way about.
And I never thought I--I would feel--I just want you to know that this...
What you did here tonight...
You don't think I knew this?
I knew this was important to you.
Of course I was going to go all out.
And I'm saying--oh crap--if I cry I'll mess up my makeup.
You don't like stuff like this.
Hey.
Tonight is important to me too.
I like making you happy and I've never had a chance to make you this happy.
I would totally marry you right now.
Wow. Then I'm really glad I splurged--
For the--

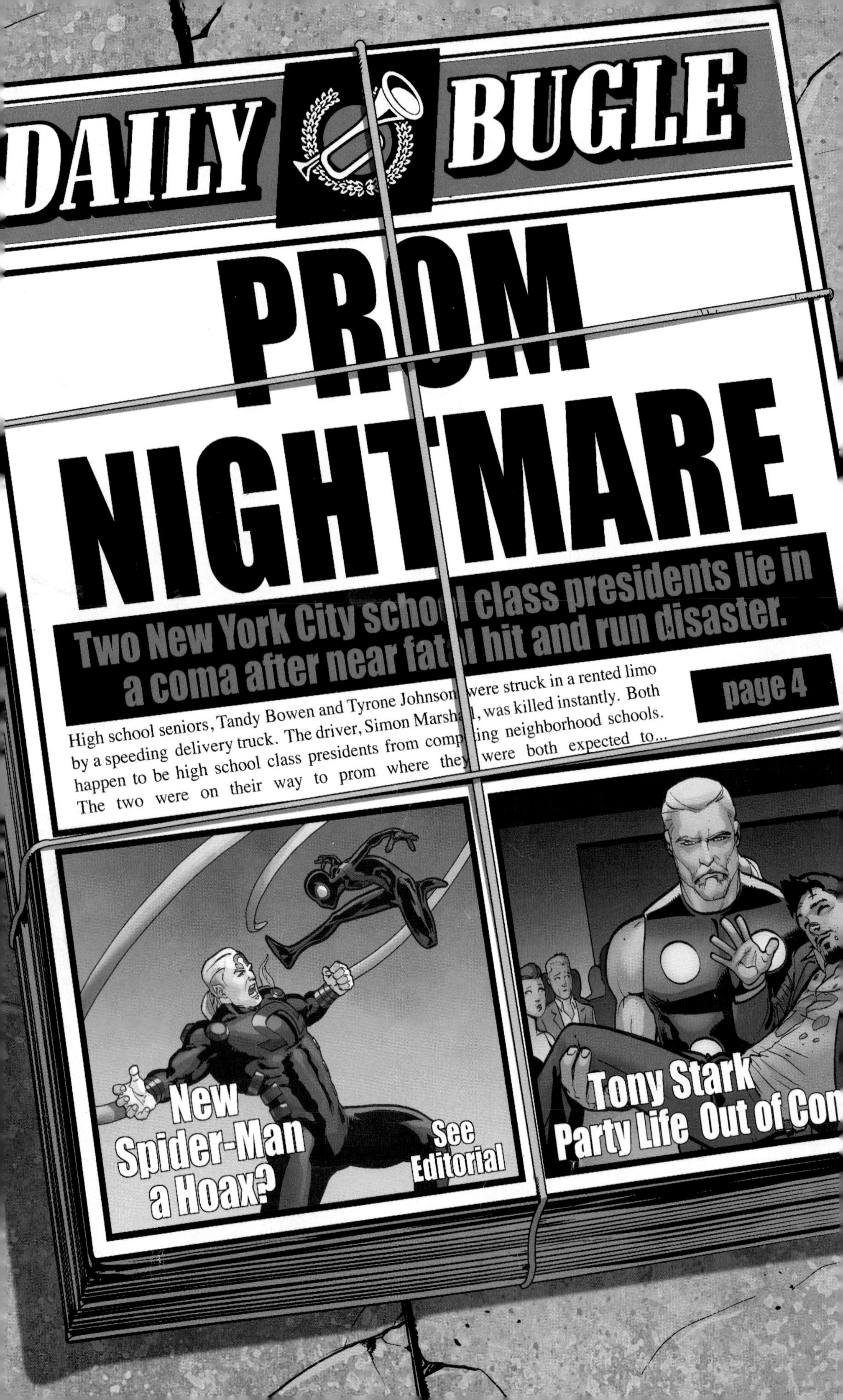
DAILY BUGLE
PROM NIGHTMARE
Two New York City school class presidents lie in a coma after near fatal hit and run disaster.
page 4
High school seniors, Tandy Bowen and Tyrone Johnson were struck in a rented limo by a speeding delivery truck. The driver, Simon Marshall, was killed instantly. Both happen to be high school class presidents from competing neighborhood schools. The two were on their way to prom where they were both expected to...
New Spider-Man a Hoax?
See Editorial
Tony Stark Party Life Out of Con

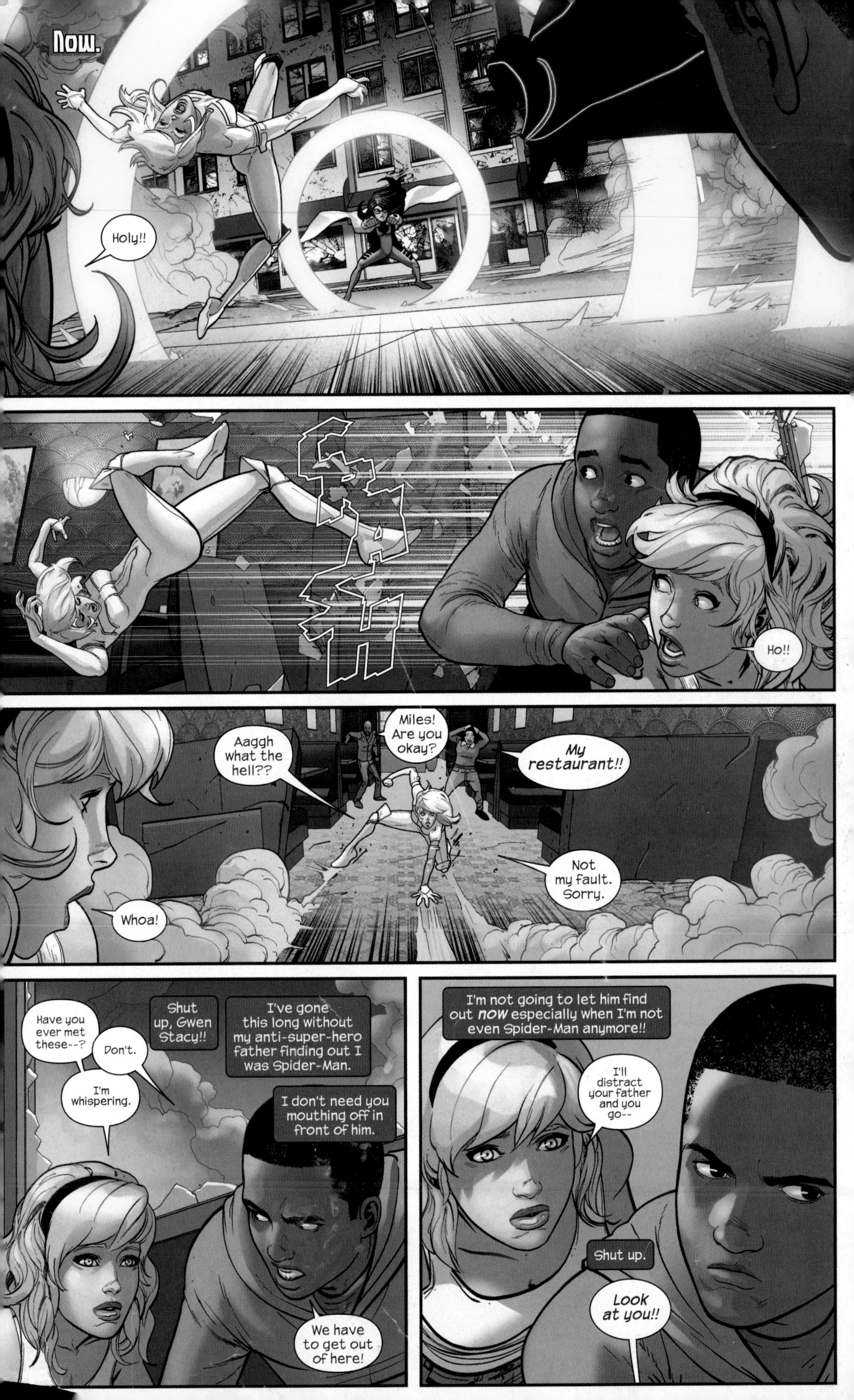
Now.
Holy!!
Ho!!
Aaggh what the hell??
Miles! Are you okay?
My restaurant!!
Not my fault. Sorry.
Whoa!
Have you ever met these--?
Shut up, Gwen Stacy!!
Don't.
I'm whispering.
I've gone this long without my anti-super-hero father finding out I was Spider-Man.
I don't need you mouthing off in front of him.
We have to get out of here!
I'm not going to let him find out NOW especially when I'm not even Spider-Man anymore!!
I'll distract your father and you go--
Shut up.
Look at you!!

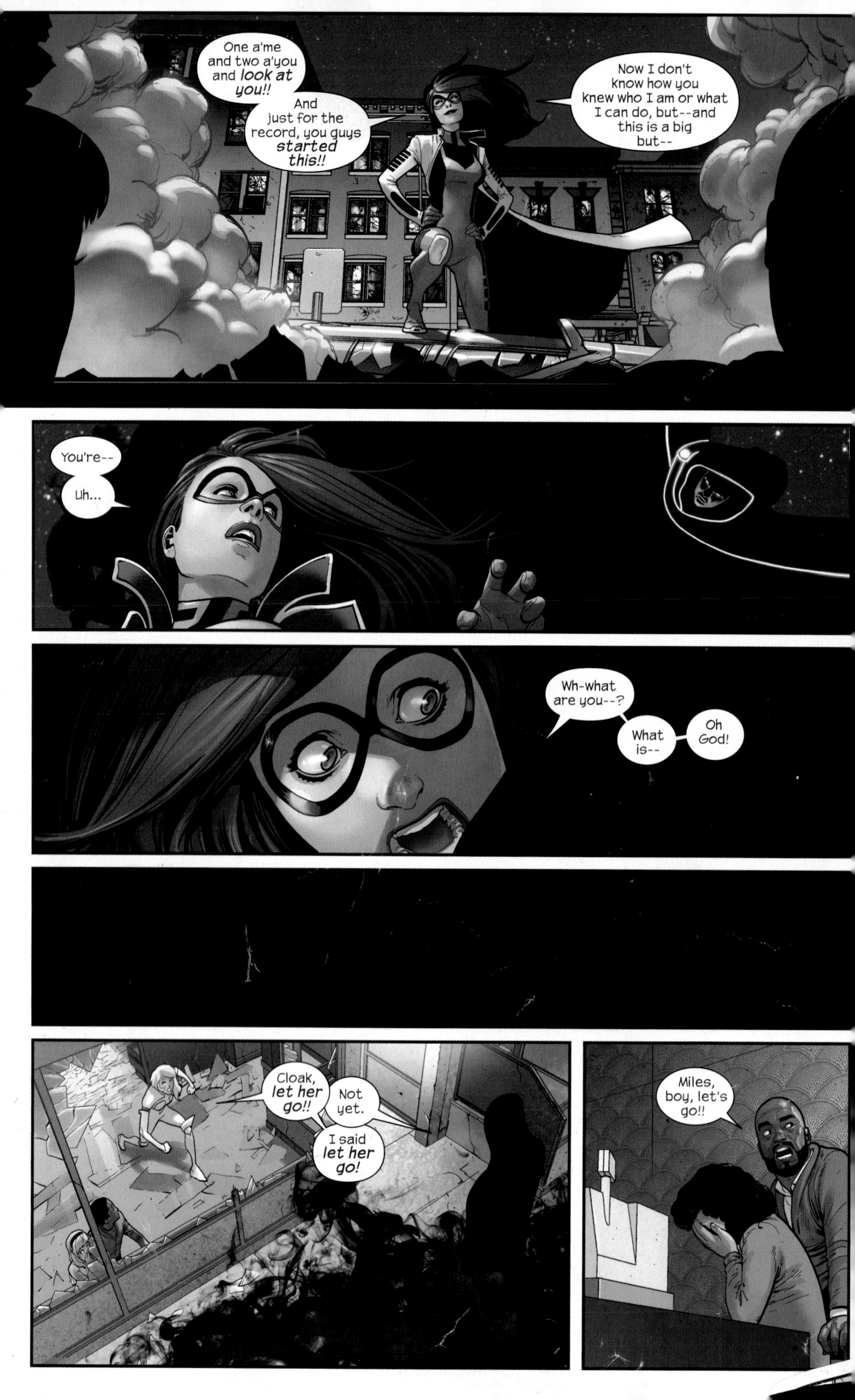
One a'me and two a'you and look at you!!
And just for the record, you guys started this!!
Now I don't know how you knew who I am or what I can do, but--and this is a big but--
You're--
Uh...
Wh-what are you--?
What is--
Oh God!
Cloak, let her go!!
Not yet.
I said let her go!
Miles, boy, let's go!!

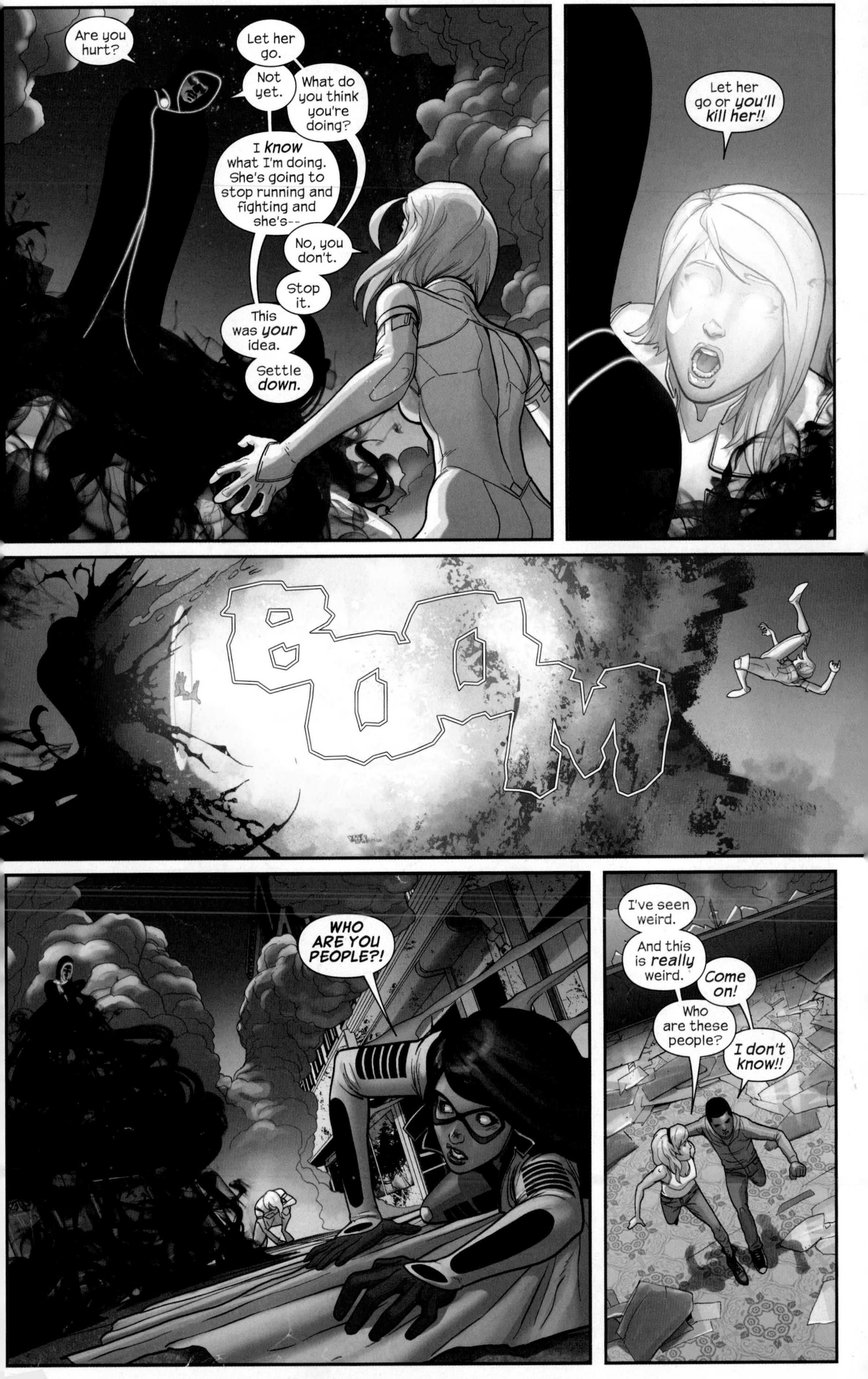

Are you hurt?
Let her go.
Not yet.
What do you think you're doing?
I *know* what I'm doing. She's going to stop running and fighting and she's--
No, you don't.
Stop it.
This was *your* idea.
Settle *down.*
Let her go or *you'll kill her!!*
BOOM
WHO ARE YOU PEOPLE?!
I've seen weird.
And this is *really* weird.
Come on!
Who are these people?
I don't know!!

Midtown Hospital.

Well, that is both sad and sweet.

That they get to share a room.

It's kind of sweet.

Why are they in the *same* room?

Oh, you know, Nathaniel, it's that holistic healing horse crap...

Probably one of their mothers thinks their spirits might somehow wake each other up or--

My mother was into that kind of thing. All the good it did her.

And no one will notice they're not here anymore while we experiment on them?

Dr. Layla Miller

Nathaniel Essex

Dr. Samuel Sterns

Dr. Arnim Zola III

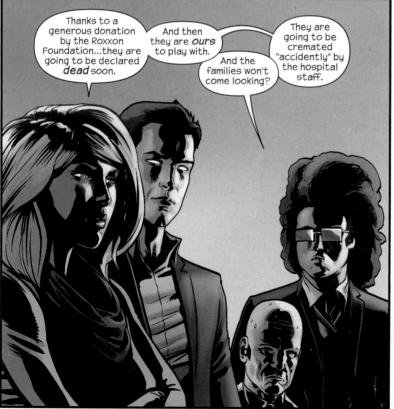

Thanks to a generous donation by the Roxxon Foundation...they are going to be declared *dead* soon.

And then they are *ours* to play with.

And the families won't come looking?

They are going to be cremated "accidently" by the hospital staff.

That is grim.

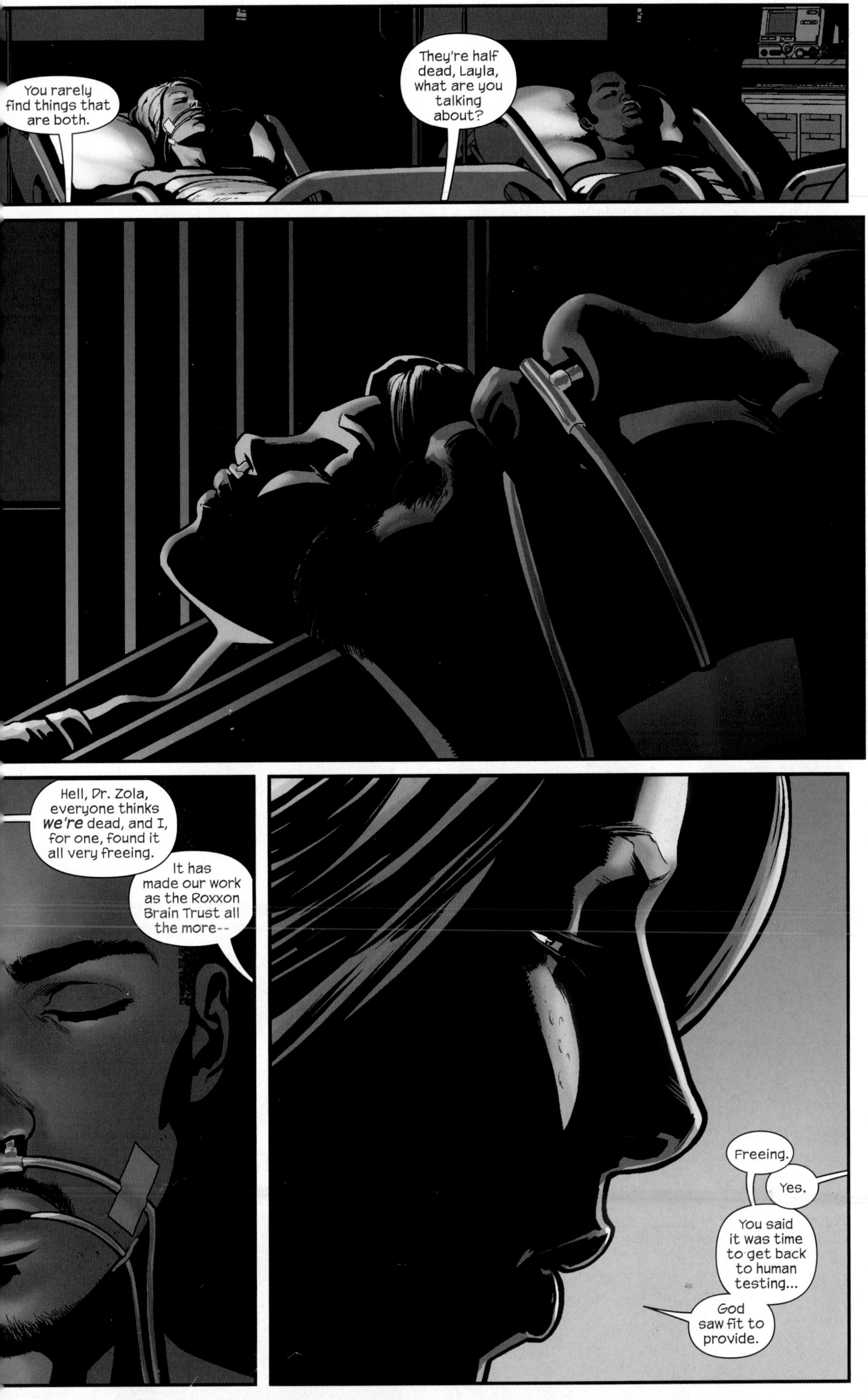
You rarely find things that are both.
They're half dead, Layla, what are you talking about?
Hell, Dr. Zola, everyone thinks *we're* dead, and I, for one, found it all very freeing.
It has made our work as the Roxxon Brain Trust all the more--
Freeing.
Yes.
You said it was time to get back to human testing...
God saw fit to provide.

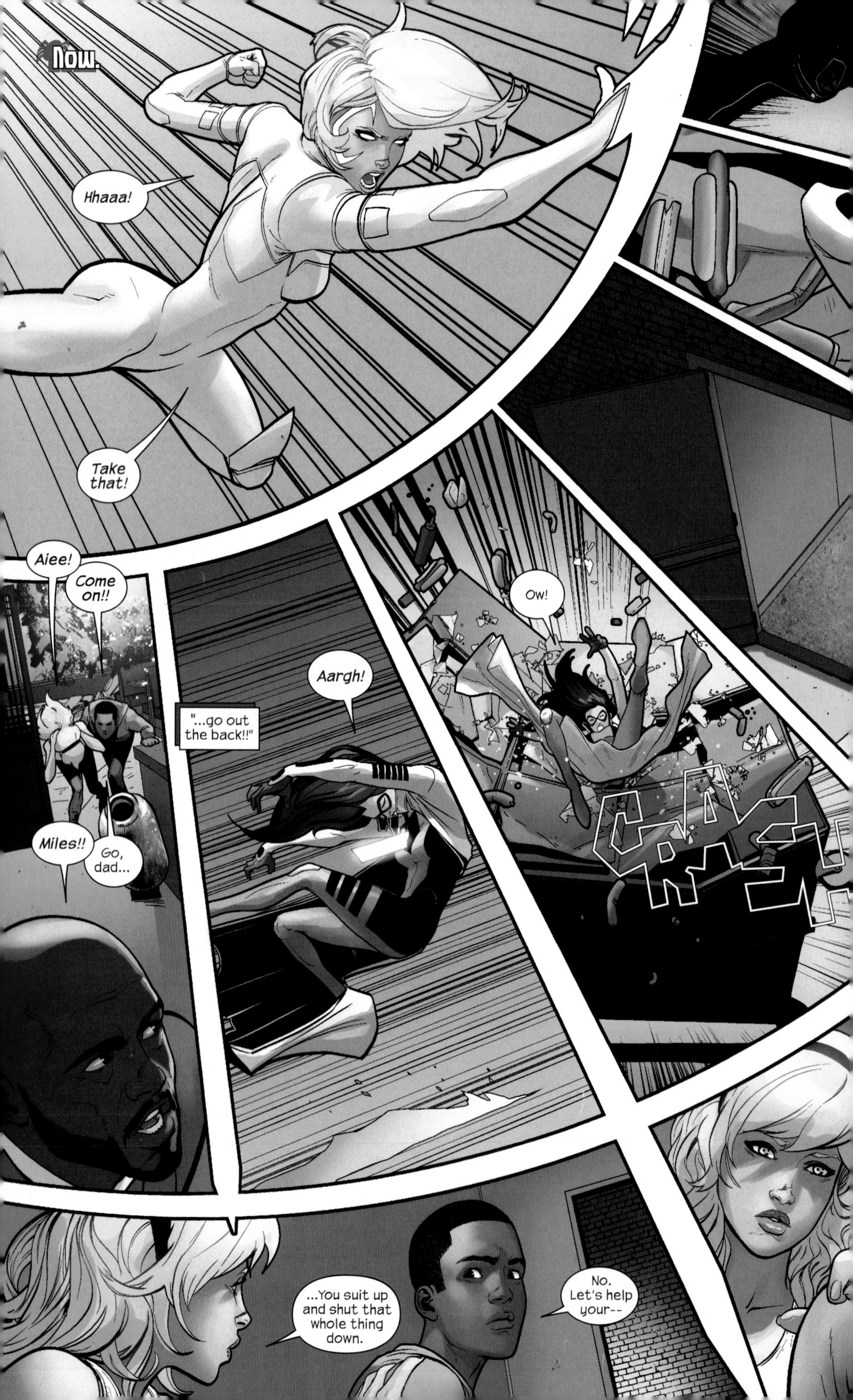
Now.
Hhaaa!
Take that!
Aiee!
Come on!!
Miles!!
Go, dad...
"...go out the back!!"
Aargh!
Ow!
CRASH
...You suit up and shut that whole thing down.
No. Let's help your--

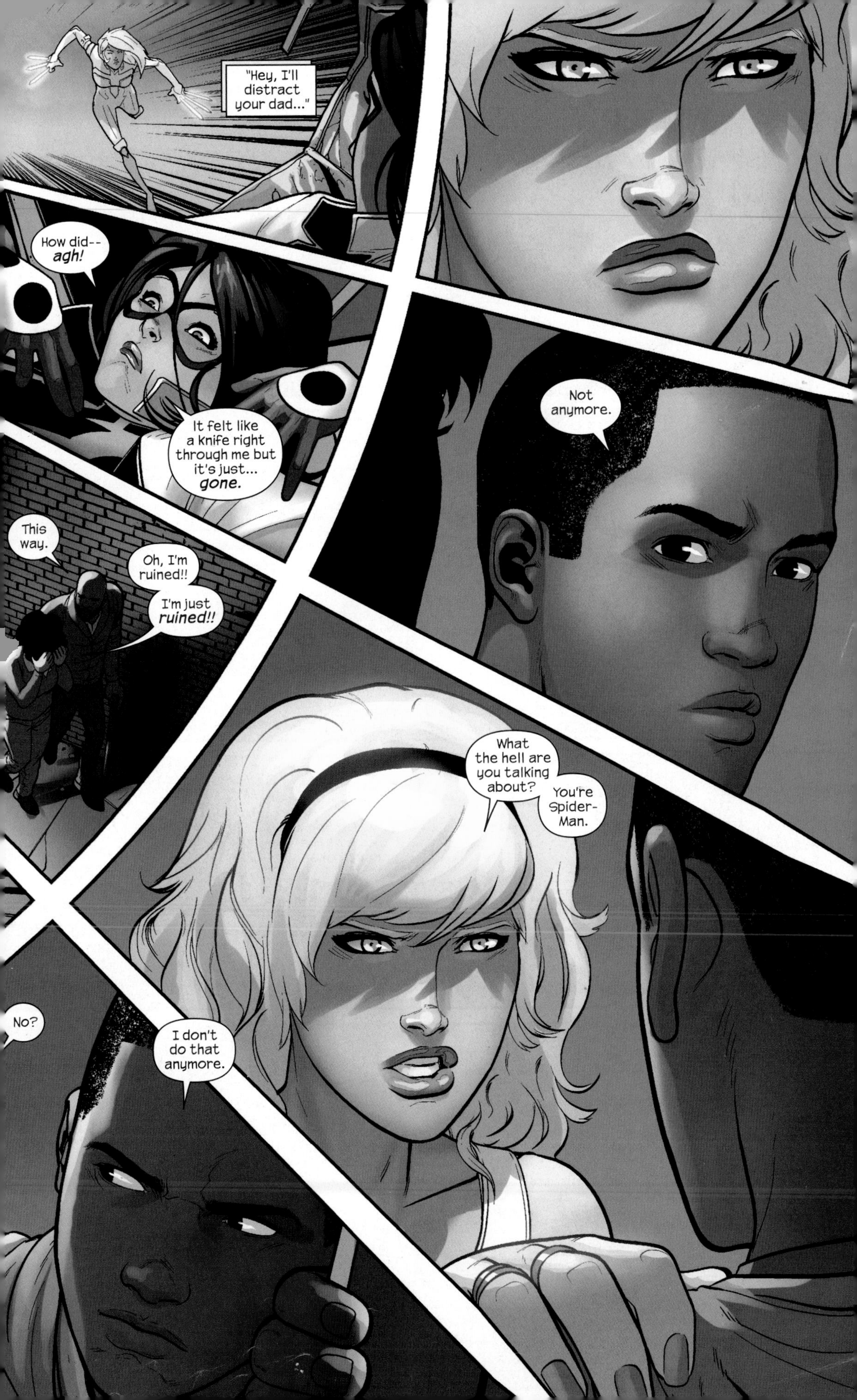
"Hey, I'll distract your dad..."
How did-- *agh!*
It felt like a knife right through me but it's just... *gone.*
This way.
Oh, I'm ruined!!
I'm just *ruined!!*
Not anymore.
What the hell are you talking about?
You're Spider-Man.
No?
I don't do that anymore.

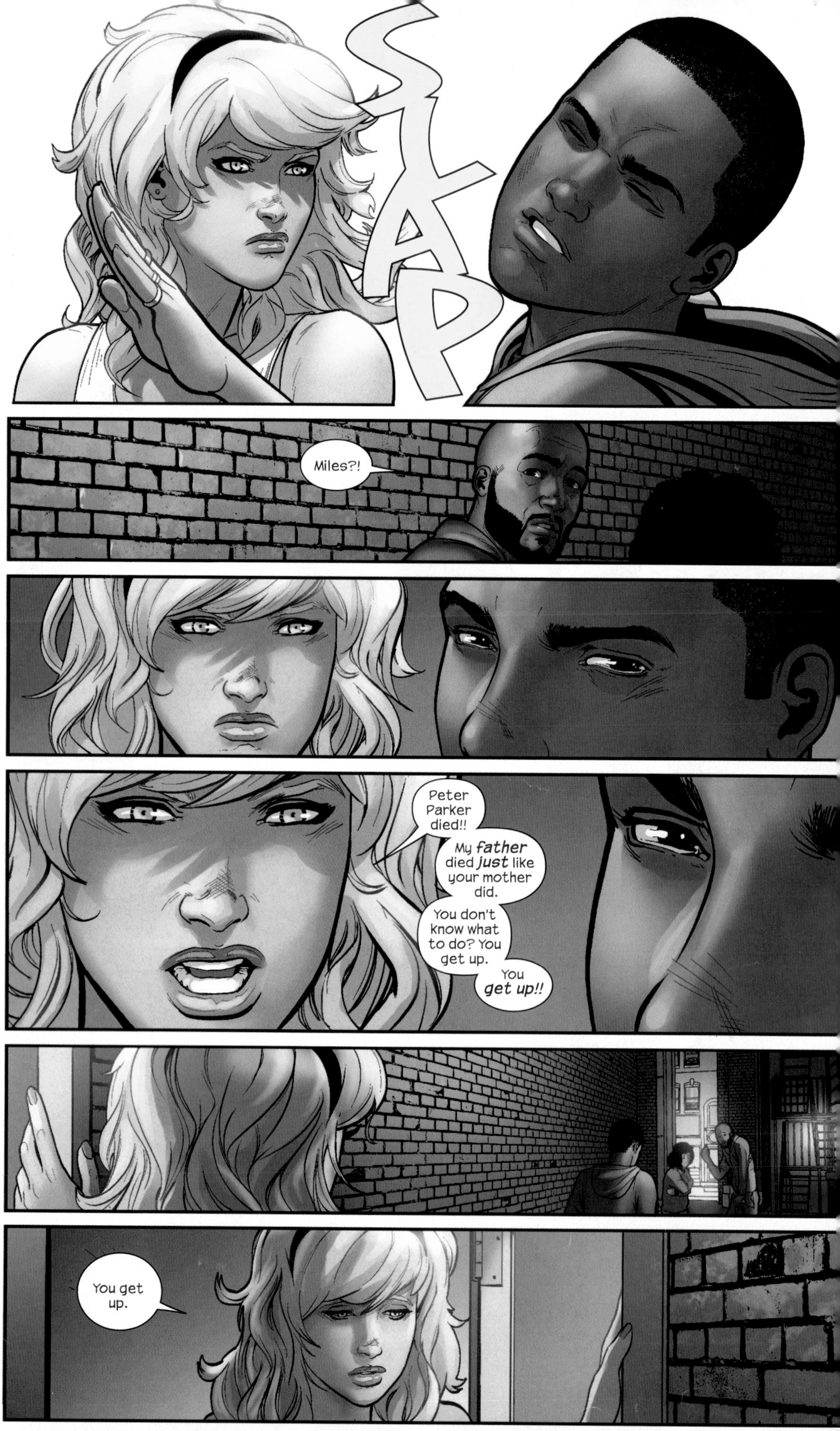
SLAP
Miles?!
Peter Parker died!!
My father died just like your mother did.
You don't know what to do? You get up.
You get up!!
You get up.

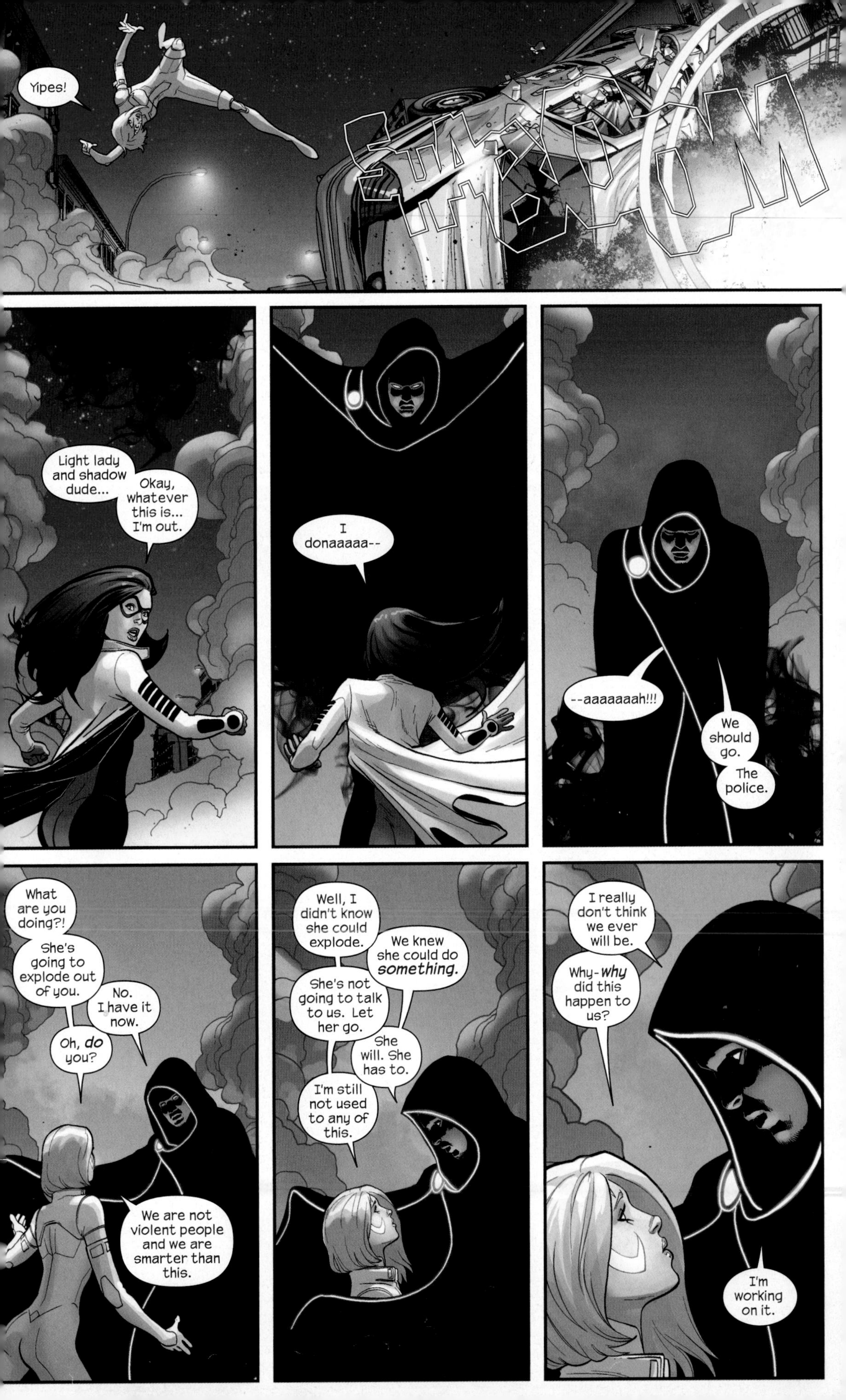
Yipes!
Light lady and shadow dude...
Okay, whatever this is... I'm out.
I donaaaaa--
--aaaaaaah!!!
We should go.
The police.
What are you doing?!
She's going to explode out of you.
No. I have it now.
Oh, *do* you?
We are not violent people and we are smarter than this.
Well, I didn't know she could explode.
We knew she could do *something.*
She's not going to talk to us. Let her go.
She will. She has to.
I'm still not used to any of this.
I really don't think we ever will be.
Why- *why* did this happen to us?
I'm working on it.

THREE DAYS AGO

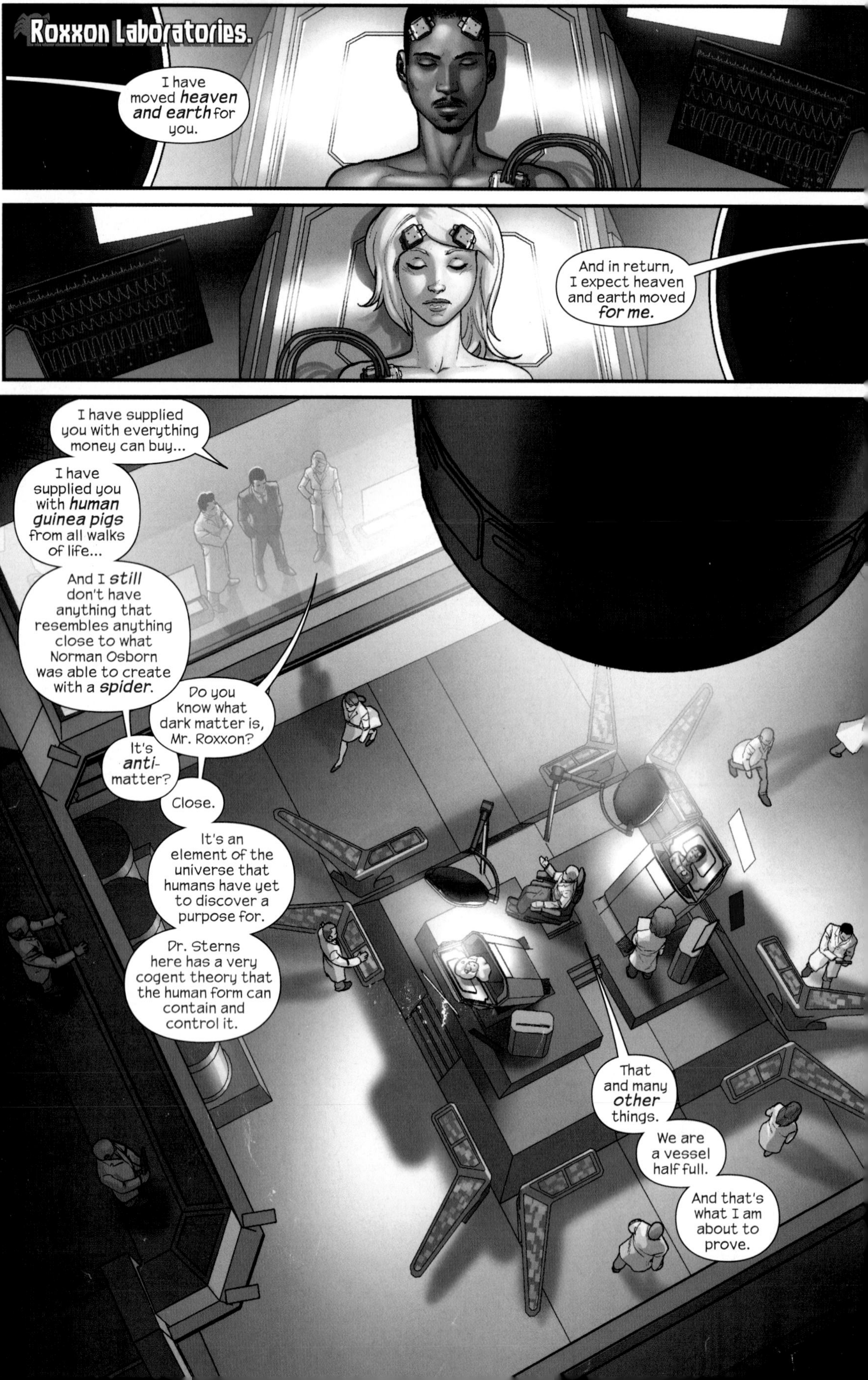
Roxxon Laboratories.
I have moved heaven and earth for you.
And in return, I expect heaven and earth moved for me.
I have supplied you with everything money can buy...
I have supplied you with human guinea pigs from all walks of life...
And I still don't have anything that resembles anything close to what Norman Osborn was able to create with a spider.
Do you know what dark matter is, Mr. Roxxon?
It's anti-matter?
Close.
It's an element of the universe that humans have yet to discover a purpose for.
Dr. Sterns here has a very cogent theory that the human form can contain and control it.
That and many other things.
We are a vessel half full.
And that's what I am about to prove.

Initiate phase 1 protocols.

Everyone at your stations.

Please make sure that all sensors and recording devices are **on** and calibrated.

Right now? This is happening right now?

That's what we called you in for, boss.

Really? **Right** now?

You have moved heaven and earth for us... it's the least we can do.

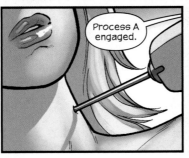

Process A engaged.

What are you injecting into the--?

Is--is-- is **that** dark matter?

It is a catalyst compound.

Vital signs are stable, Zola.

I think we are a go for Process B.

We already **have** dark matter inside of us.

Everything does. All things do.

It's the thing in between the things that make us **us**.

So is the **theory**...

You see...and I mean no offense, Mr. Roxxon, but the problem with your experiments up until now is that you keep trying to duplicate what Norman **Osborn** did.

What Norman Osborn created with his fractured Oz formula...

What the Parkers created with the symbiotes years ago...

Why would you try to duplicate failure?

Spider-Man was Osborn's penicillin, his accident...

But what it did show us, inarguably, was that there are energies inside all of us.

Untapped potential.

Things we can't even perceive yet.

Um, I think we have a--

Uh-oh.

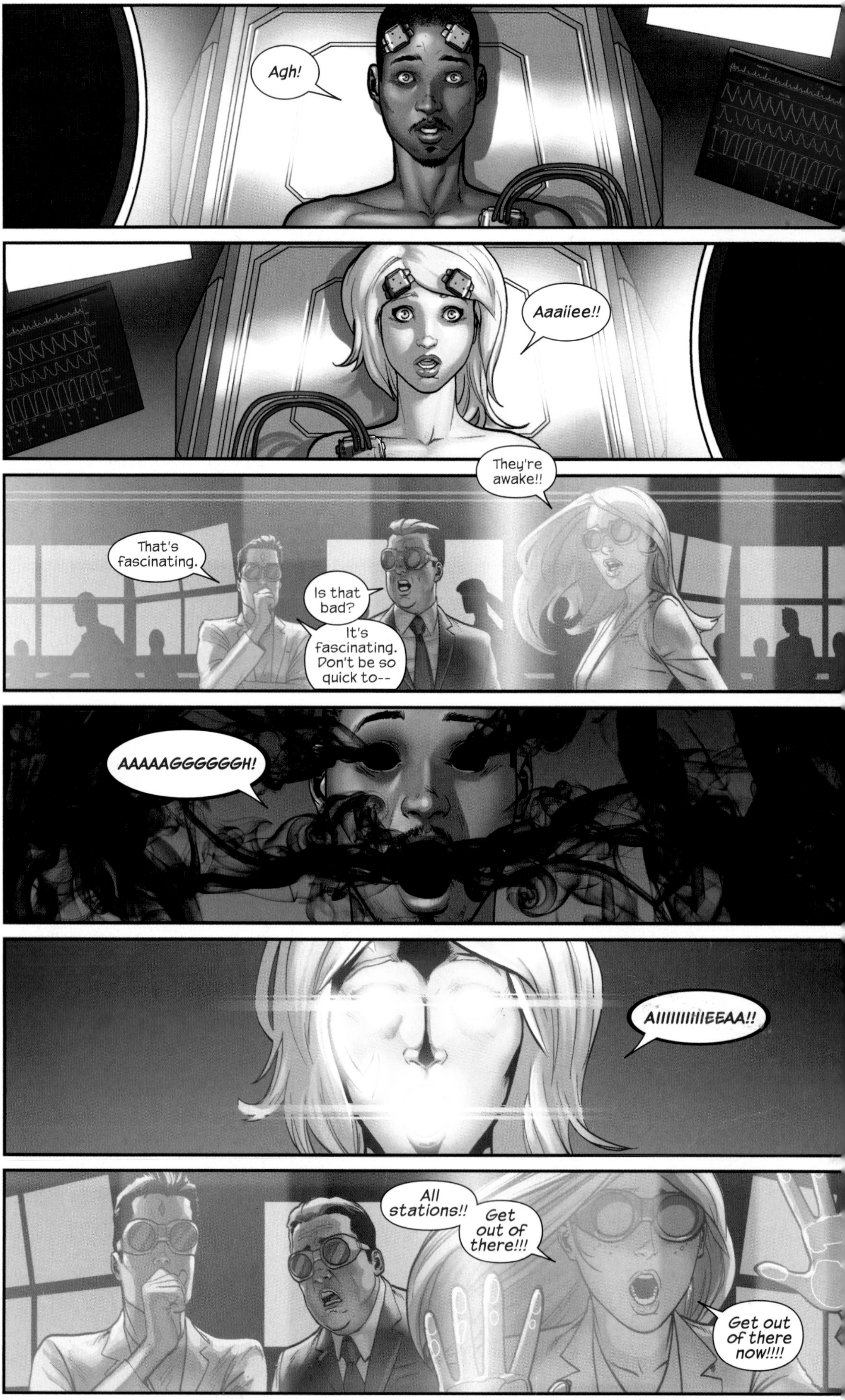
Agh!
Aaaiiee!!
They're awake!!
That's fascinating.
Is that bad?
It's fascinating. Don't be so quick to--
AAAAAGGGGGGH!
AIIIIIIIIIIEEAA!!
All stations!!
Get out of there!!!
Get out of there now!!!!

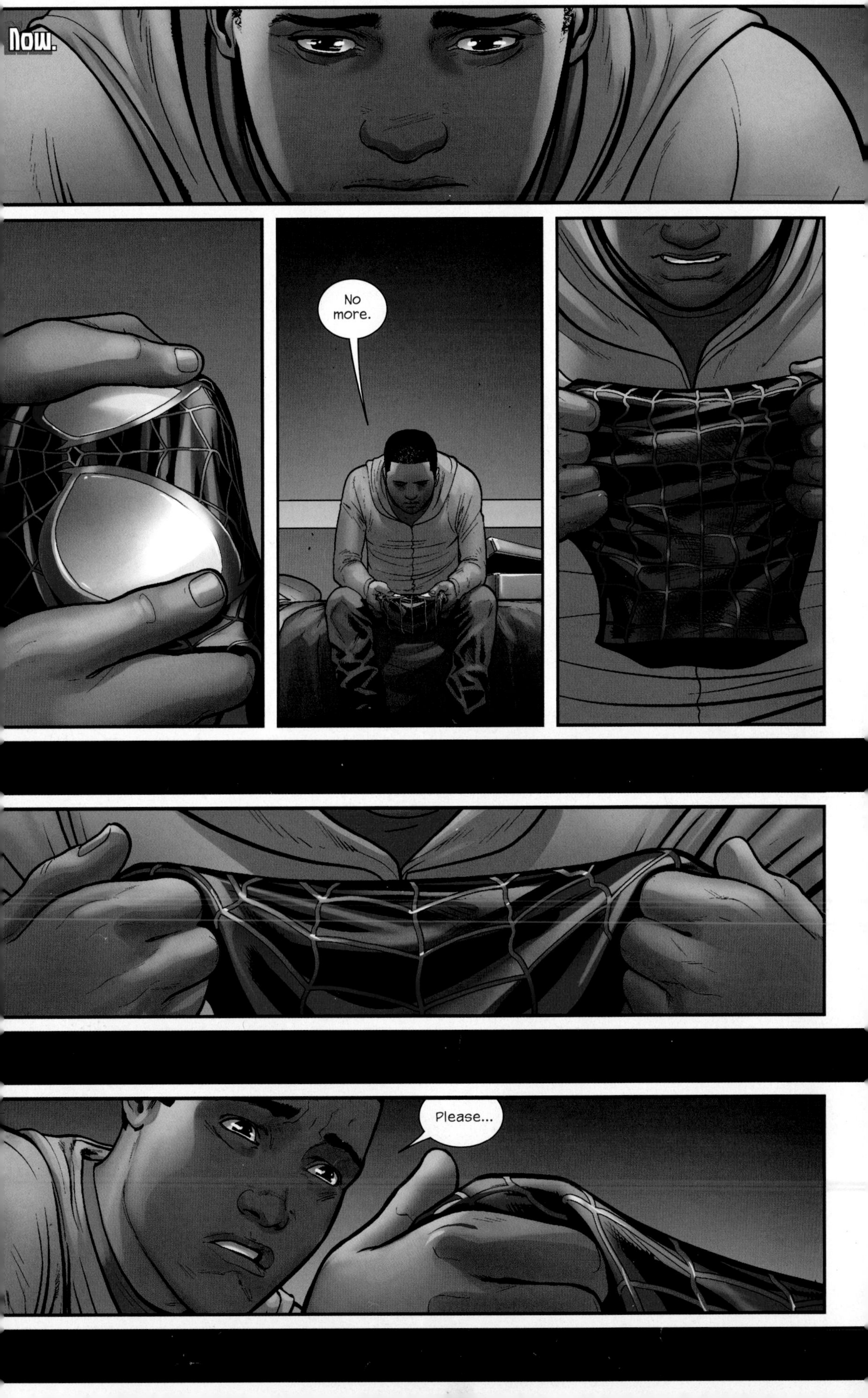
Now.
No more.
Please...

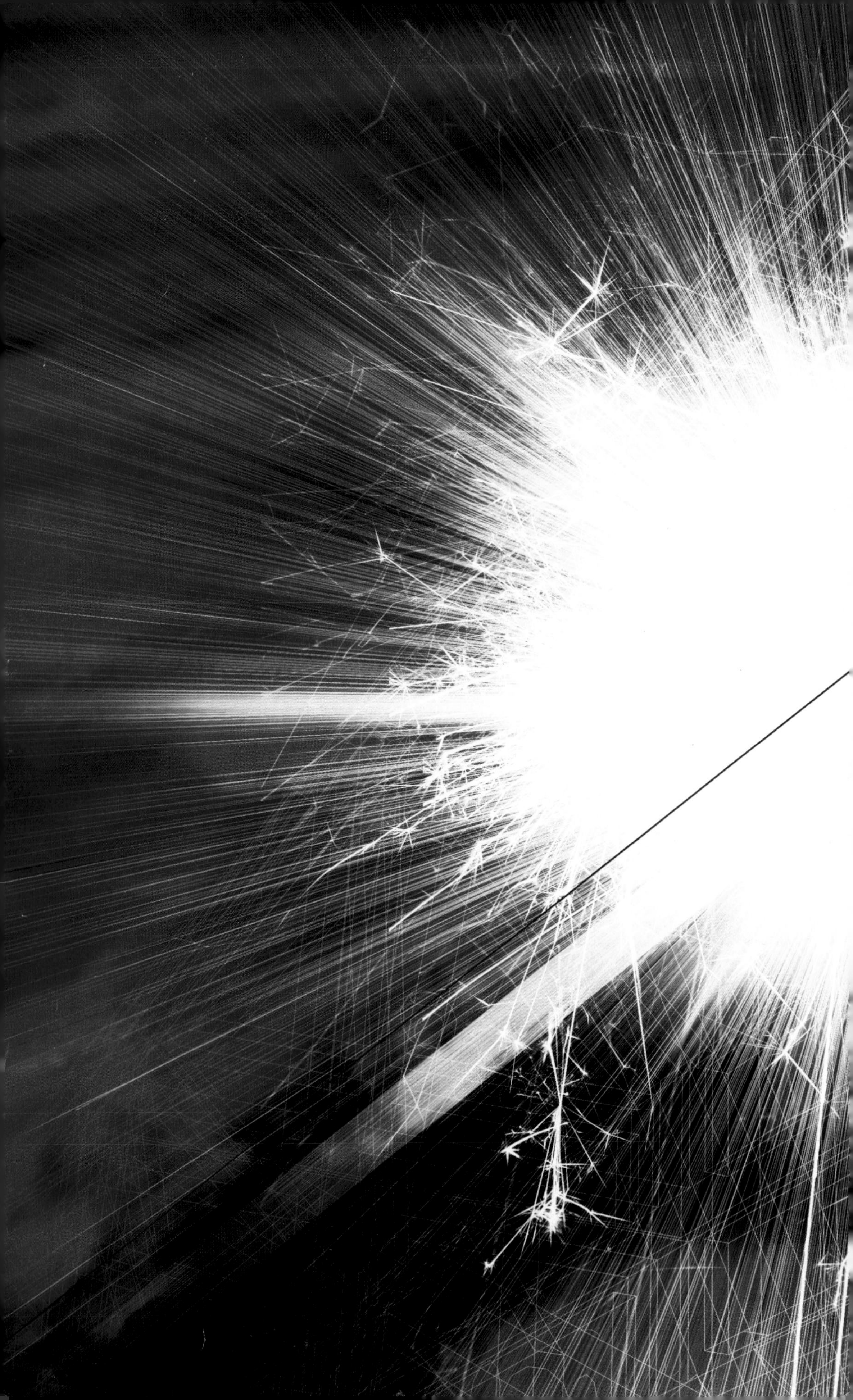

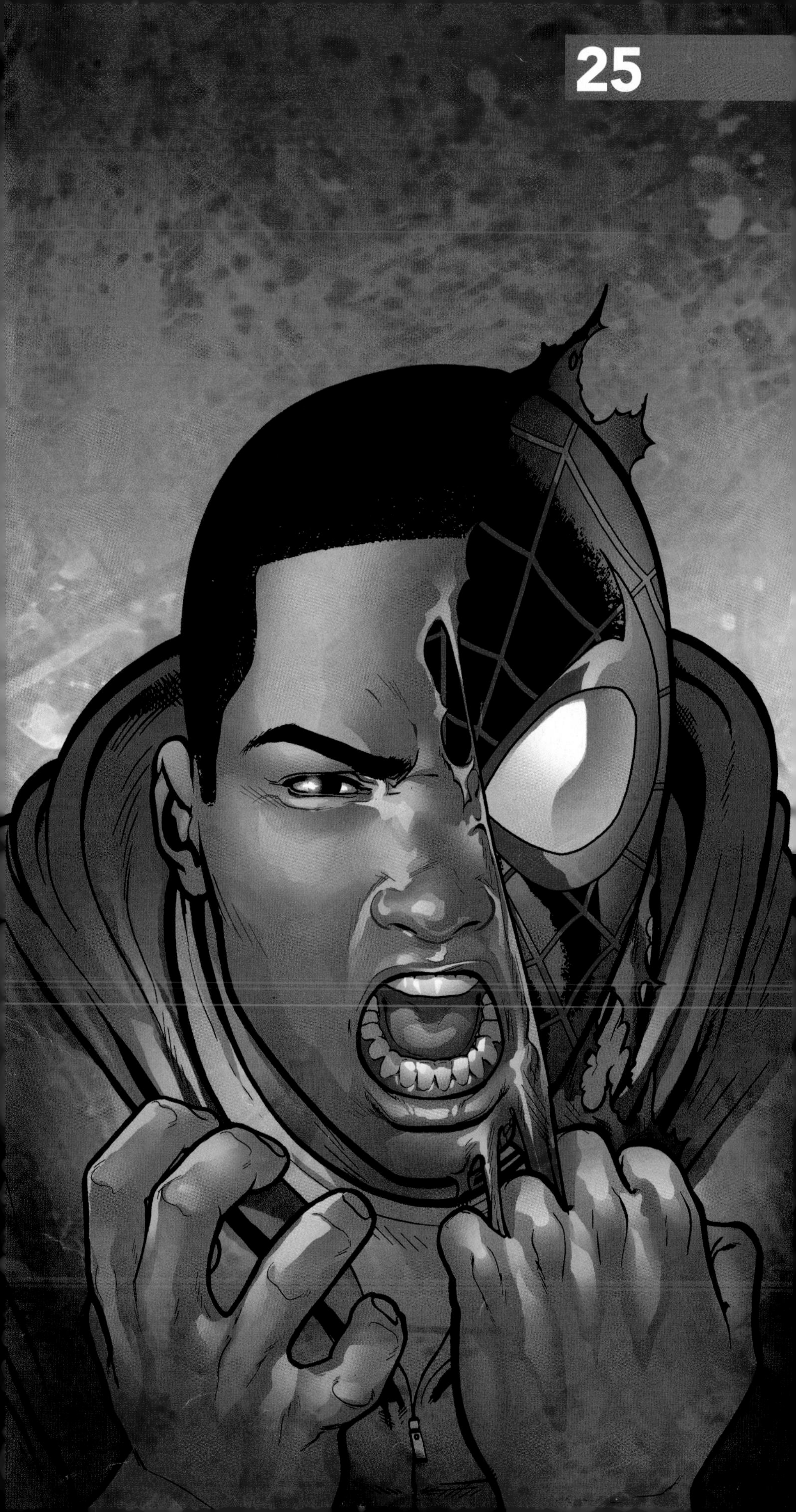
25

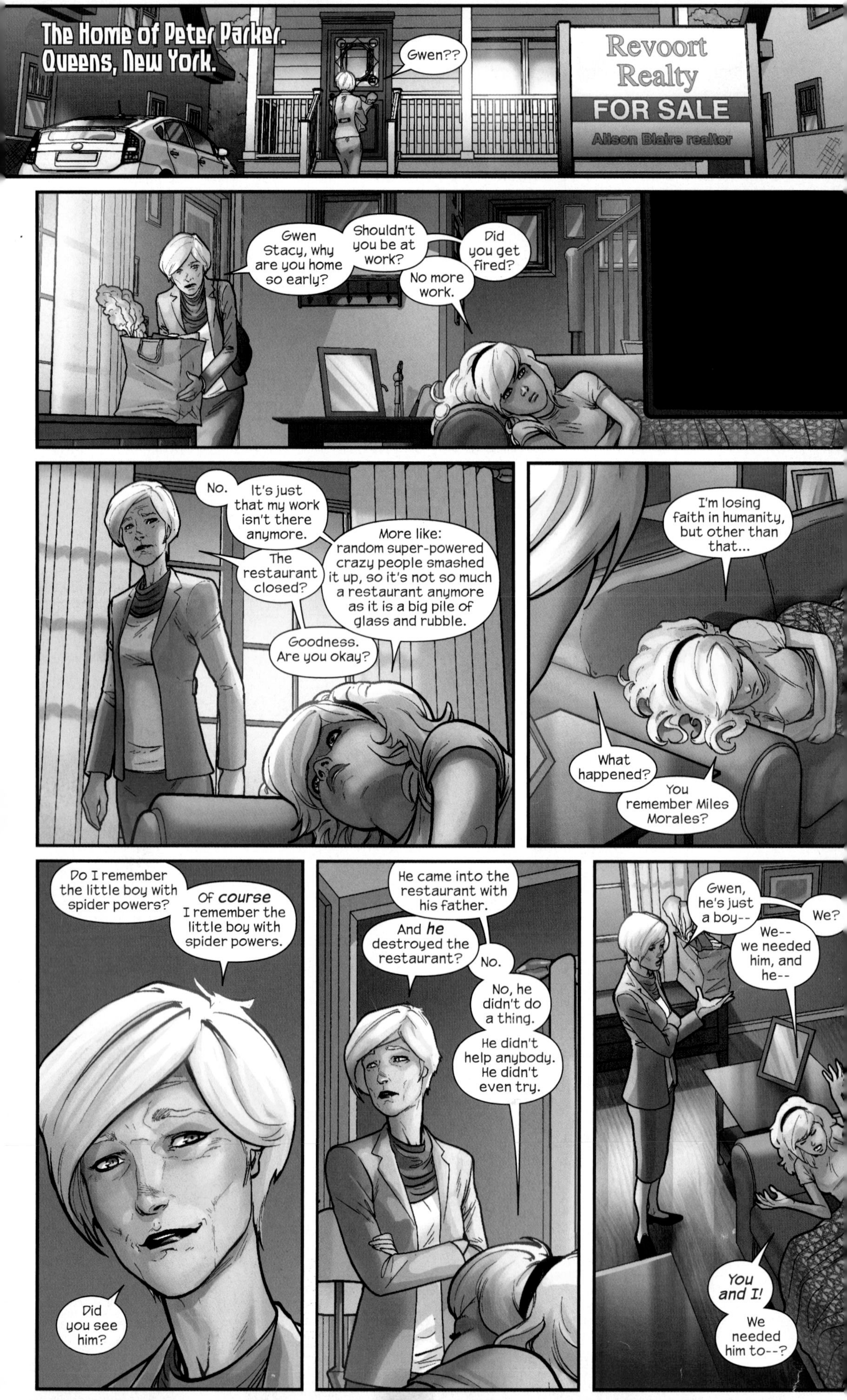
The Home of Peter Parker.
Queens, New York.
Gwen??
Revoort Realty
FOR SALE
Alison Blaire realtor
Gwen Stacy, why are you home so early?
Shouldn't you be at work?
Did you get fired?
No more work.
No.
It's just that my work isn't there anymore.
The restaurant closed?
More like: random super-powered crazy people smashed it up, so it's not so much a restaurant anymore as it is a big pile of glass and rubble.
Goodness. Are you okay?
I'm losing faith in humanity, but other than that...
What happened?
You remember Miles Morales?
Do I remember the little boy with spider powers?
Of *course* I remember the little boy with spider powers.
Did you see him?
He came into the restaurant with his father.
And *he* destroyed the restaurant?
No.
No, he didn't do a thing.
He didn't help anybody. He didn't even try.
Gwen, he's just a boy--
We?
We-- we needed him, and he--
You and I!
We needed him to--?

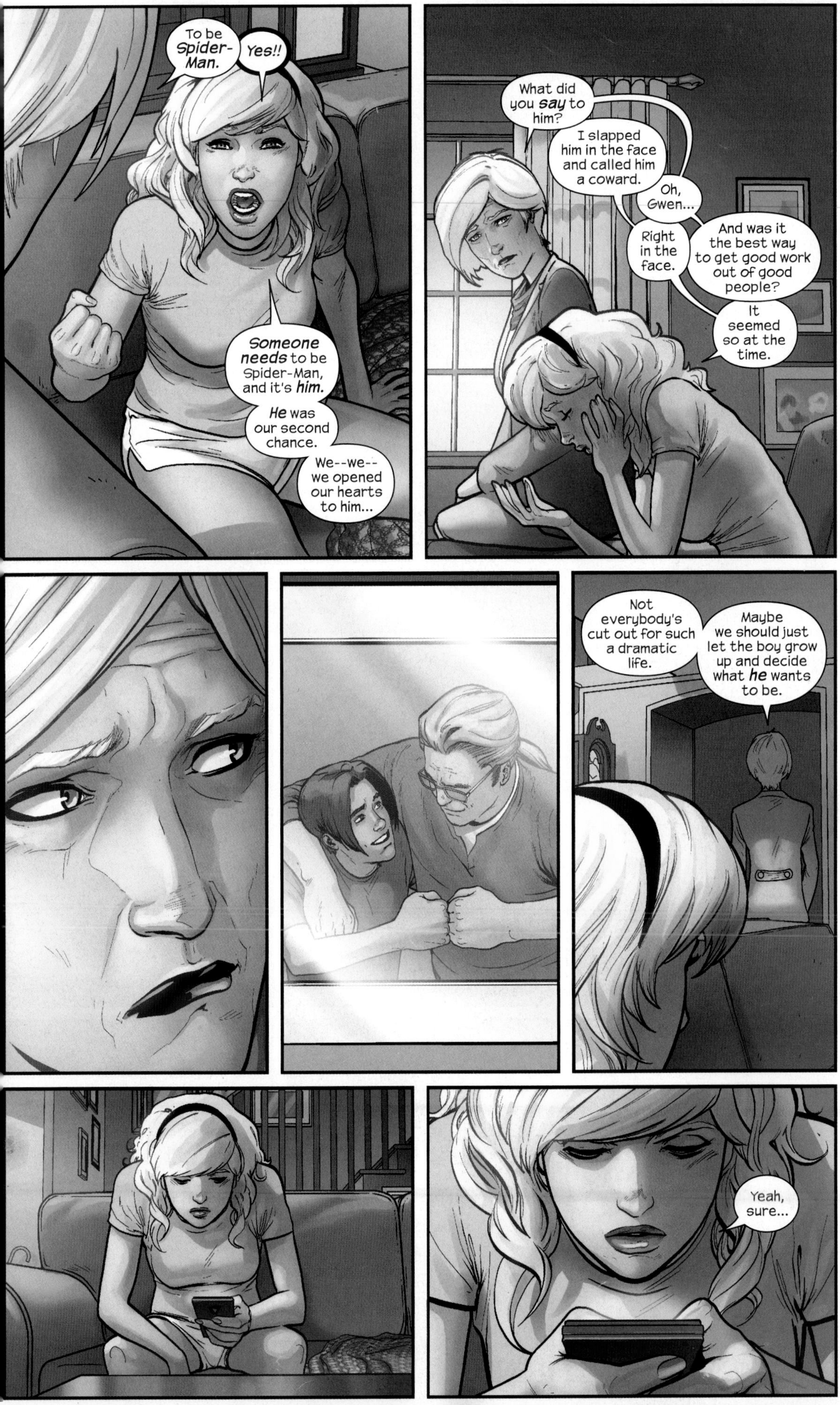
To be Spider-Man.
Yes!!
Someone needs to be Spider-Man, and it's him.
He was our second chance.
We--we--we opened our hearts to him...
What did you say to him?
I slapped him in the face and called him a coward.
Oh, Gwen...
Right in the face.
And was it the best way to get good work out of good people?
It seemed so at the time.
Not everybody's cut out for such a dramatic life.
Maybe we should just let the boy grow up and decide what he wants to be.
Yeah, sure...

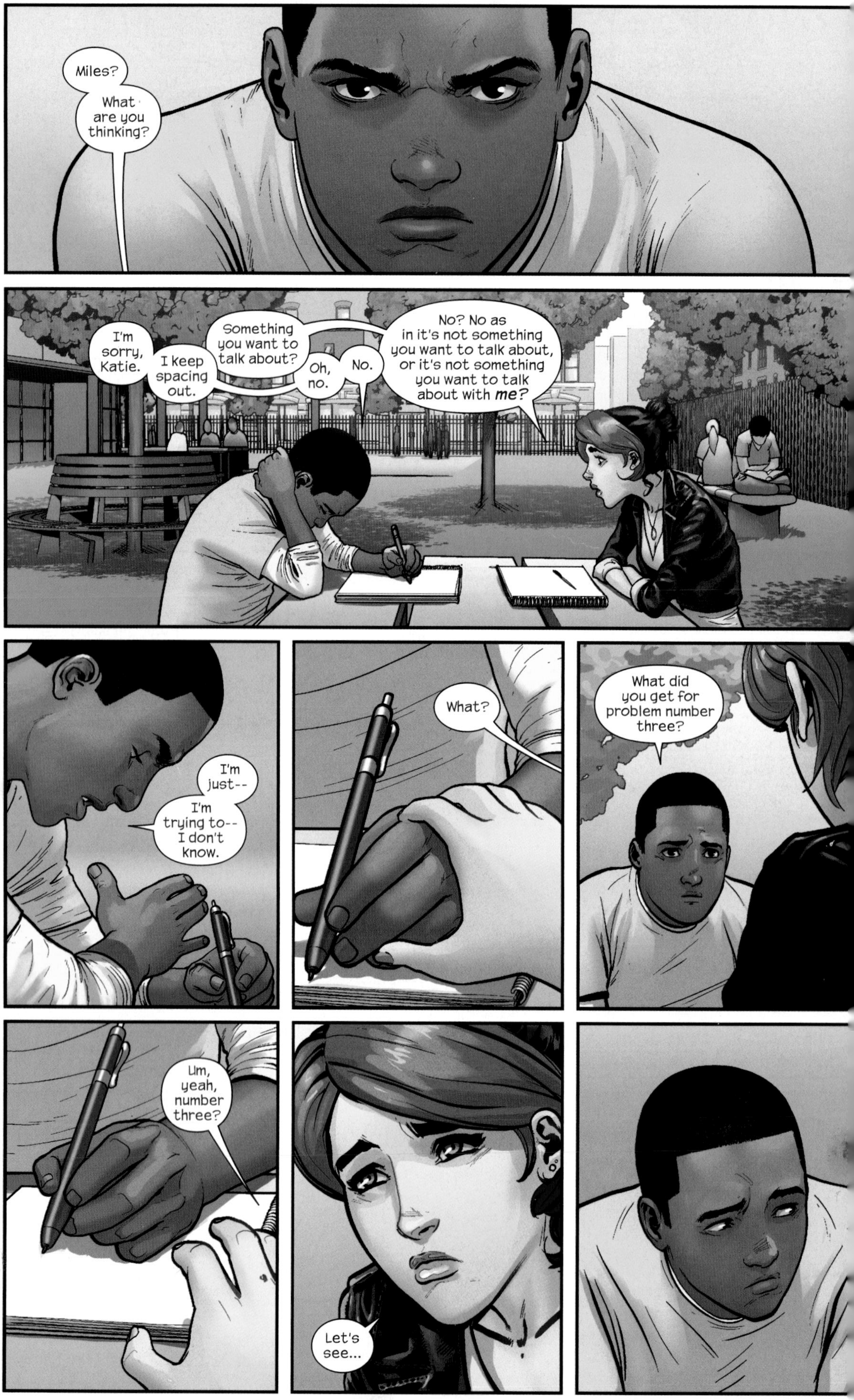
Miles?
What are you thinking?
I'm sorry, Katie.
I keep spacing out.
Something you want to talk about?
Oh, no.
No.
No? No as in it's not something you want to talk about, or it's not something you want to talk about with *me?*
I'm just--
I'm trying to-- I don't know.
What?
What did you get for problem number three?
Um, yeah, number three?
Let's see...

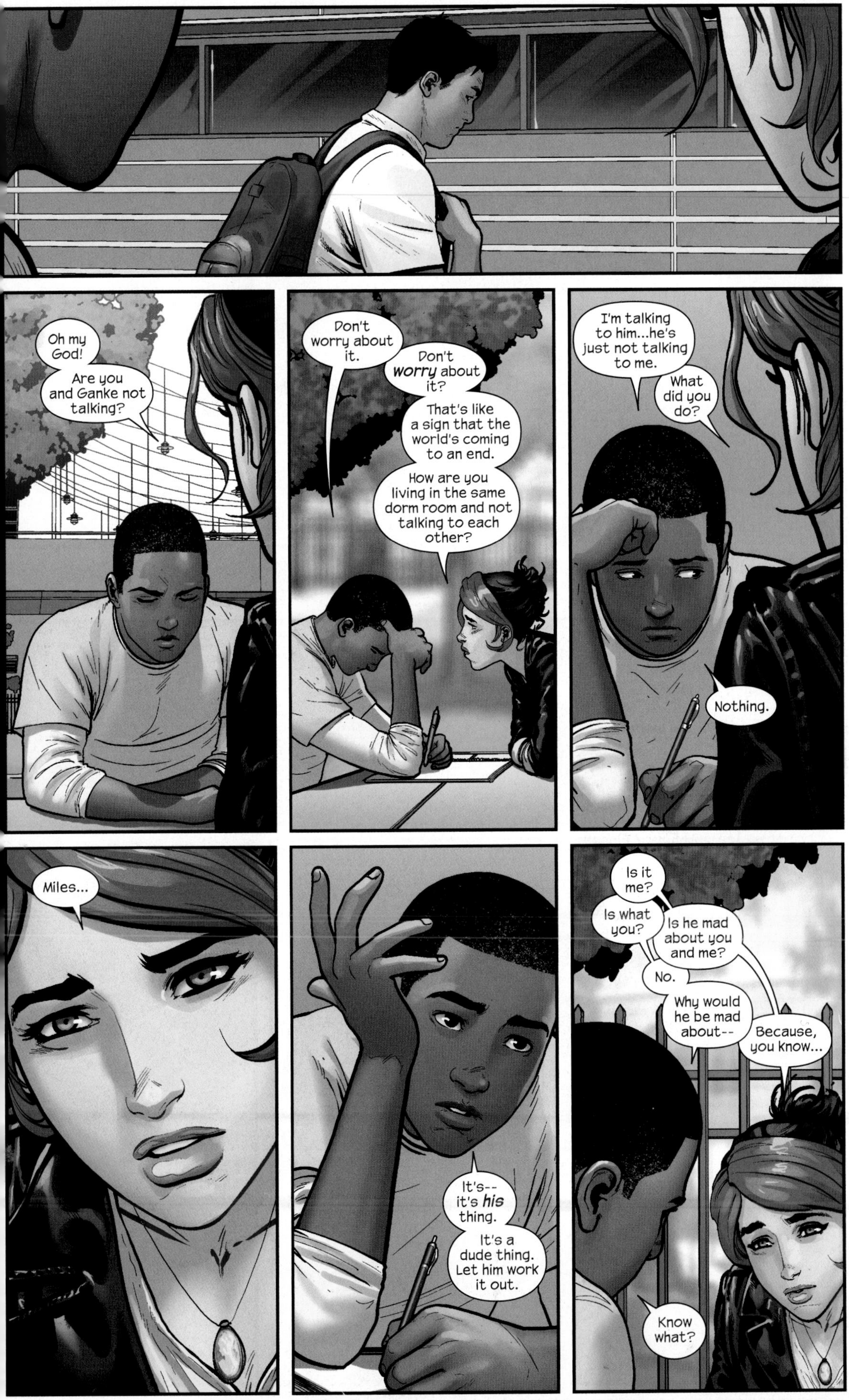

Oh my God!
Are you and Ganke not talking?
Don't worry about it.
Don't *worry* about it?
That's like a sign that the world's coming to an end.
How are you living in the same dorm room and not talking to each other?
I'm talking to him...he's just not talking to me.
What did you do?
Nothing.
Miles...
It's-- it's *his* thing.
It's a dude thing. Let him work it out.
Is it me?
Is what you?
Is he mad about you and me?
No.
Why would he be mad about--
Because, you know...
Know what?

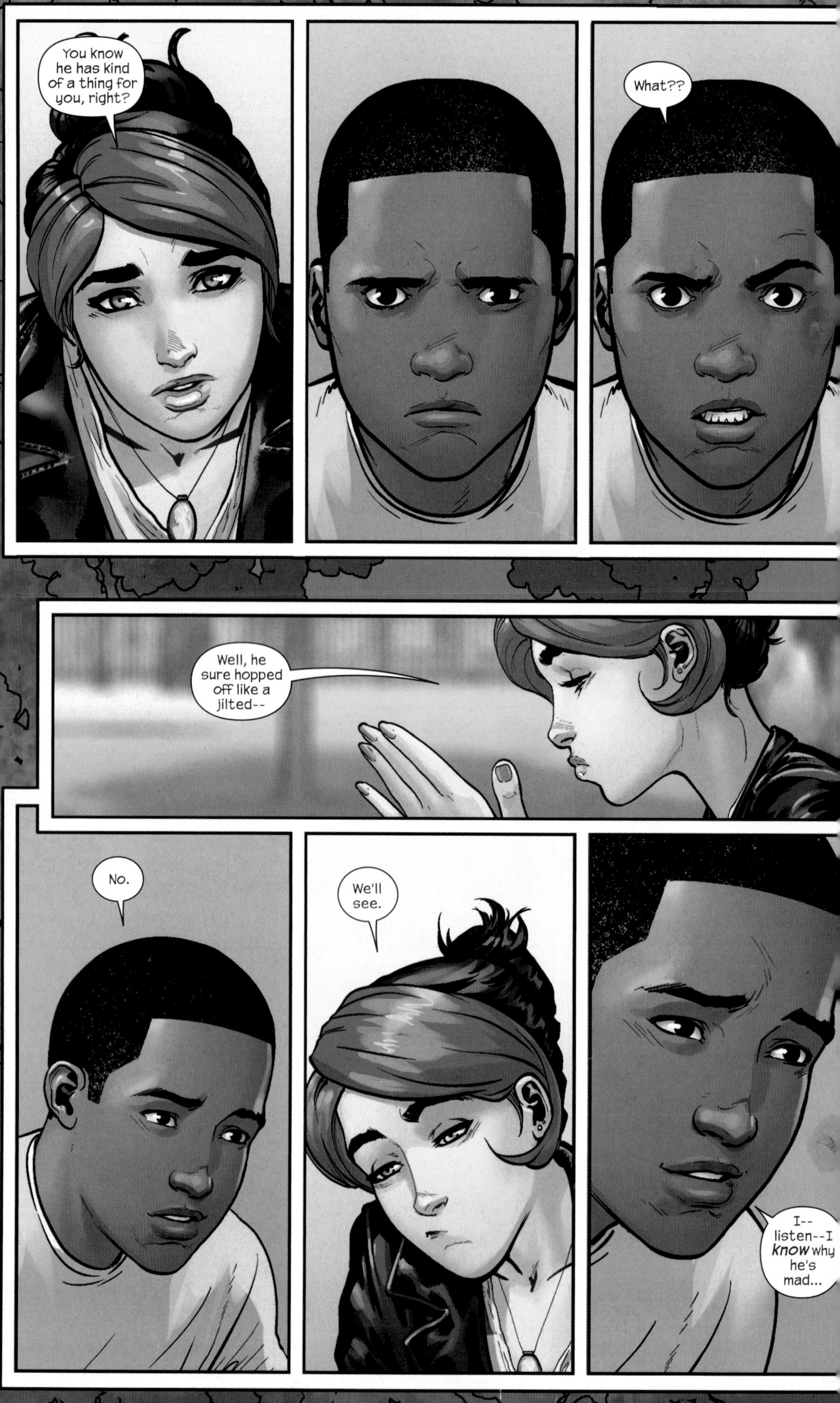
You know he has kind of a thing for you, right?
What??
Well, he sure hopped off like a jilted--
No.
We'll see.
I-- listen--I *KNOW* why he's mad...

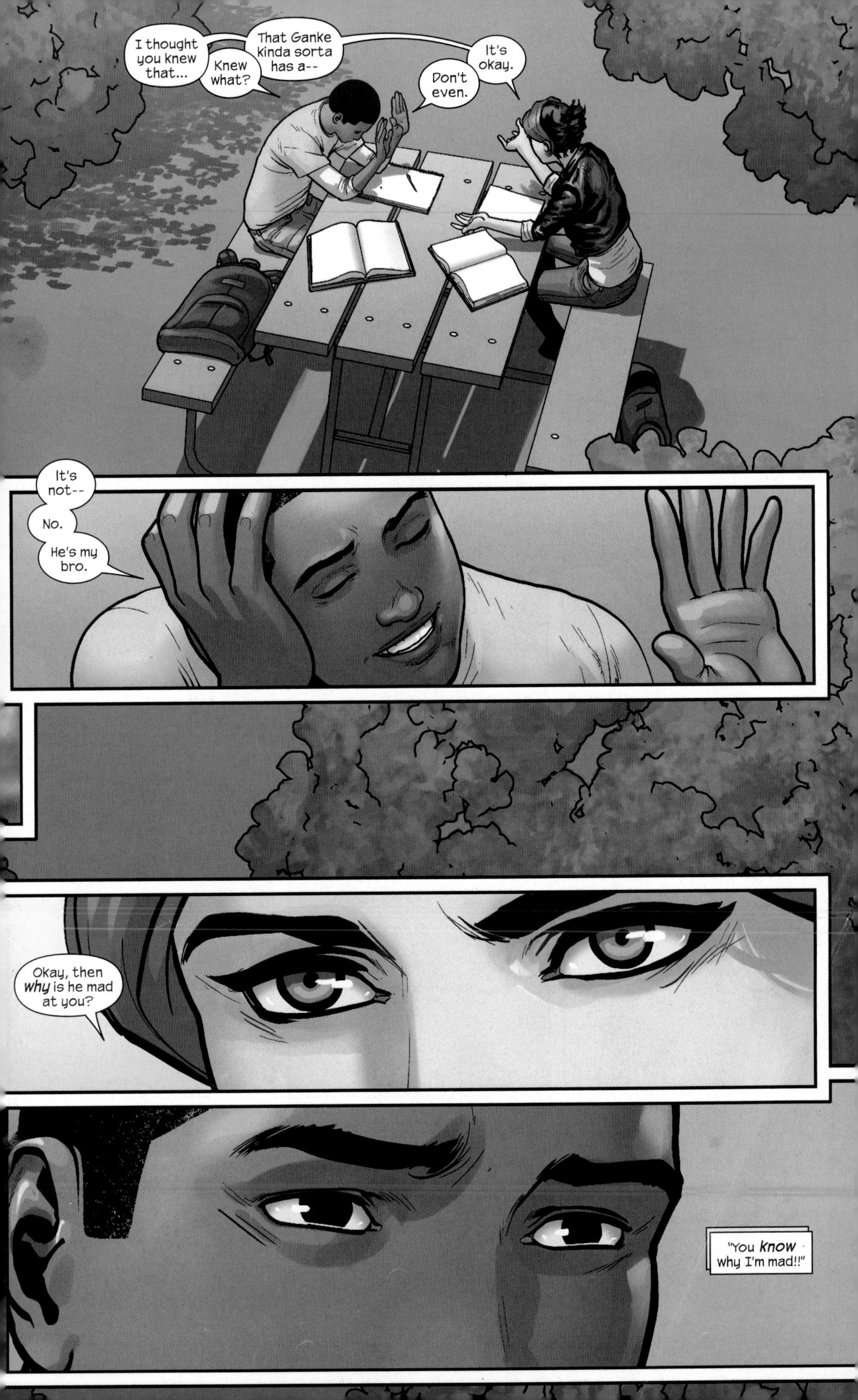

I thought you knew that...
Knew what?
That Ganke kinda sorta has a--
Don't even.
It's okay.
It's not--
No.
He's my bro.
Okay, then *why* is he mad at you?
"You *know* why I'm mad!!"

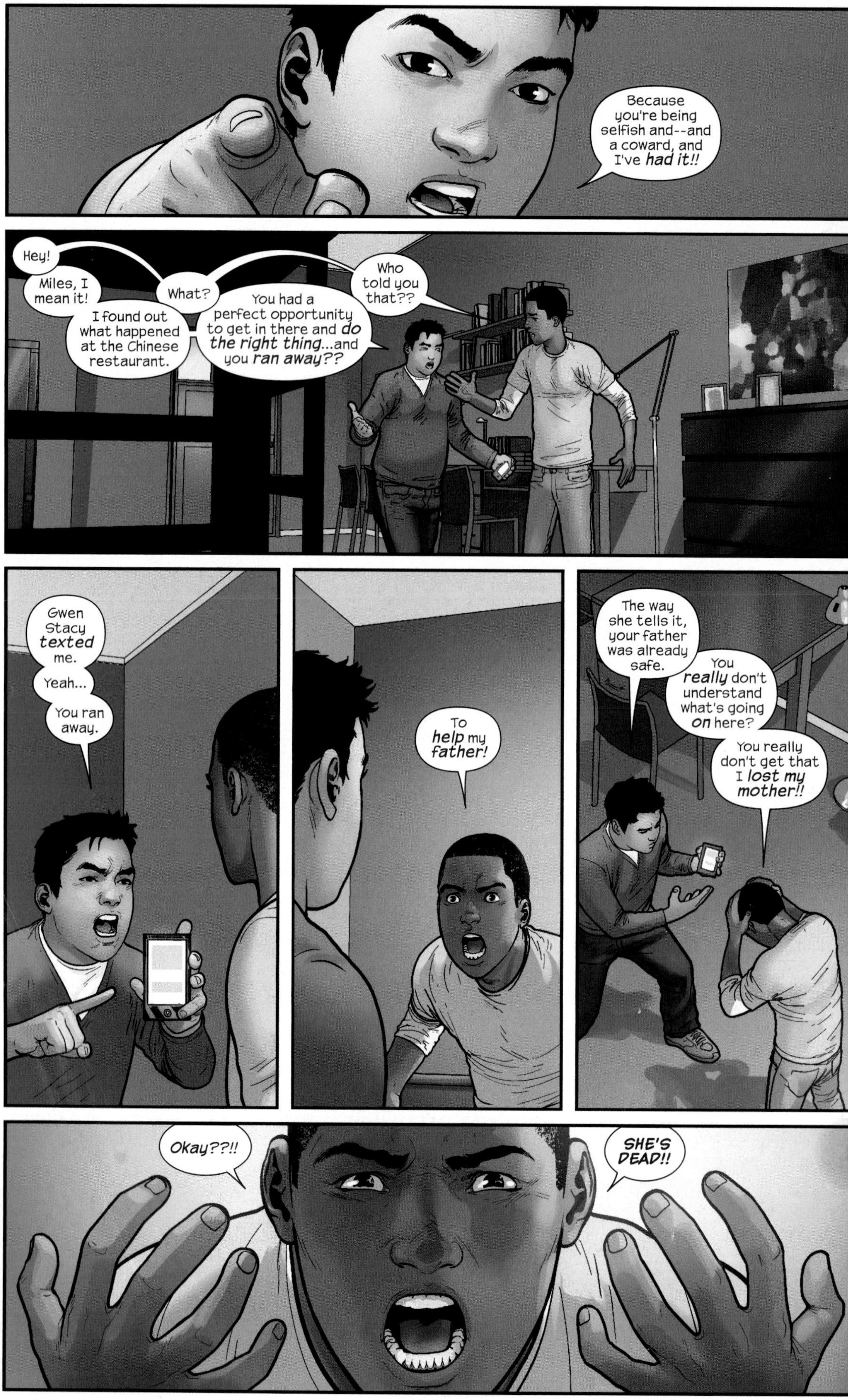
Because you're being selfish and--and a coward, and I've *had it!!*
Hey!
Miles, I mean it!
What?
I found out what happened at the Chinese restaurant.
You had a perfect opportunity to get in there and *do the right thing*...and you *ran away??*
Who told you that??
Gwen Stacy *texted* me.
Yeah...
You ran away.
To *help* my *father!*
The way she tells it, your father was already safe.
You *really* don't understand what's going *on* here?
You really don't get that I *lost my mother!!*
Okay??!!
SHE'S DEAD!!

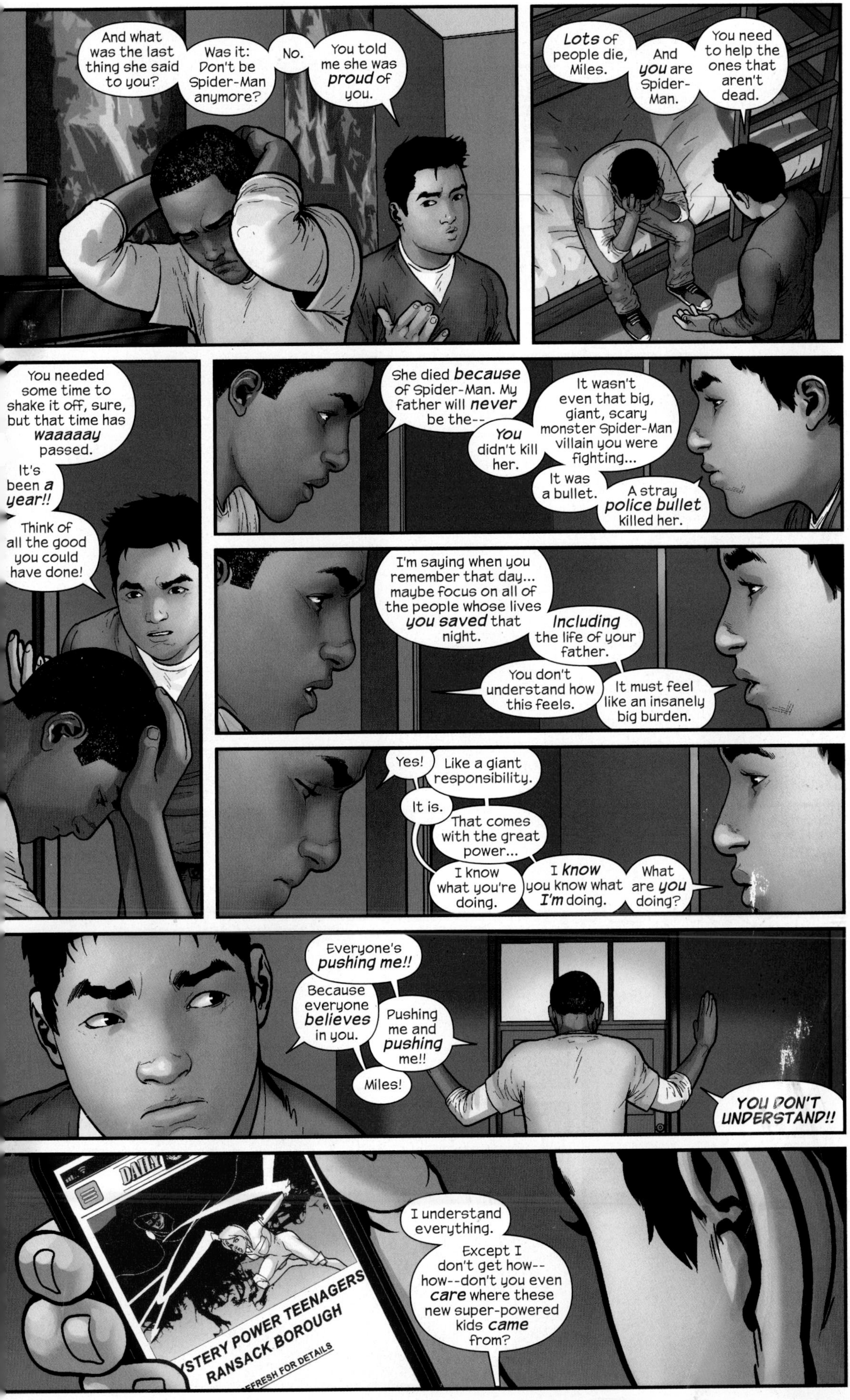
And what was the last thing she said to you?
Was it: Don't be Spider-Man anymore?
No.
You told me she was *proud* of you.
Lots of people die, Miles.
And *you* are Spider-Man.
You need to help the ones that aren't dead.
You needed some time to shake it off, sure, but that time has *waaaaay* passed.
It's been *a year!!*
Think of all the good you could have done!
She died *because* of Spider-Man. My father will *never* be the--
You didn't kill her.
It wasn't even that big, giant, scary monster Spider-Man villain you were fighting...
It was a bullet.
A stray *police bullet* killed her.
I'm saying when you remember that day... maybe focus on all of the people whose lives *you saved* that night.
Including the life of your father.
You don't understand how this feels.
It must feel like an insanely big burden.
Yes!
Like a giant responsibility.
It is.
That comes with the great power...
I know what you're doing.
I *know* you know what *I'm* doing.
What are *you* doing?
Everyone's *pushing me!!*
Because everyone *believes* in you.
Pushing me and *pushing* me!!
Miles!
YOU DON'T UNDERSTAND!!
YSTERY POWER TEENAGERS
RANSACK BOROUGH
EFRESH FOR DETAILS
I understand everything.
Except I don't get how--how--don't you even *care* where these new super-powered kids *came* from?

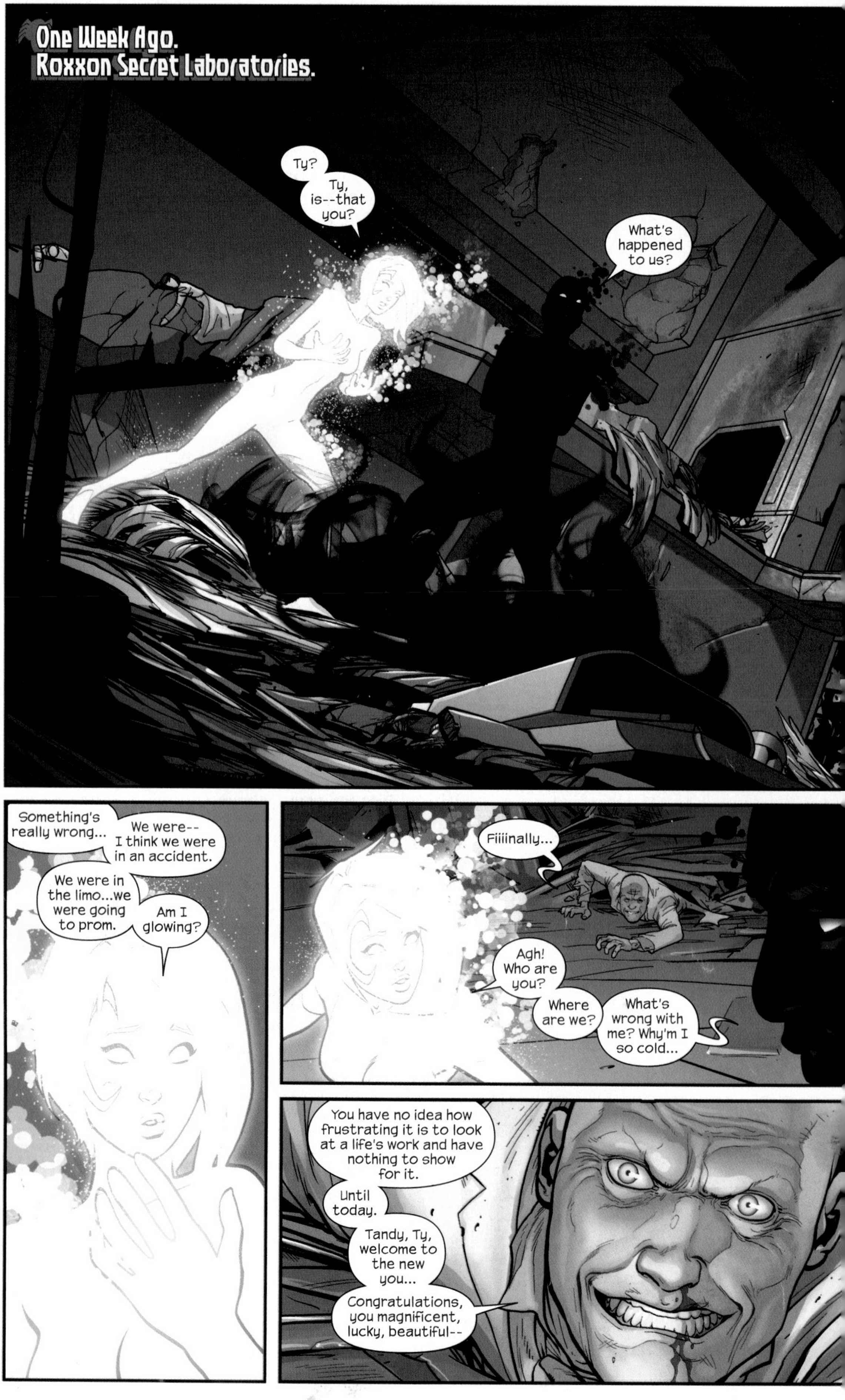
One Week Ago.
Roxxon Secret Laboratories.
Ty?
Ty, is--that you?
What's happened to us?
Something's really wrong...
We were-- I think we were in an accident.
We were in the limo...we were going to prom.
Am I glowing?
Fiiiinally...
Agh! Who are you?
Where are we?
What's wrong with me? Why'm I so cold...
You have no idea how frustrating it is to look at a life's work and have nothing to show for it.
Until today.
Tandy, Ty, welcome to the new you...
Congratulations, you magnificent, lucky, beautiful--

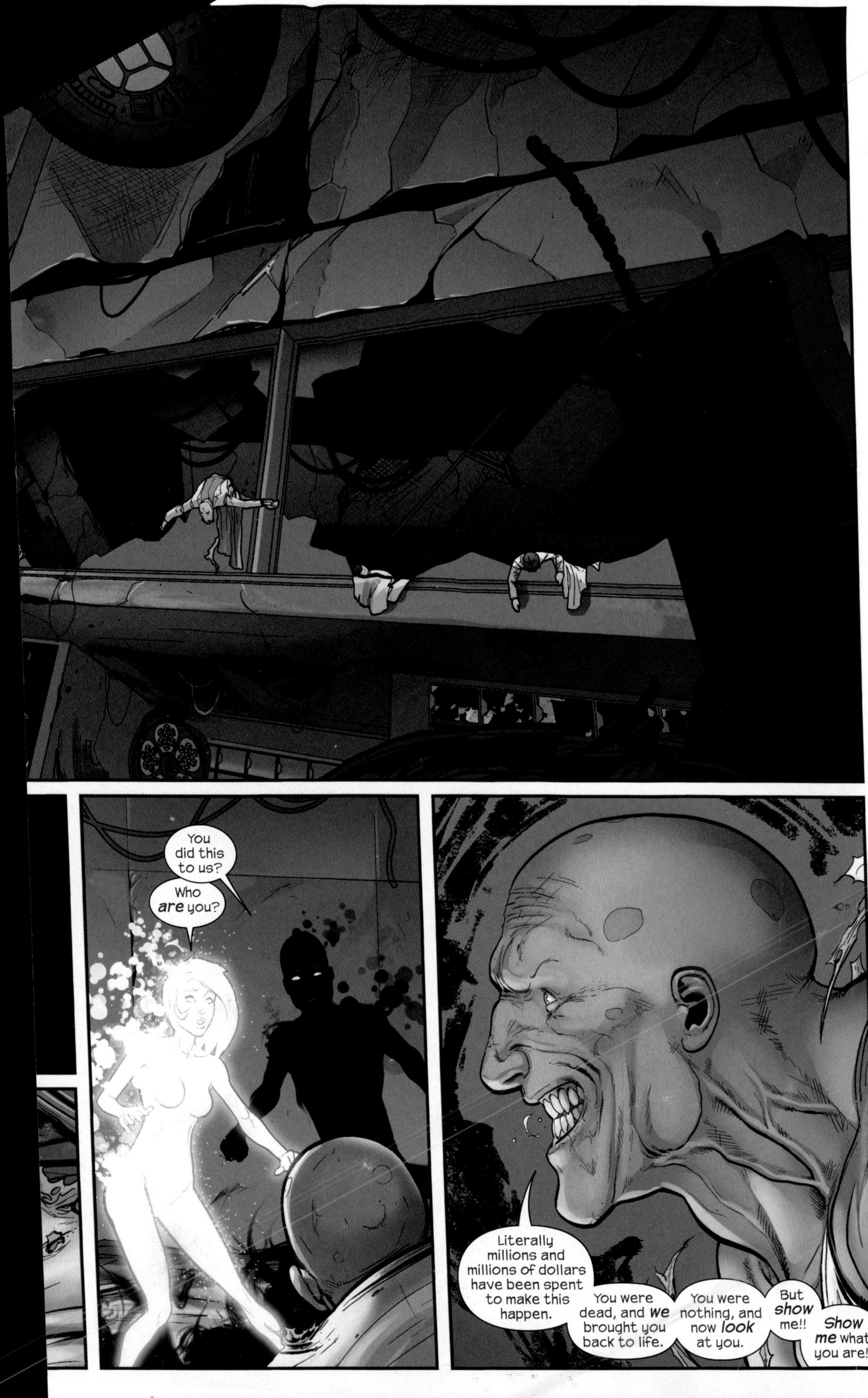
You did this to us?
Who are you?
Literally millions and millions of dollars have been spent to make this happen.
You were dead, and we brought you back to life.
You were nothing, and now look at you.
But show me!!
Show me what you are!!

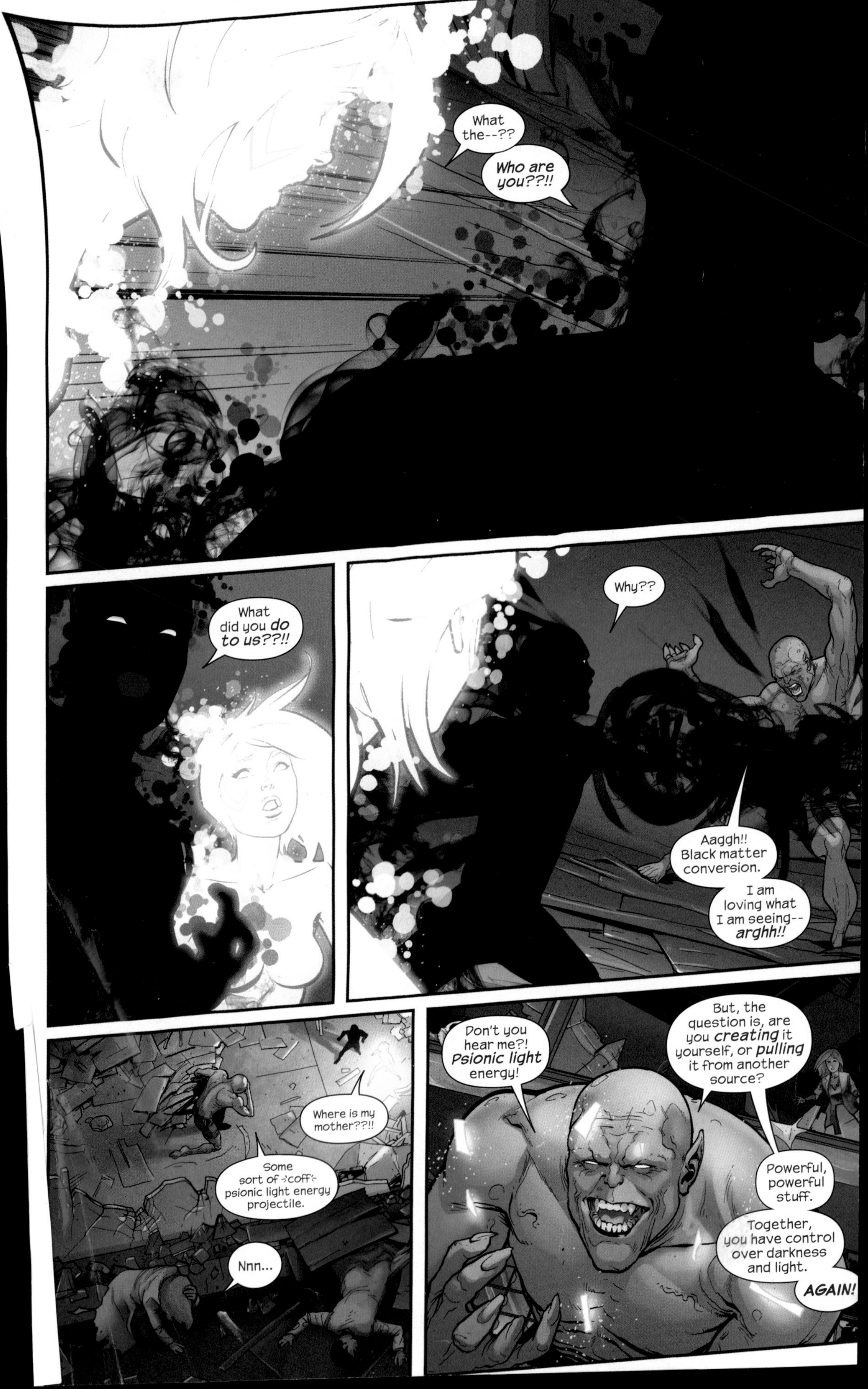
What the--??
Who are you??!!
What did you do to us??!!
Why??
Aaggh!! Black matter conversion.
I am loving what I am seeing-- arghh!!
Where is my mother??!!
Some sort of -coff- psionic light energy projectile.
Nnn...
Don't you hear me?! Psionic light energy!
But, the question is, are you creating it yourself, or pulling it from another source?
Powerful, powerful stuff.
Together, you have control over darkness and light.
AGAIN!

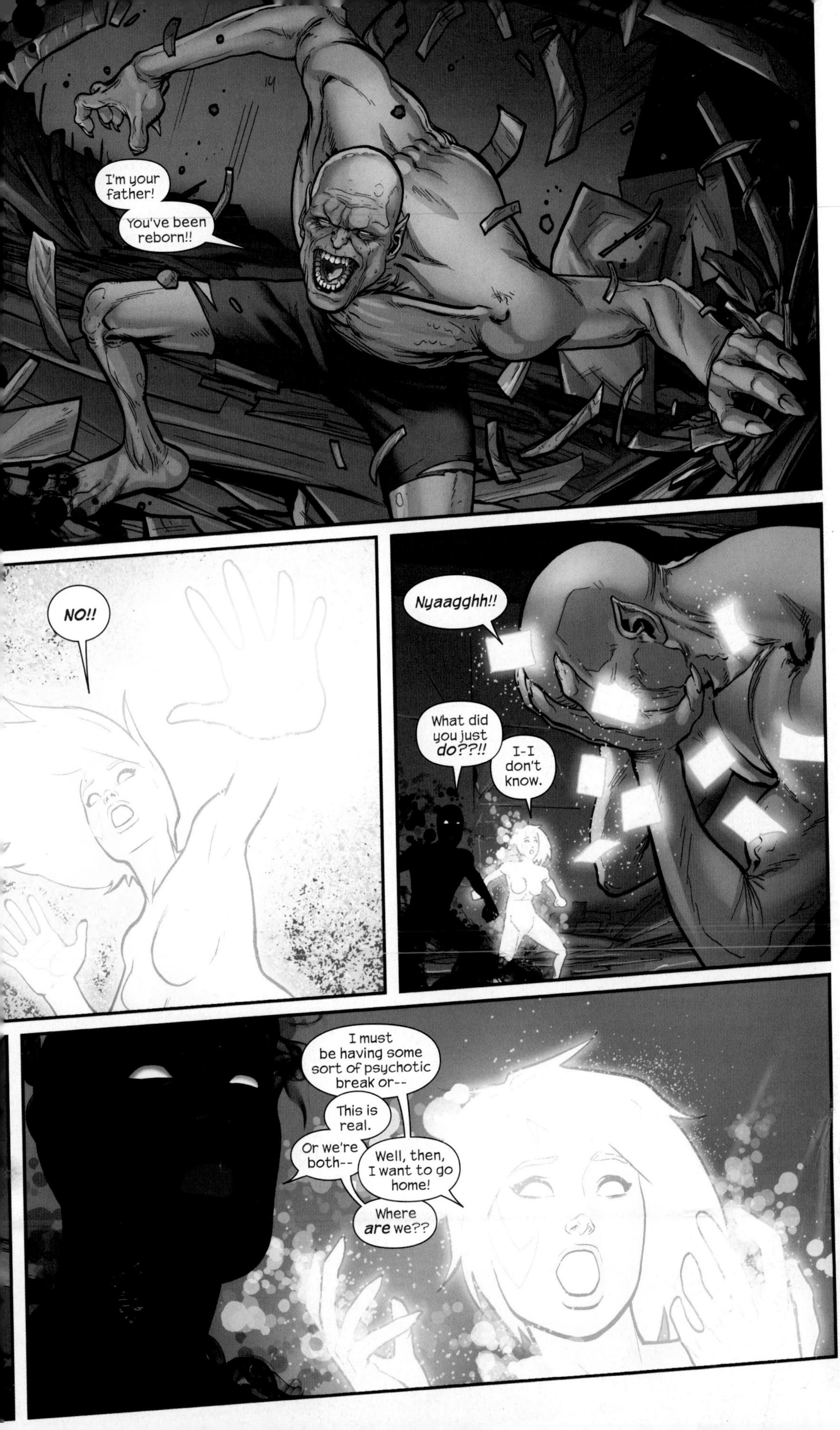

I'm your father!
You've been reborn!!
NO!!
Nyaagghh!!
What did you just do??!!
I-I don't know.
I must be having some sort of psychotic break or--
This is real.
Or we're both--
Well, then, I want to go home!
Where are we??

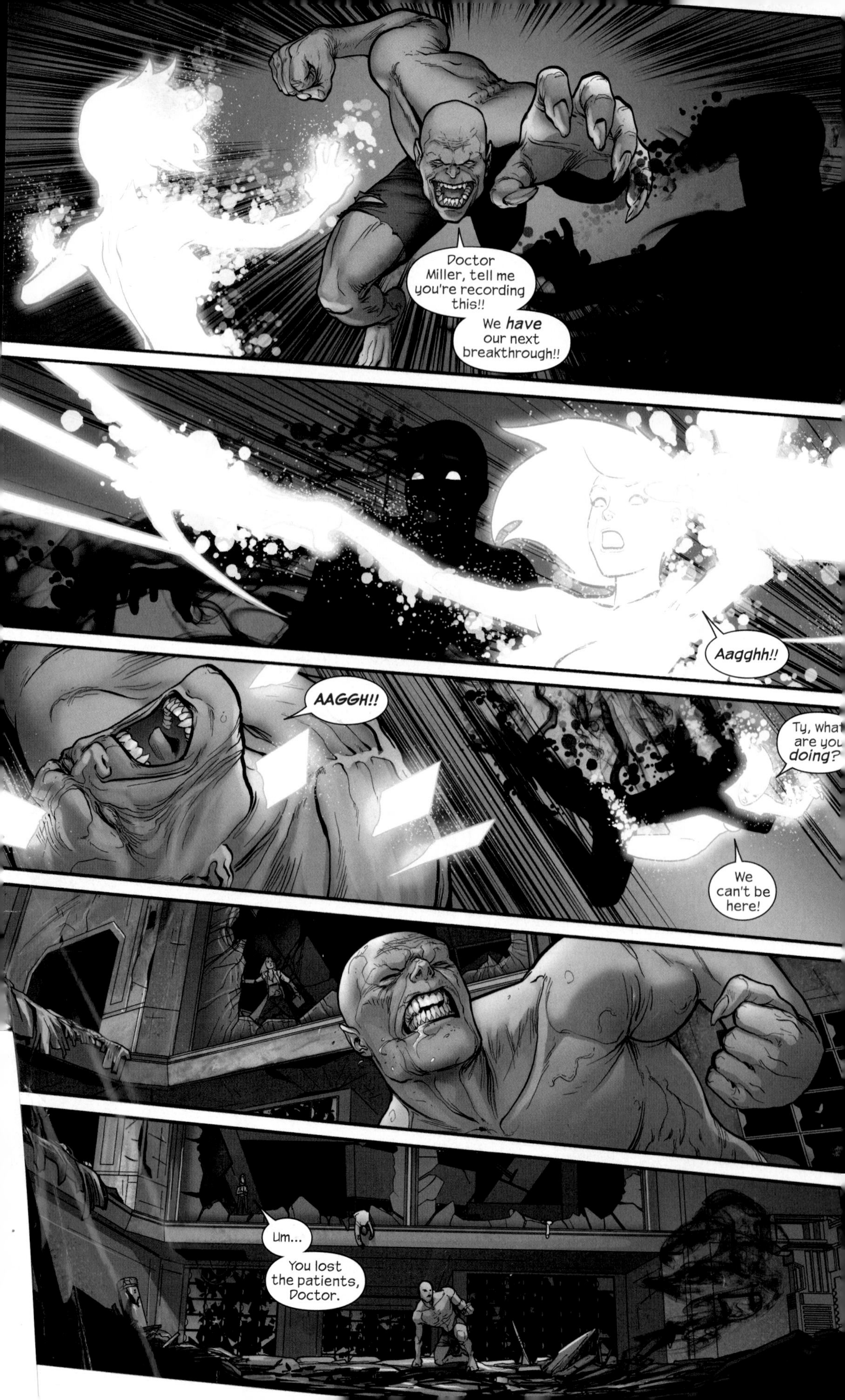
Doctor Miller, tell me you're recording this!!
We **have** our next breakthrough!!
Aagghh!!
AAGGH!!
Ty, what are you **doing**?
We can't be here!
Um...
You lost the patients, Doctor.

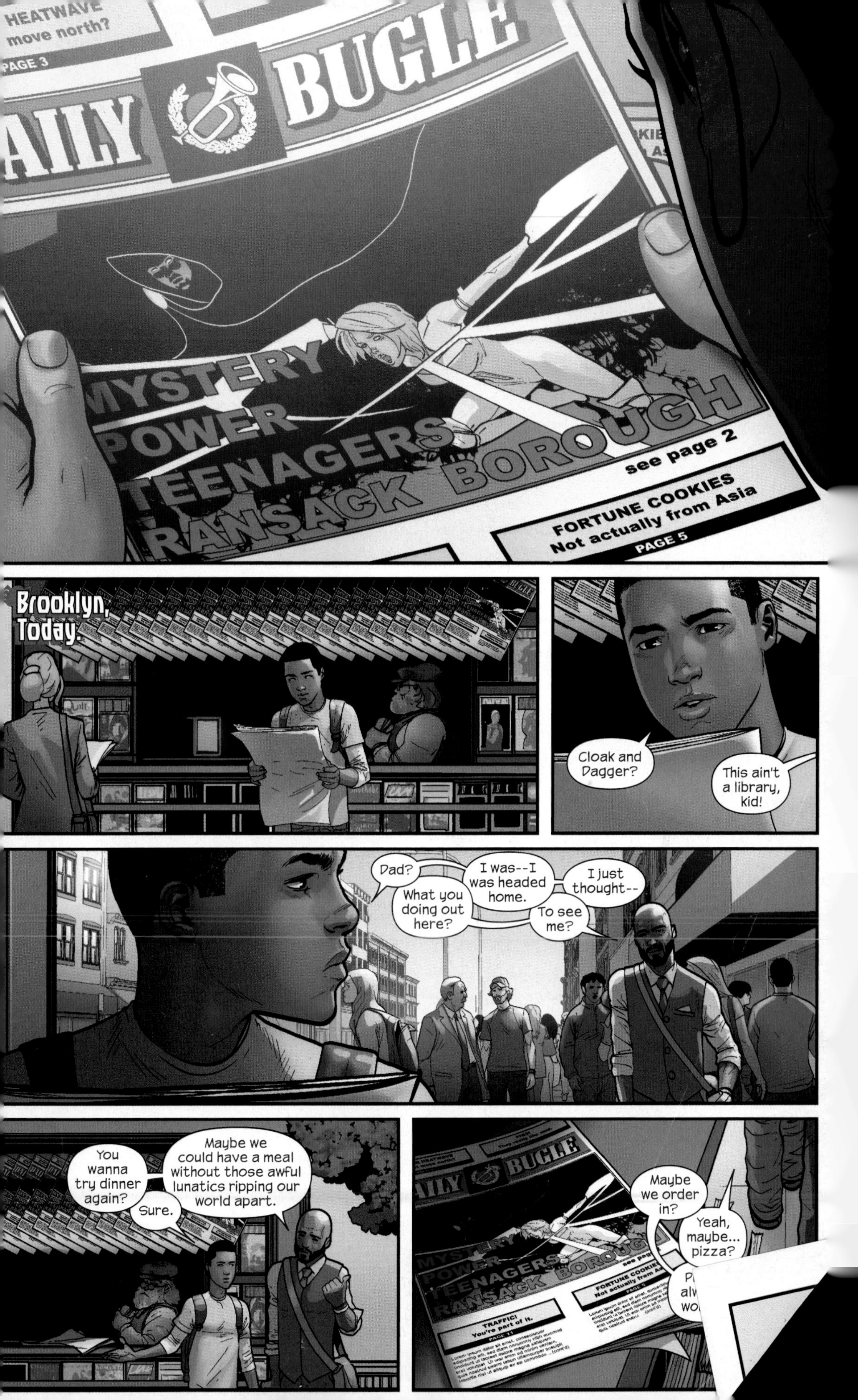

HEATWAVE
move north?
PAGE 3
AILY BUGLE
MYSTERY POWER TEENAGERS RANSACK BOROUGH
see page 2
FORTUNE COOKIES
Not actually from Asia
PAGE 5
Brooklyn, Today.
Cloak and Dagger?
This ain't a library, kid!
Dad?
What you doing out here?
I was--I was headed home.
To see me?
I just thought--
You wanna try dinner again?
Sure.
Maybe we could have a meal without those awful lunatics ripping our world apart.
Maybe we order in?
Yeah, maybe... pizza?
TRAFFIC!
You're part of it.
PAGE 11

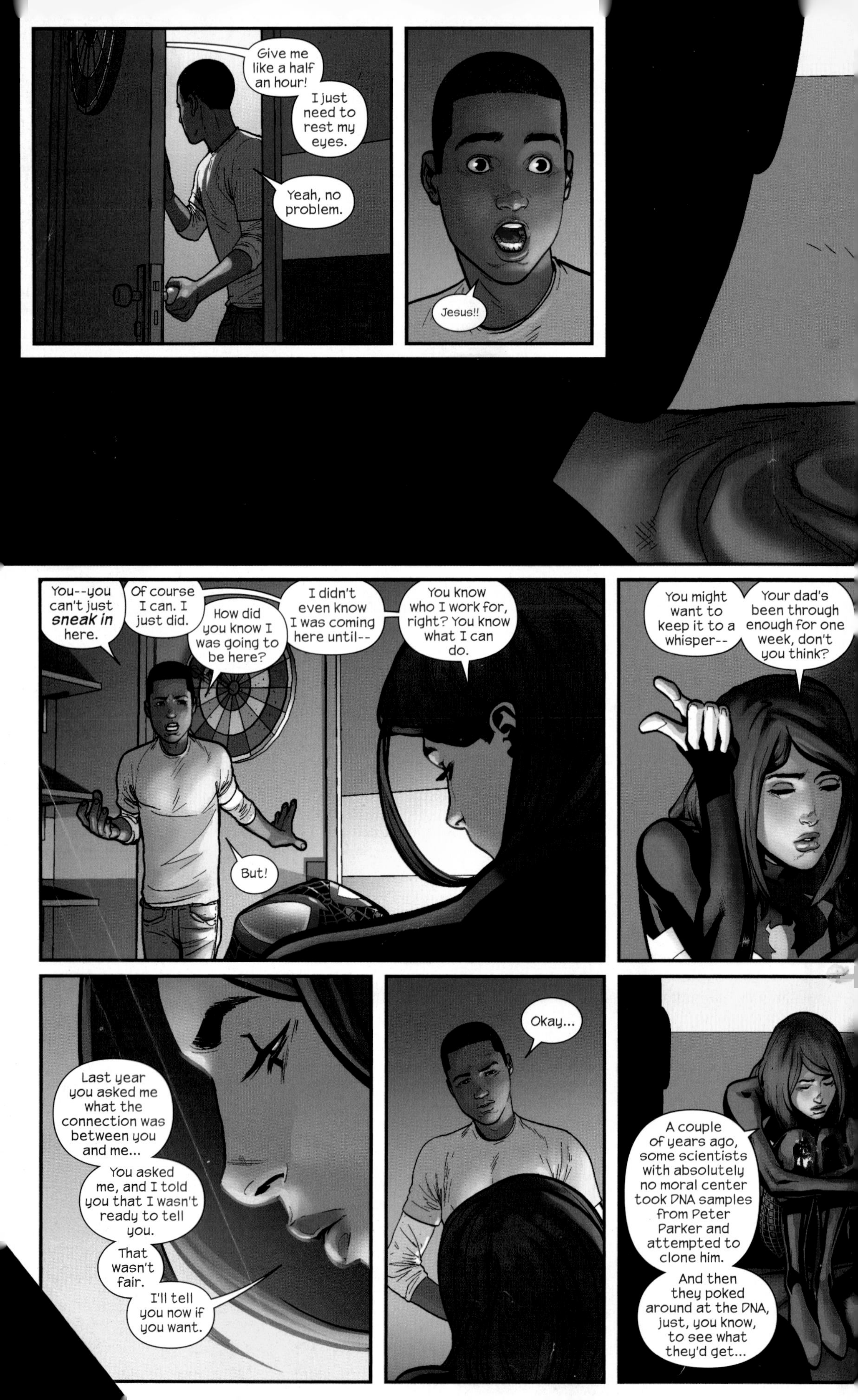

Give me like a half an hour!
I just need to rest my eyes.
Yeah, no problem.
Jesus!!
You--you can't just *sneak in* here.
Of course I can. I just did.
How did you know I was going to be here?
I didn't even know I was coming here until--
You know who I work for, right? You know what I can do.
But!
You might want to keep it to a whisper--
Your dad's been through enough for one week, don't you think?
Last year you asked me what the connection was between you and me...
You asked me, and I told you that I wasn't ready to tell you.
That wasn't fair.
I'll tell you now if you want.
Okay...
A couple of years ago, some scientists with absolutely no moral center took DNA samples from Peter Parker and attempted to clone him.
And then they poked around at the DNA, just, you know, to see what they'd get...

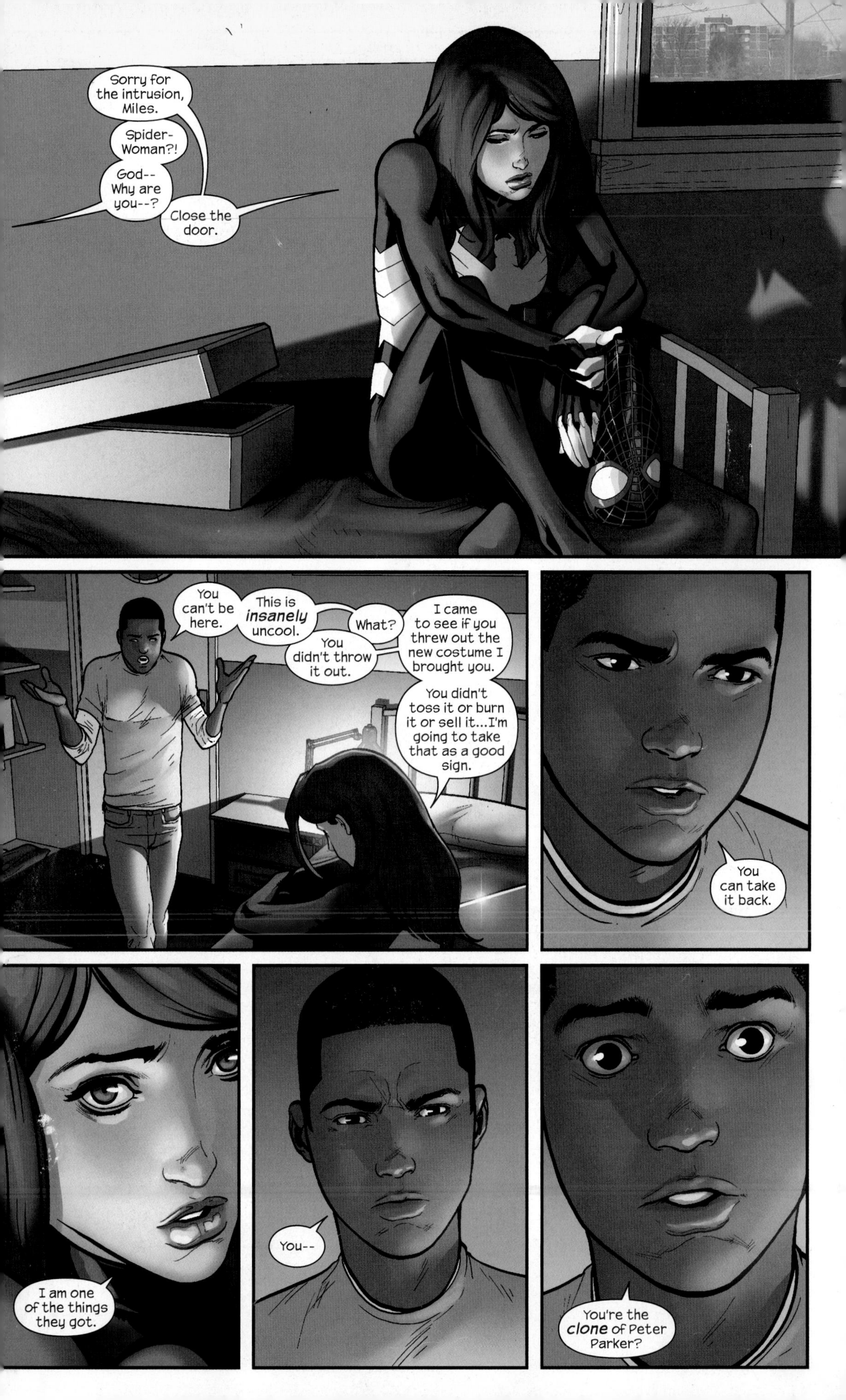
Sorry for the intrusion, Miles.
Spider-Woman?!
God-- Why are you--?
Close the door.
You can't be here.
This is *insanely* uncool.
What?
I came to see if you threw out the new costume I brought you.
You didn't throw it out.
You didn't toss it or burn it or sell it...I'm going to take that as a good sign.
You can take it back.
I am one of the things they got.
You--
You're the *clone* of Peter Parker?

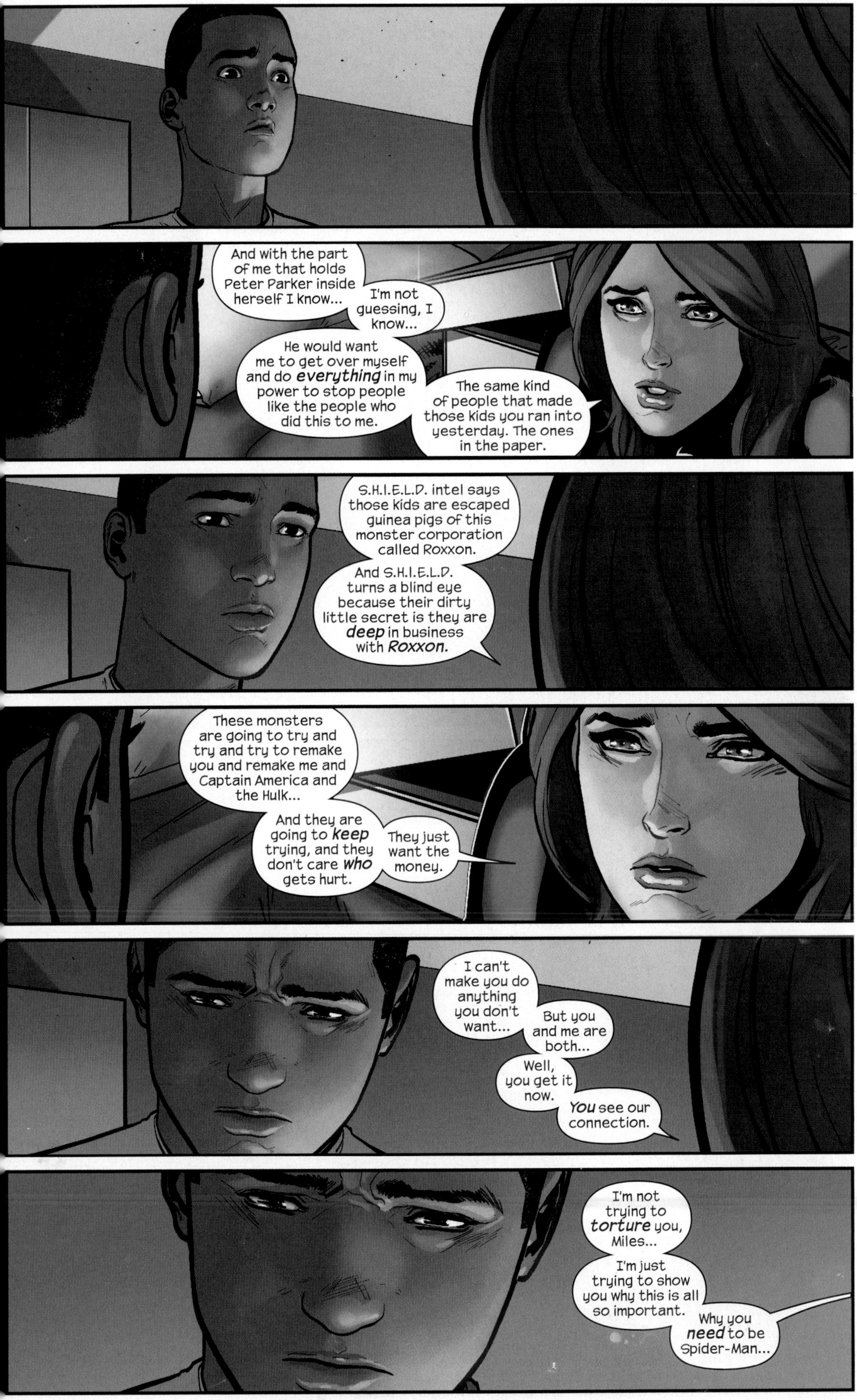

And with the part of me that holds Peter Parker inside herself I know...
I'm not guessing, I know...
He would want me to get over myself and do everything in my power to stop people like the people who did this to me.
The same kind of people that made those kids you ran into yesterday. The ones in the paper.
S.H.I.E.L.D. intel says those kids are escaped guinea pigs of this monster corporation called Roxxon.
And S.H.I.E.L.D. turns a blind eye because their dirty little secret is they are deep in business with Roxxon.
These monsters are going to try and try and try to remake you and remake me and Captain America and the Hulk...
And they are going to keep trying, and they don't care who gets hurt.
They just want the money.
I can't make you do anything you don't want...
But you and me are both...
Well, you get it now.
You see our connection.
I'm not trying to torture you, Miles...
I'm just trying to show you why this is all so important.
Why you need to be Spider-Man...

A doctor!! *I need a doctor!!*
Look at you.
Look what you can do.
Why there needs to be a Spider-Man.
had to go back to school. Forgot about a test. Call you tomorrow.

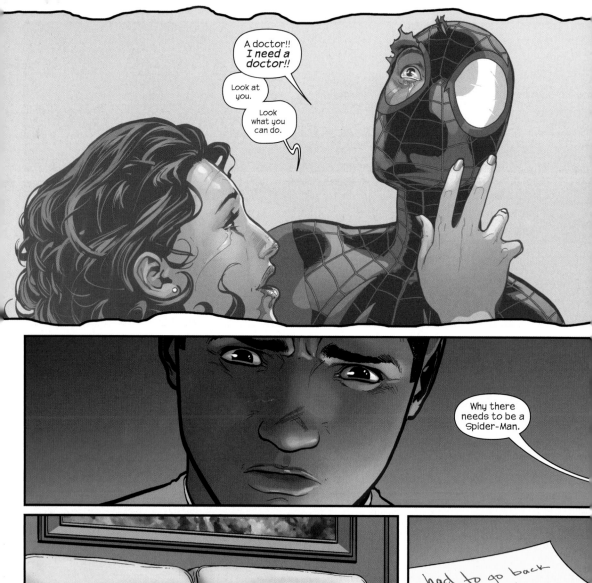

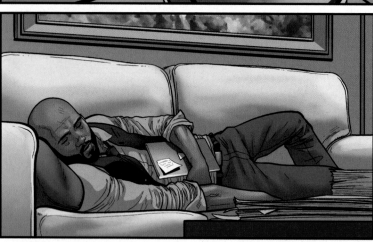

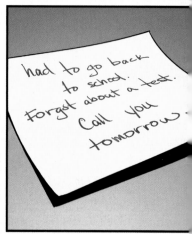

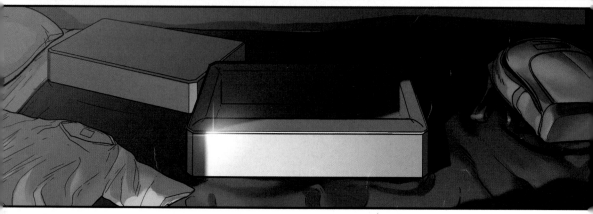

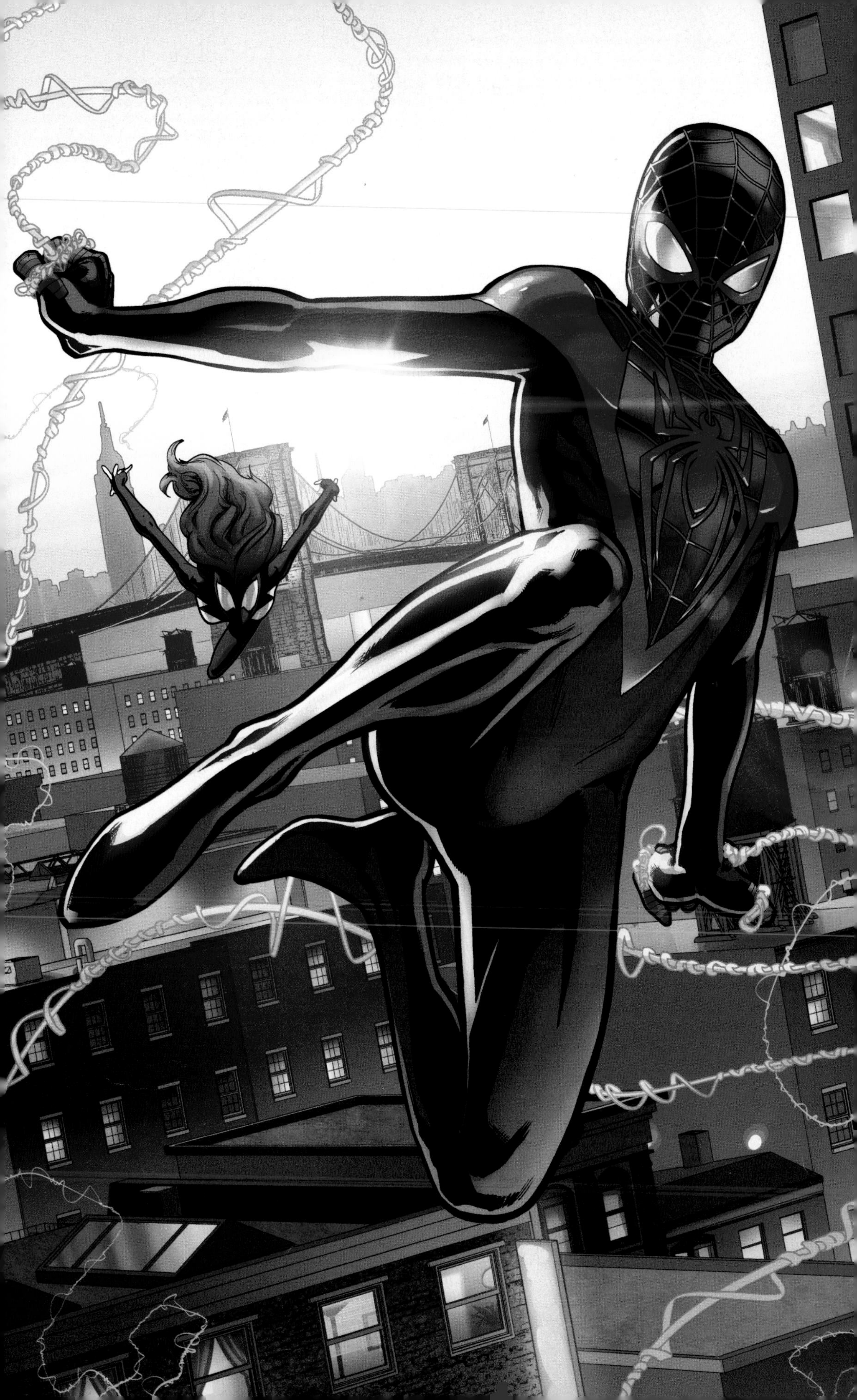

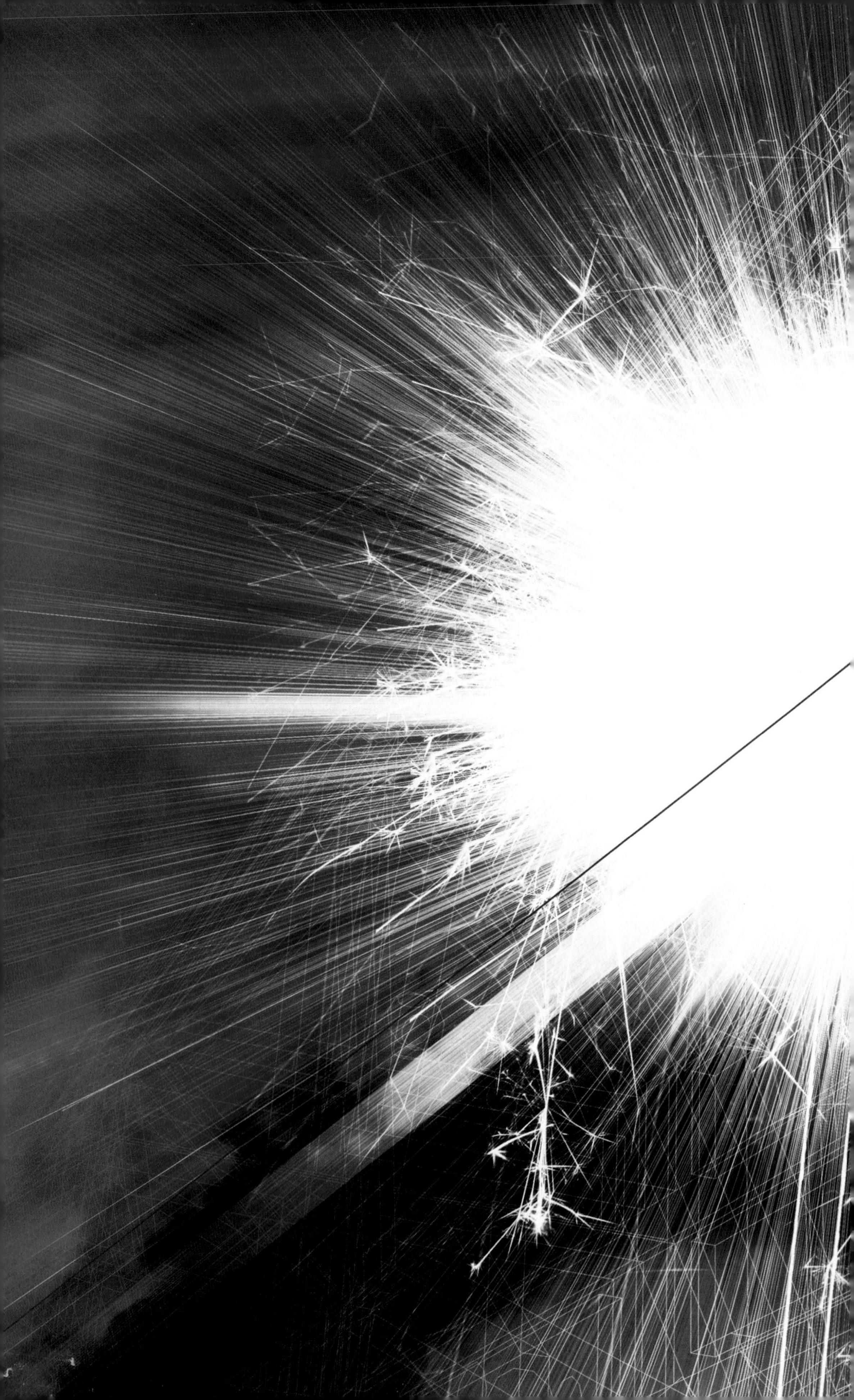

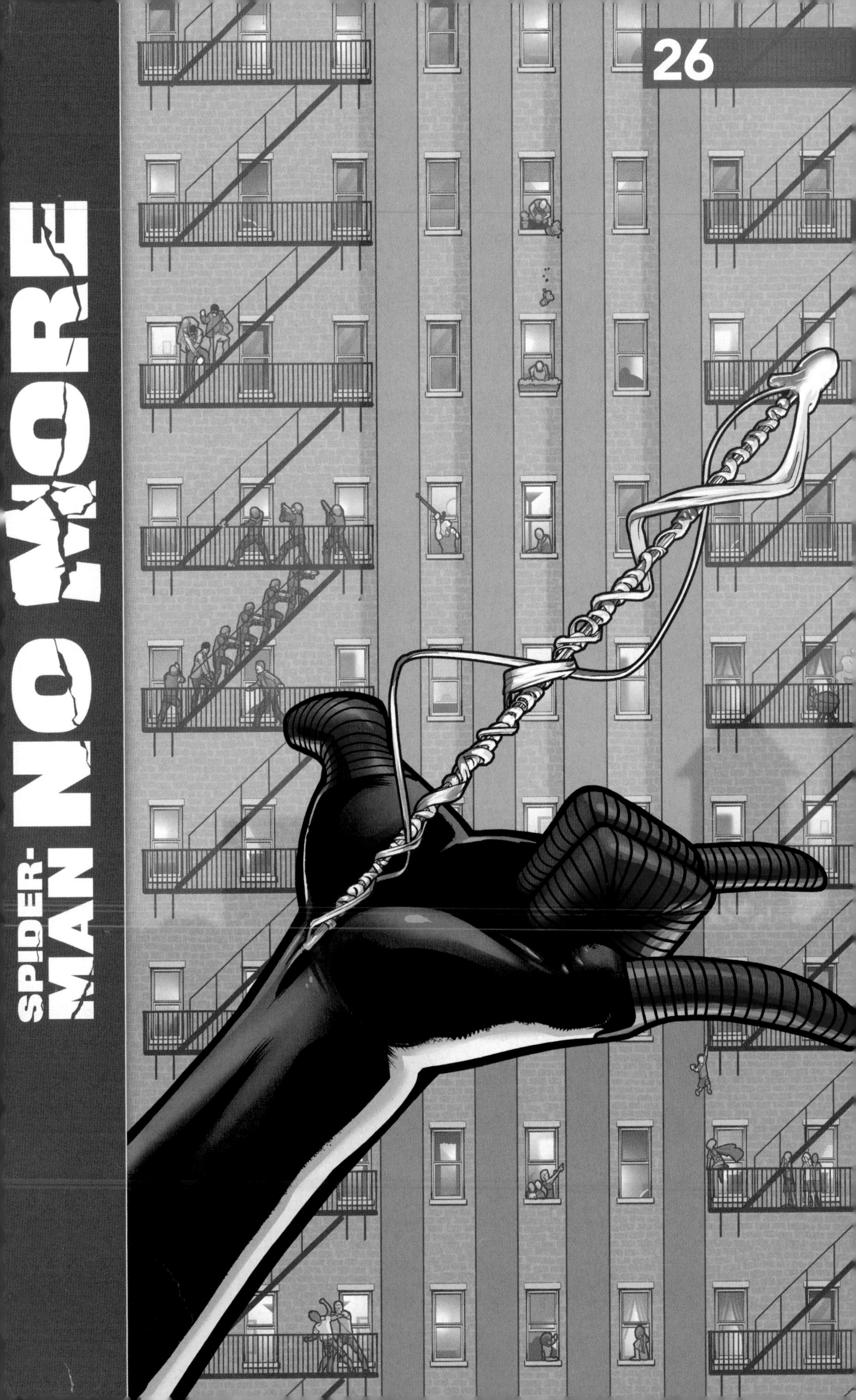
SPIDER-MAN NO MORE
26

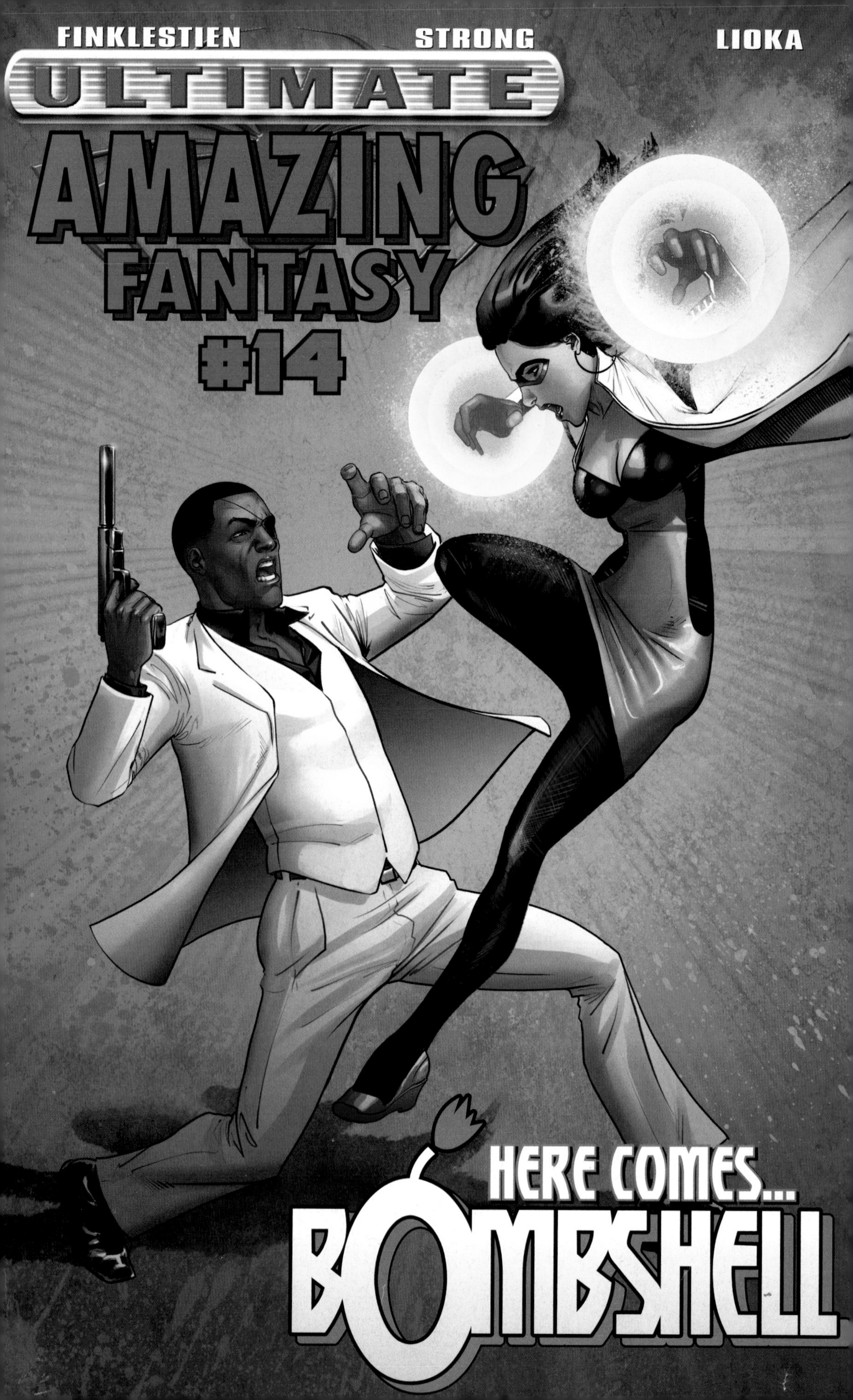
FINKLESTIEN
STRONG
LIOKA
ULTIMATE
AMAZING
FANTASY
#14
HERE COMES...
BOMBSHELL

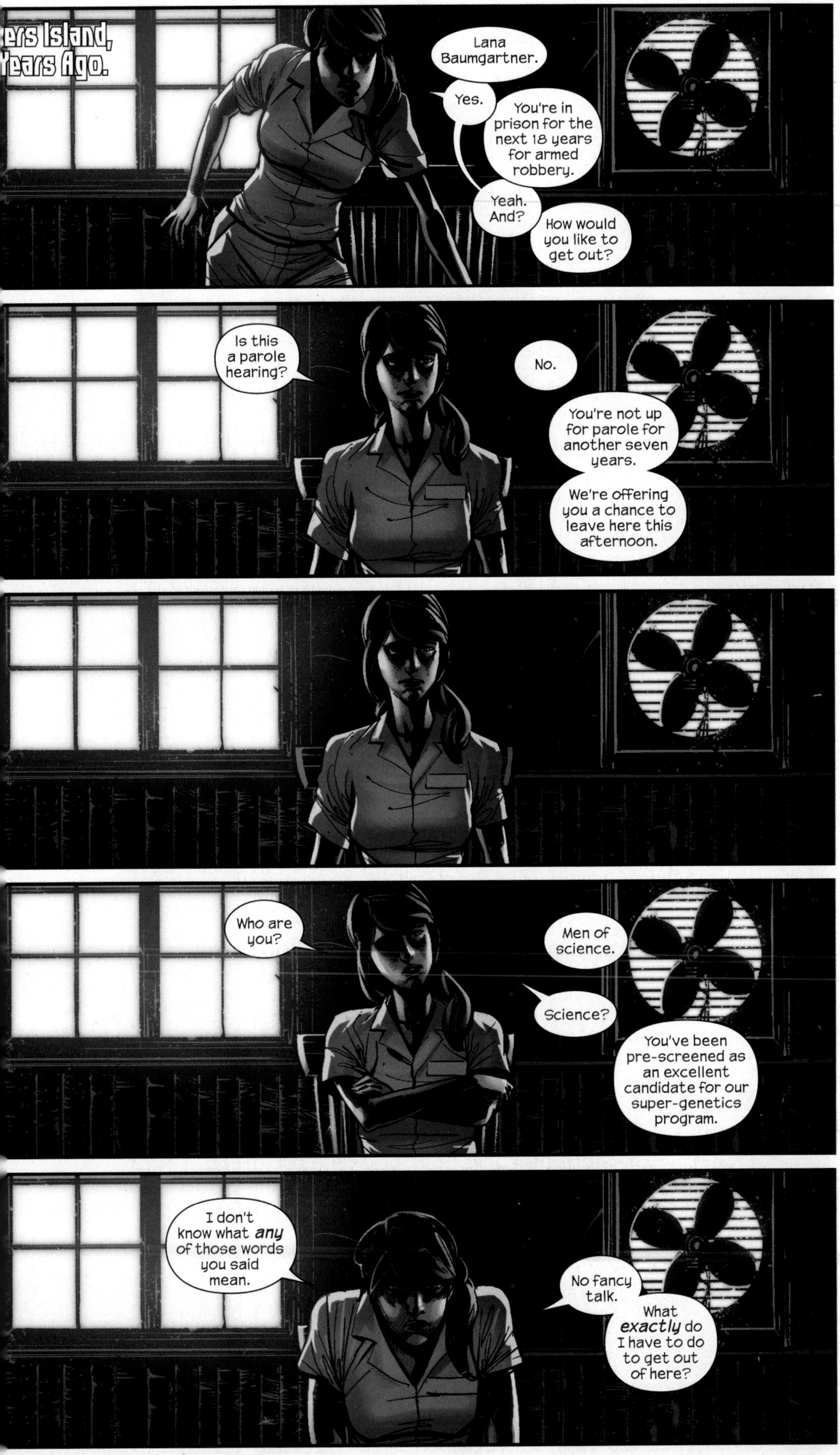

...ers Island, ...Years Ago.
Lana Baumgartner.
Yes.
You're in prison for the next 18 years for armed robbery.
Yeah. And?
How would you like to get out?
Is this a parole hearing?
No.
You're not up for parole for another seven years.
We're offering you a chance to leave here this afternoon.
Who are you?
Men of science.
Science?
You've been pre-screened as an excellent candidate for our super-genetics program.
I don't know what *any* of those words you said mean.
No fancy talk.
What *exactly* do I have to do to get out of here?

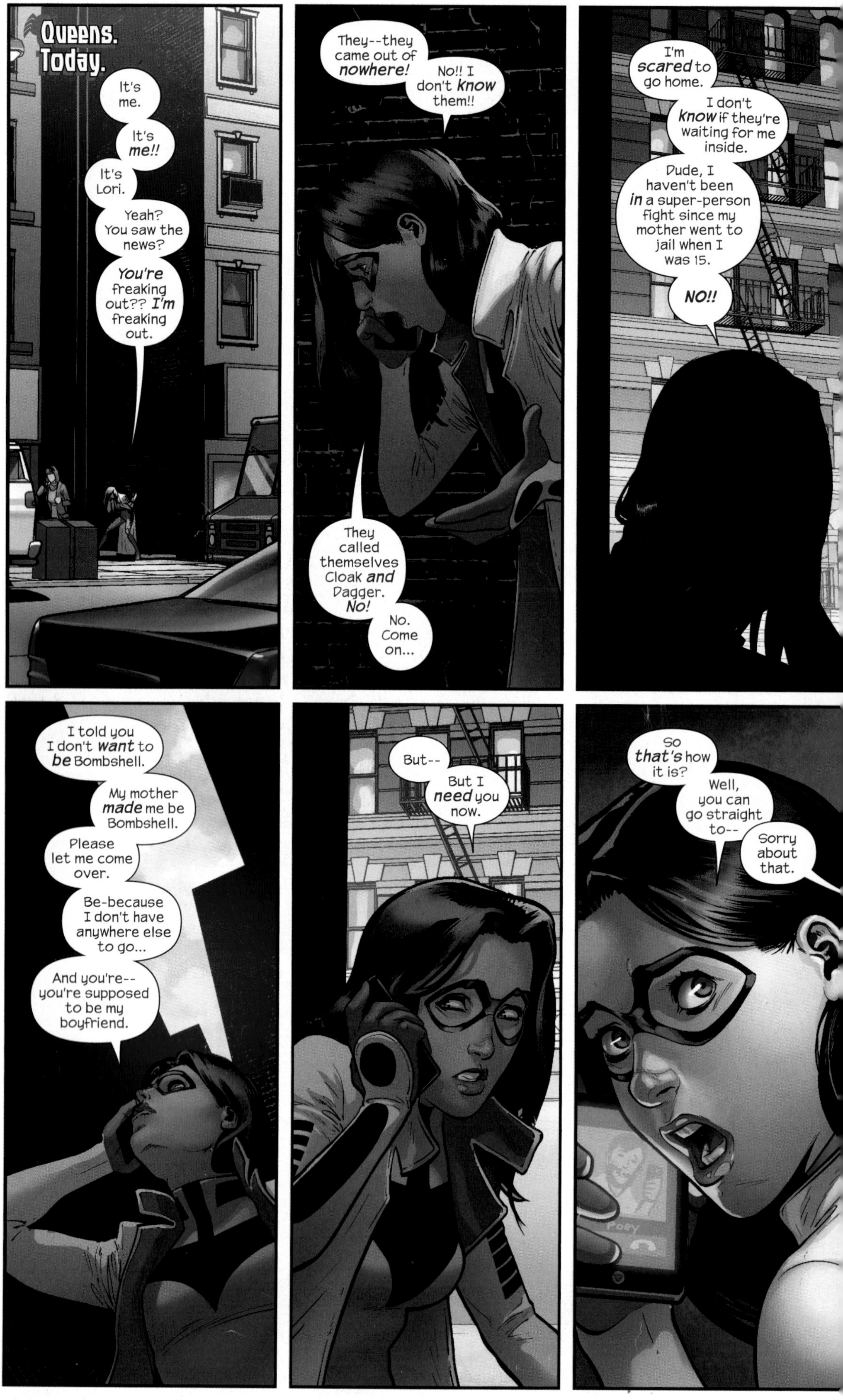
Queens. Today.
It's me.
It's me!!
It's Lori.
Yeah? You saw the news?
You're freaking out?? I'm freaking out.
They--they came out of nowhere!
No!! I don't know them!!
They called themselves Cloak and Dagger. No!
No. Come on...
I'm scared to go home.
I don't know if they're waiting for me inside.
Dude, I haven't been in a super-person fight since my mother went to jail when I was 15.
NO!!
I told you I don't want to be Bombshell.
My mother made me be Bombshell.
Please let me come over.
Be-because I don't have anywhere else to go...
And you're--you're supposed to be my boyfriend.
But--
But I need you now.
So that's how it is?
Well, you can go straight to--
Sorry about that.

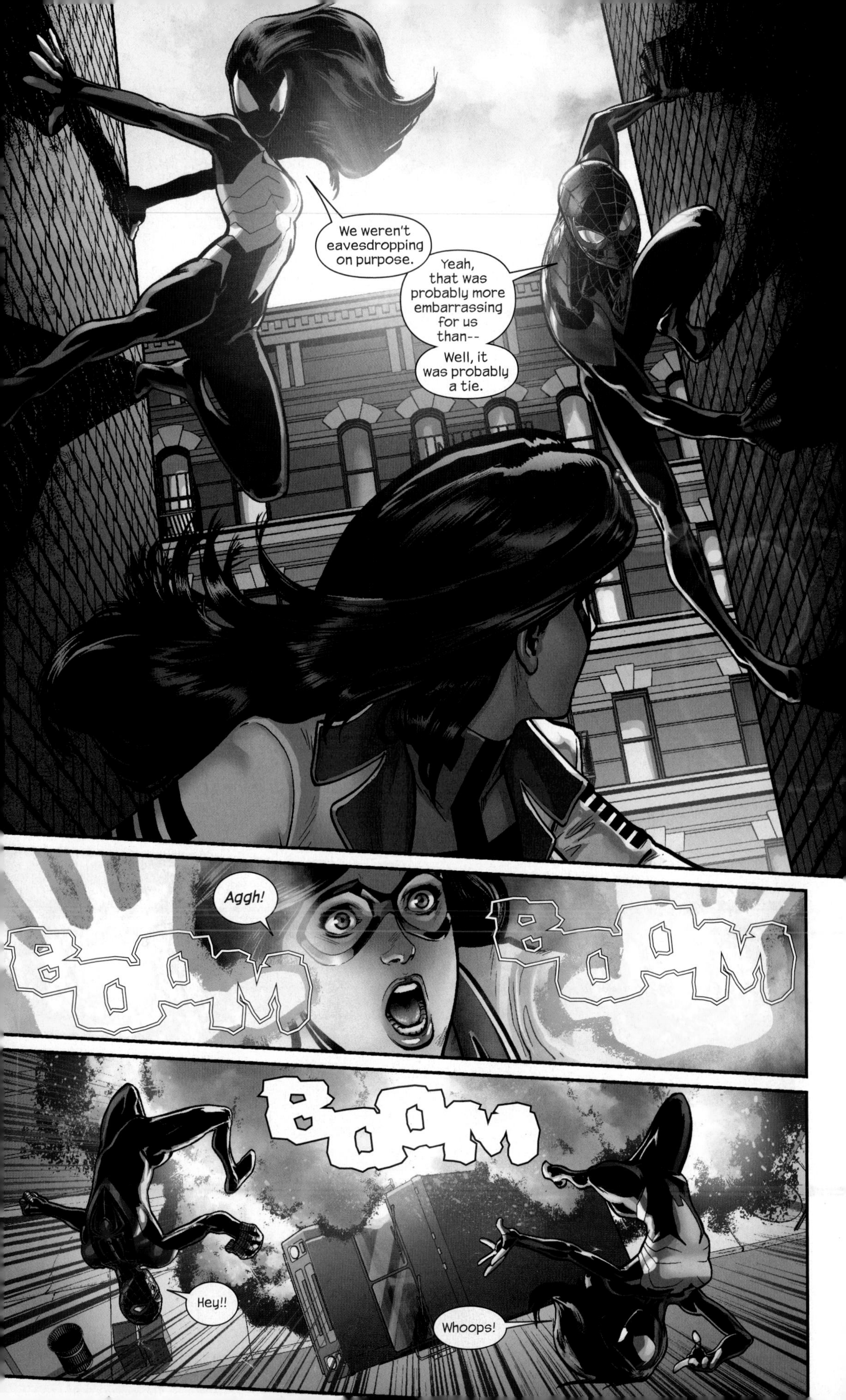
We weren't eavesdropping on purpose.
Yeah, that was probably more embarrassing for us than--
Well, it was probably a tie.
Aggh!
BOOM
BOOM
BOOM
Hey!!
Whoops!

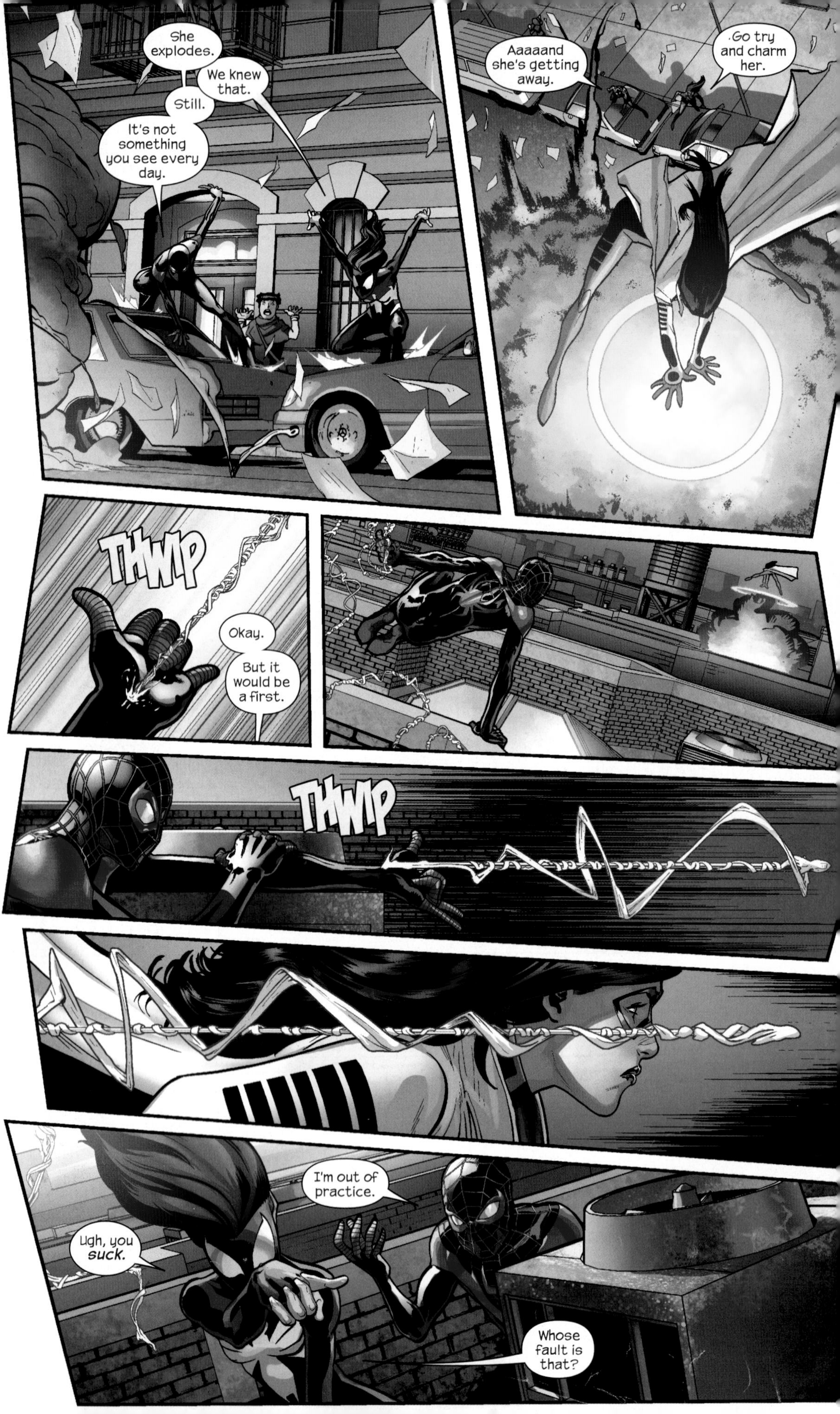
She explodes.
We knew that.
Still.
It's not something you see every day.
Aaaaand she's getting away.
Go try and charm her.
THWIP
Okay.
But it would be a first.
THWIP
I'm out of practice.
Ugh, you suck.
Whose fault is that?

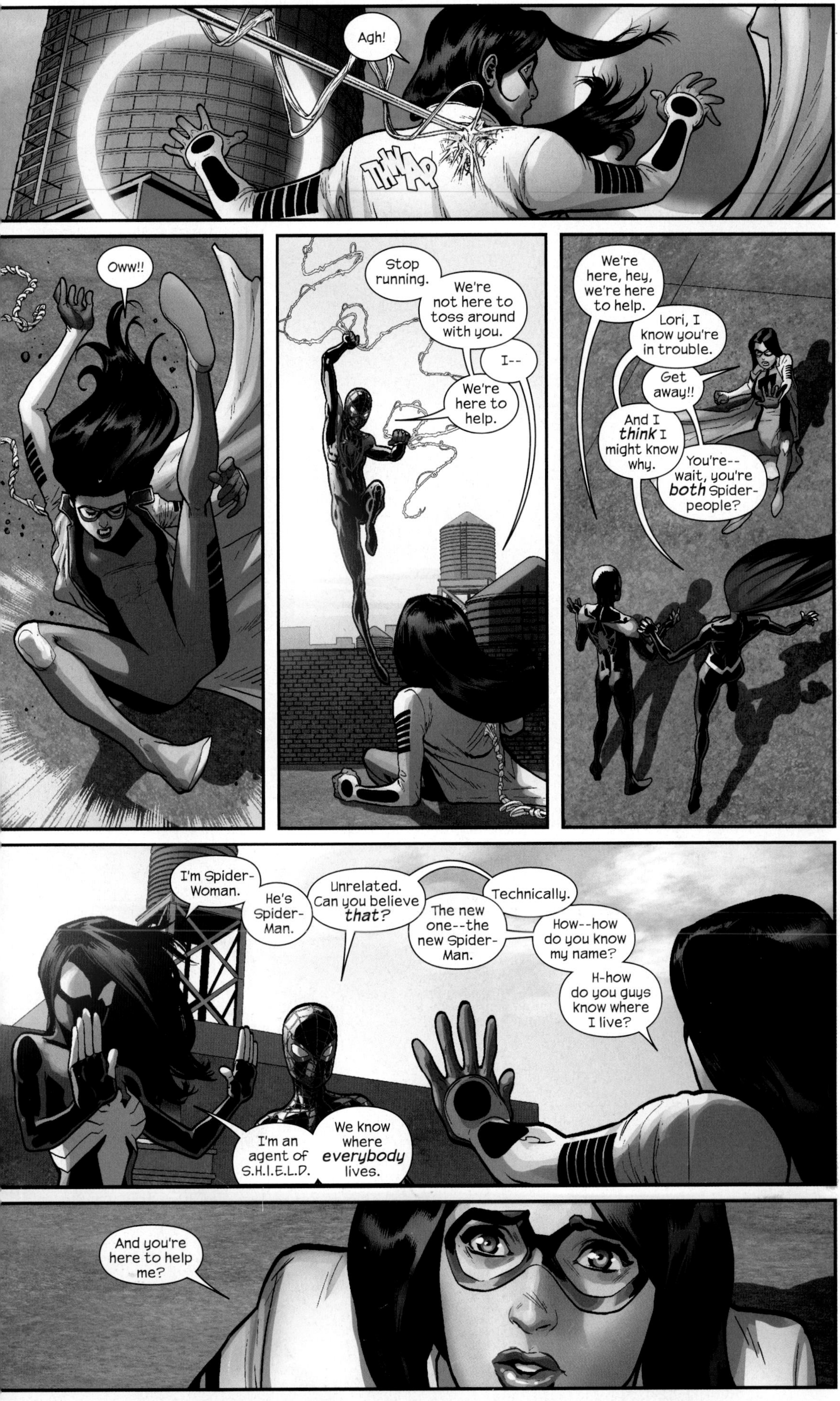

Agh!
THWAP
Oww!!
Stop running.
We're not here to toss around with you.
I--
We're here to help.
We're here, hey, we're here to help.
Lori, I know you're in trouble.
Get away!!
And I *think* I might know why.
You're-- wait, you're *both* Spider-people?
I'm Spider-Woman.
He's Spider-Man.
Unrelated. Can you believe *that?*
Technically.
The new one--the new Spider-Man.
How--how do you know my name?
H-how do you guys know where I live?
I'm an agent of S.H.I.E.L.D.
We know where *everybody* lives.
And you're here to help me?

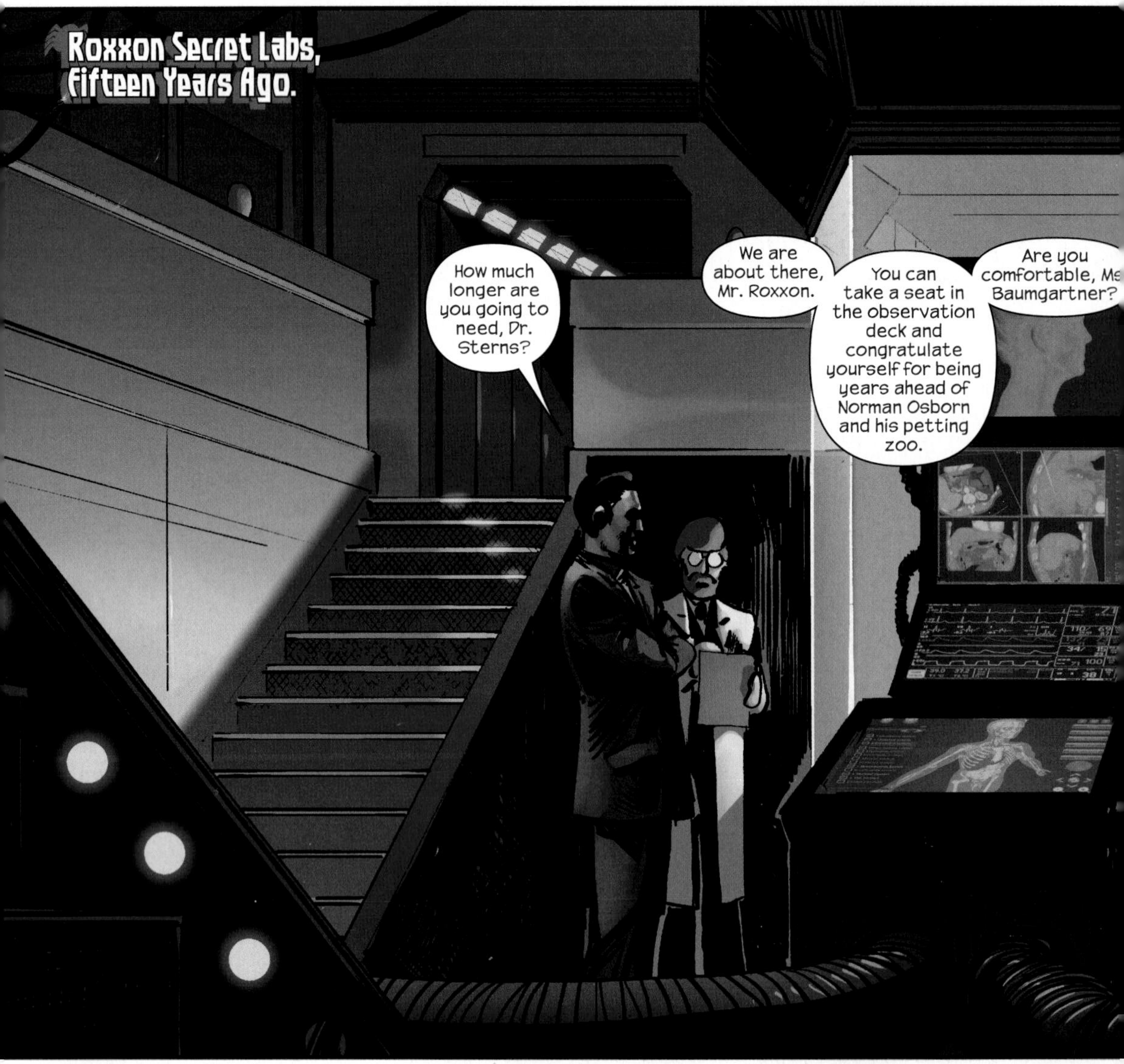
Roxxon Secret Labs, Fifteen Years Ago.
How much longer are you going to need, Dr. Sterns?
We are about there, Mr. Roxxon.
You can take a seat in the observation deck and congratulate yourself for being years ahead of Norman Osborn and his petting zoo.
Are you comfortable, Ms Baumgartner?

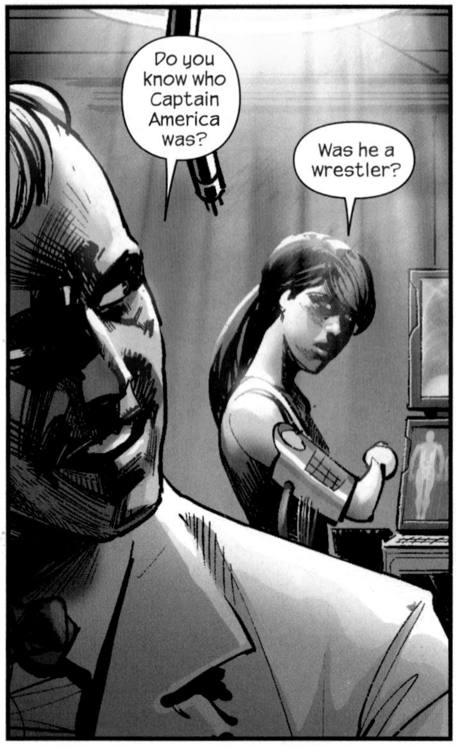
Do you know who Captain America was?
Was he a wrestler?

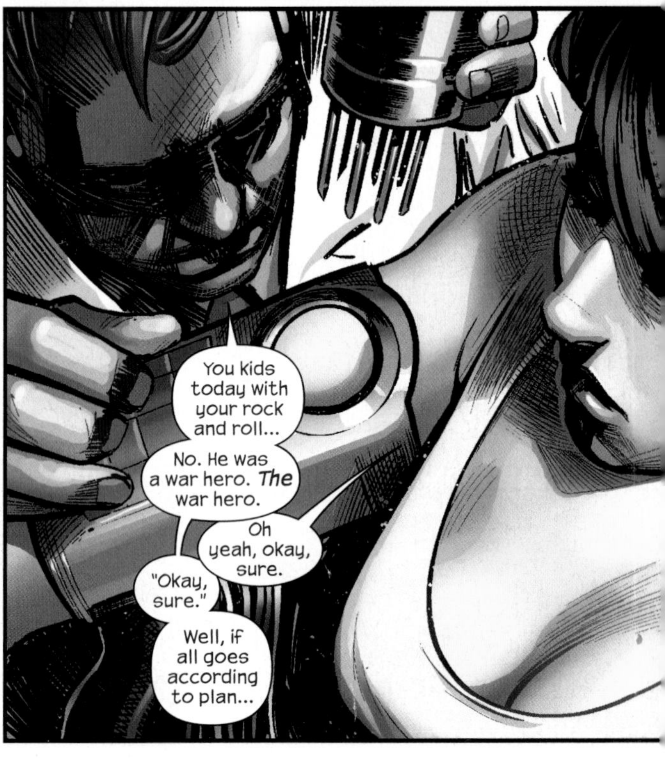
You kids today with your rock and roll...
No. He was a war hero. The war hero.
Oh yeah, okay, sure.
"Okay, sure."
Well, if all goes according to plan...

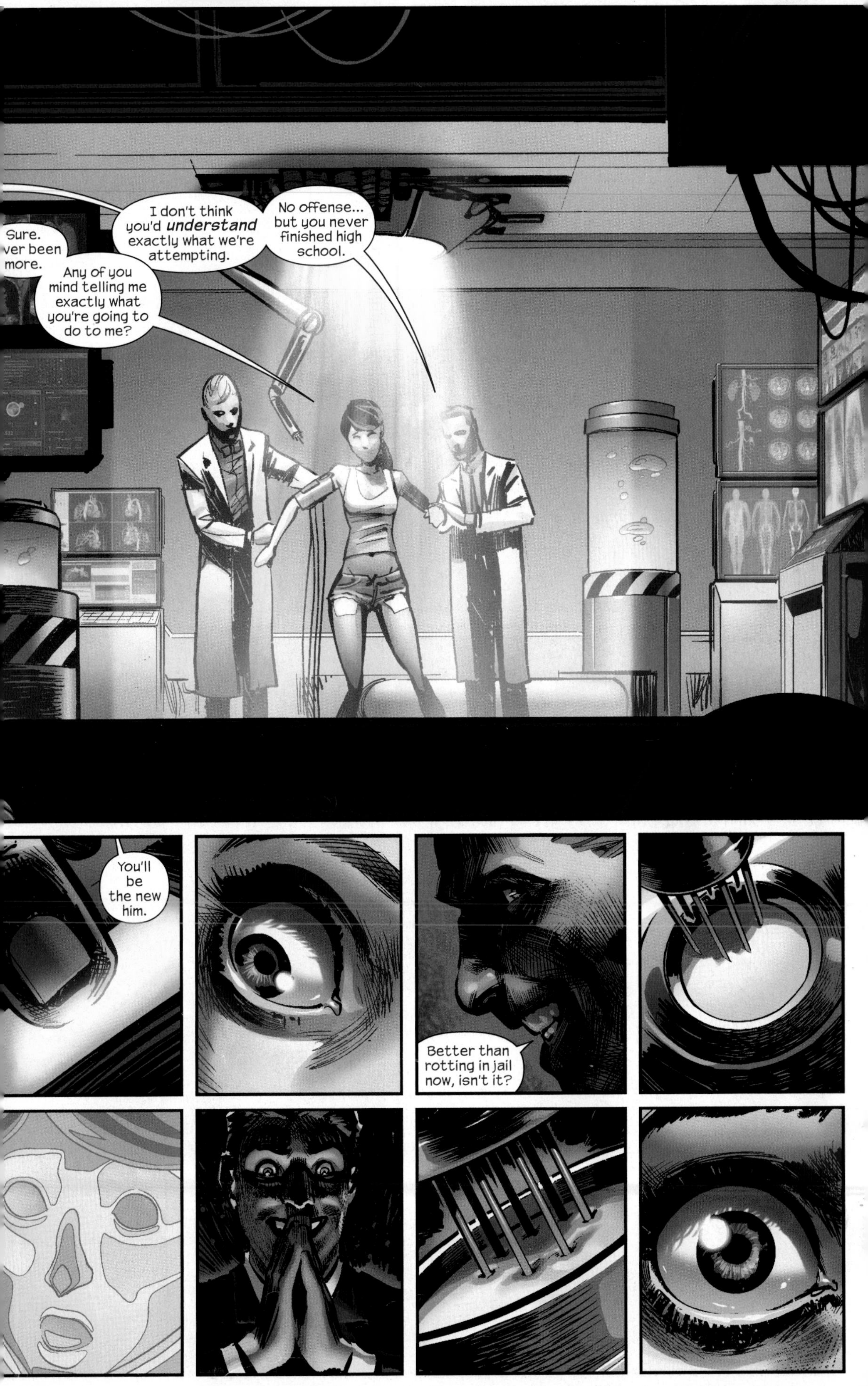
Sure.
ver been
more.
Any of you mind telling me exactly what you're going to do to me?
I don't think you'd understand exactly what we're attempting.
No offense... but you never finished high school.
You'll be the new him.
Better than rotting in jail now, isn't it?

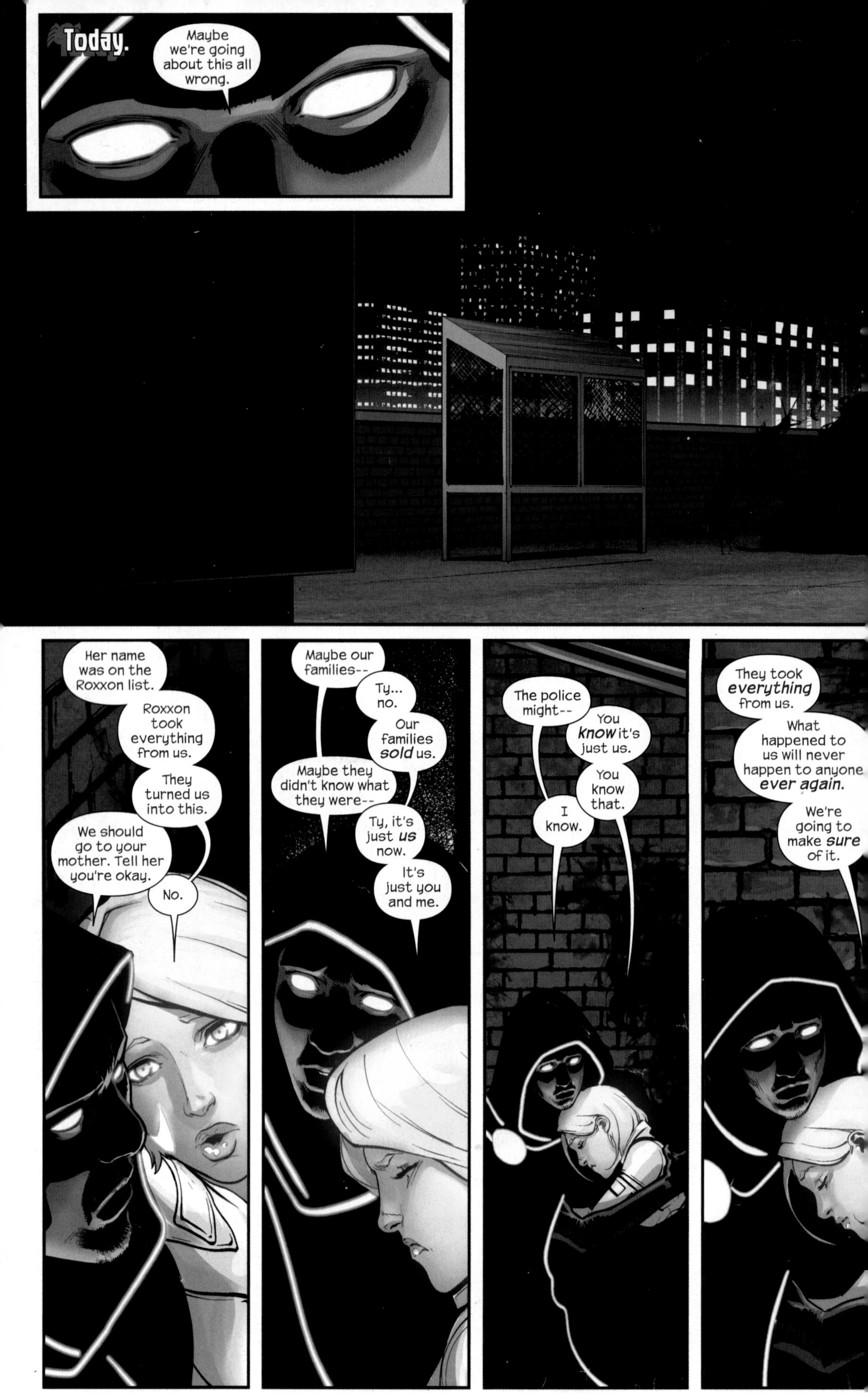
Today.
Maybe we're going about this all wrong.
Her name was on the Roxxon list.
Roxxon took everything from us.
They turned us into this.
We should go to your mother. Tell her you're okay.
No.
Maybe our families--
Ty... no.
Our families sold us.
Maybe they didn't know what they were--
Ty, it's just us now.
It's just you and me.
The police might--
You know it's just us.
You know that.
I know.
They took everything from us.
What happened to us will never happen to anyone ever again.
We're going to make sure of it.

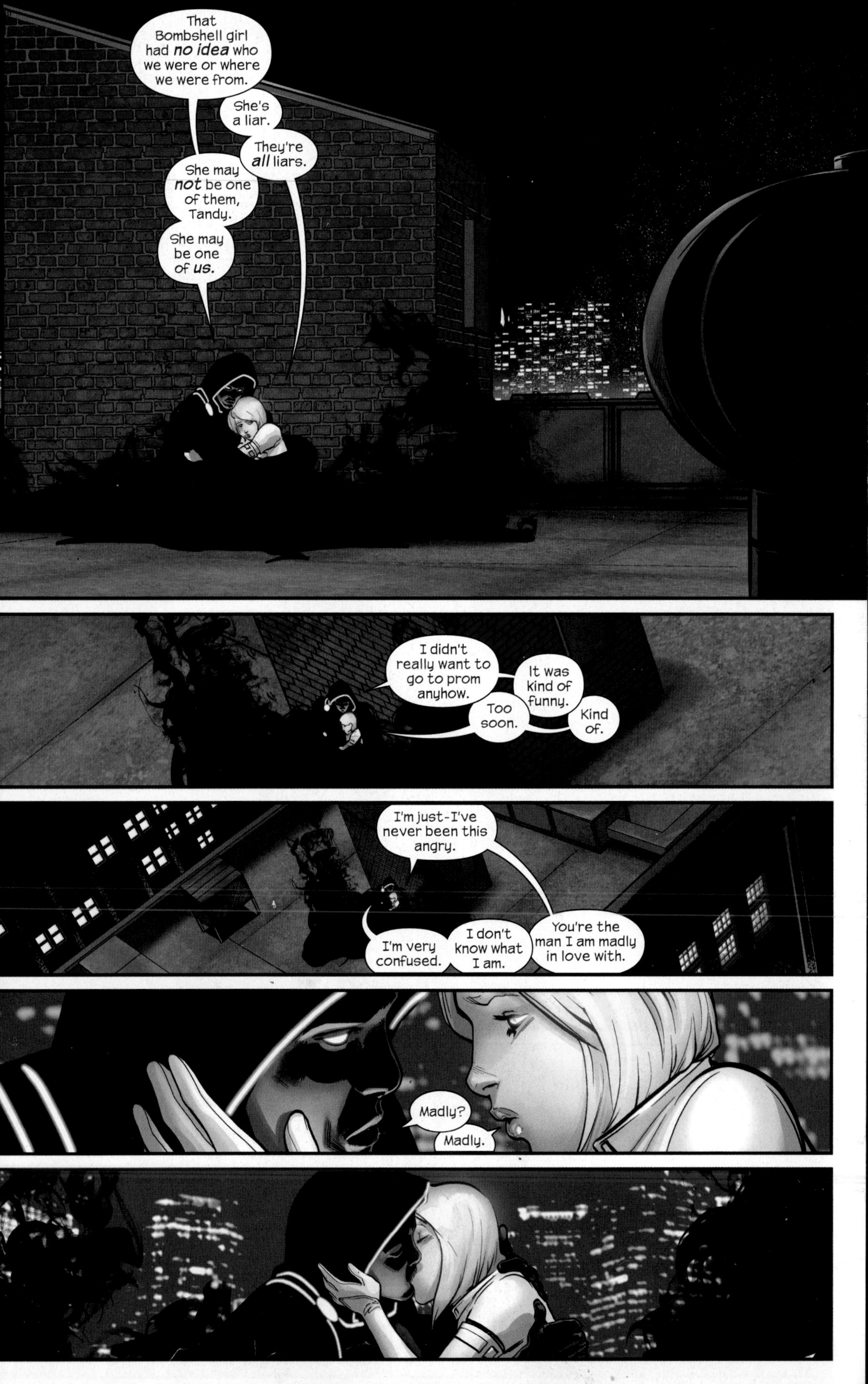
That Bombshell girl had *no idea* who we were or where we were from.
She's a liar.
They're *all* liars.
She may *not* be one of them, Tandy.
She may be one of *us.*
I didn't really want to go to prom anyhow.
It was kind of funny.
Too soon.
Kind of.
I'm just-I've never been this angry.
I'm very confused.
I don't know what I am.
You're the man I am madly in love with.
Madly?
Madly.

SUMMER HEATWAVE
Why not move north?
PAGE 3

PIGS!
They really like mud.
PAGE 15

DAILY BUGLE

MYSTERY POWER TEENAGERS RANSACK BOROUGH

see page 2

TRAFFIC!
You're part of it.
PAGE 11

FORTUNE COOKIES
Not actually from Asia
PAGE 5

Lorem ipsum dolor sit amet, consectetuer adipiscing elit, sed diam nonummy nibh euismod tincidunt ut laoreet dolore magna aliquam erat volutpat. Ut wisi enim ad minim veniam, quis nostrud exerci tation ullamcorper suscipit lobortis nisl ut aliquip ex ea commodo . (cont'd)

Lorem ipsum dolor sit amet, consectetuer adipiscing elit, sed diam nonummy nibh euismod tincidunt ut laoreet dolore magna aliquam erat volutpat. Ut wisi enim ad minim veniam, quis nostrud exerci . (cont'd)

And there is it.

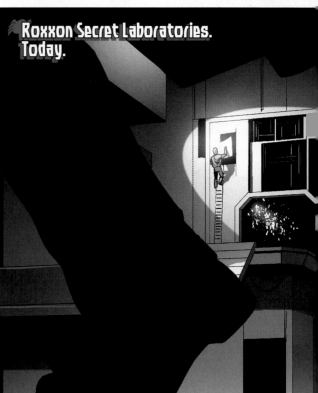

Roxxon Secret Laboratories. Today.

What would you have me do?

I told you that I could have members of my team out there hunting, but you--

We could go now.

That's not what I *pay you* to do, Dr. Miller!!

You're scientists... not bounty hunters.

I understand that, but we *have skills* that might get the job done.

No.

Then why are you here?

Mr. Roxxon, you're not seeing the big picture here.

You have-- we have brought you *amazing* results.

Are you not *in awe* of what we discovered here??!!

We took two comatose, half-dead teenagers and created walking, talking portals of energy unlike anything we have ever *seen* on this planet.

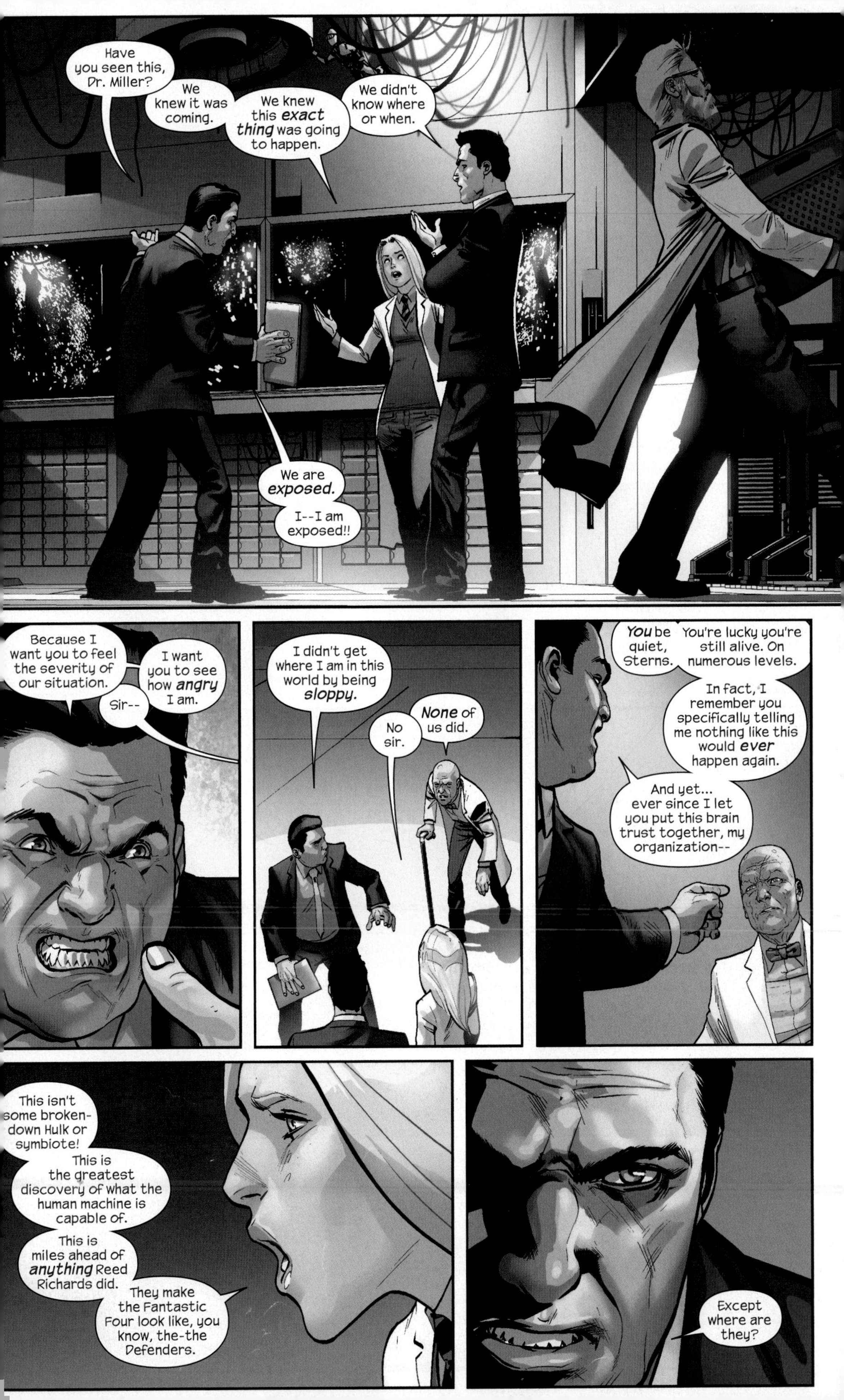
Have you seen this, Dr. Miller?
We knew it was coming.
We knew this exact thing was going to happen.
We didn't know where or when.
We are exposed.
I--I am exposed!!
Because I want you to feel the severity of our situation.
I want you to see how angry I am.
Sir--
I didn't get where I am in this world by being sloppy.
No sir.
None of us did.
You be quiet, Sterns.
You're lucky you're still alive. On numerous levels.
In fact, I remember you specifically telling me nothing like this would ever happen again.
And yet... ever since I let you put this brain trust together, my organization--
This isn't some broken-down Hulk or symbiote!
This is the greatest discovery of what the human machine is capable of.
This is miles ahead of anything Reed Richards did.
They make the Fantastic Four look like, you know, the-the Defenders.
Except where are they?

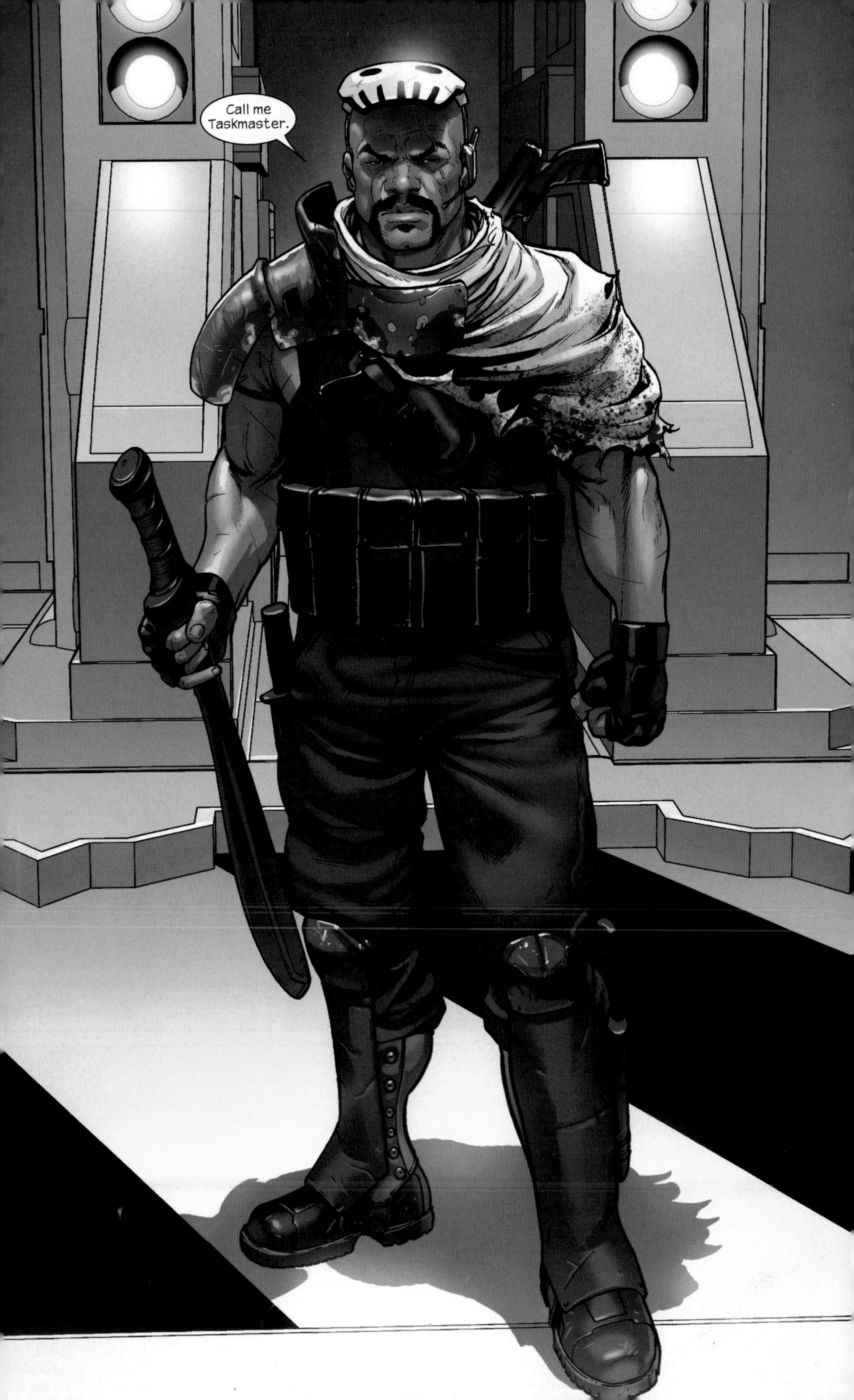
Call me Taskmaster.

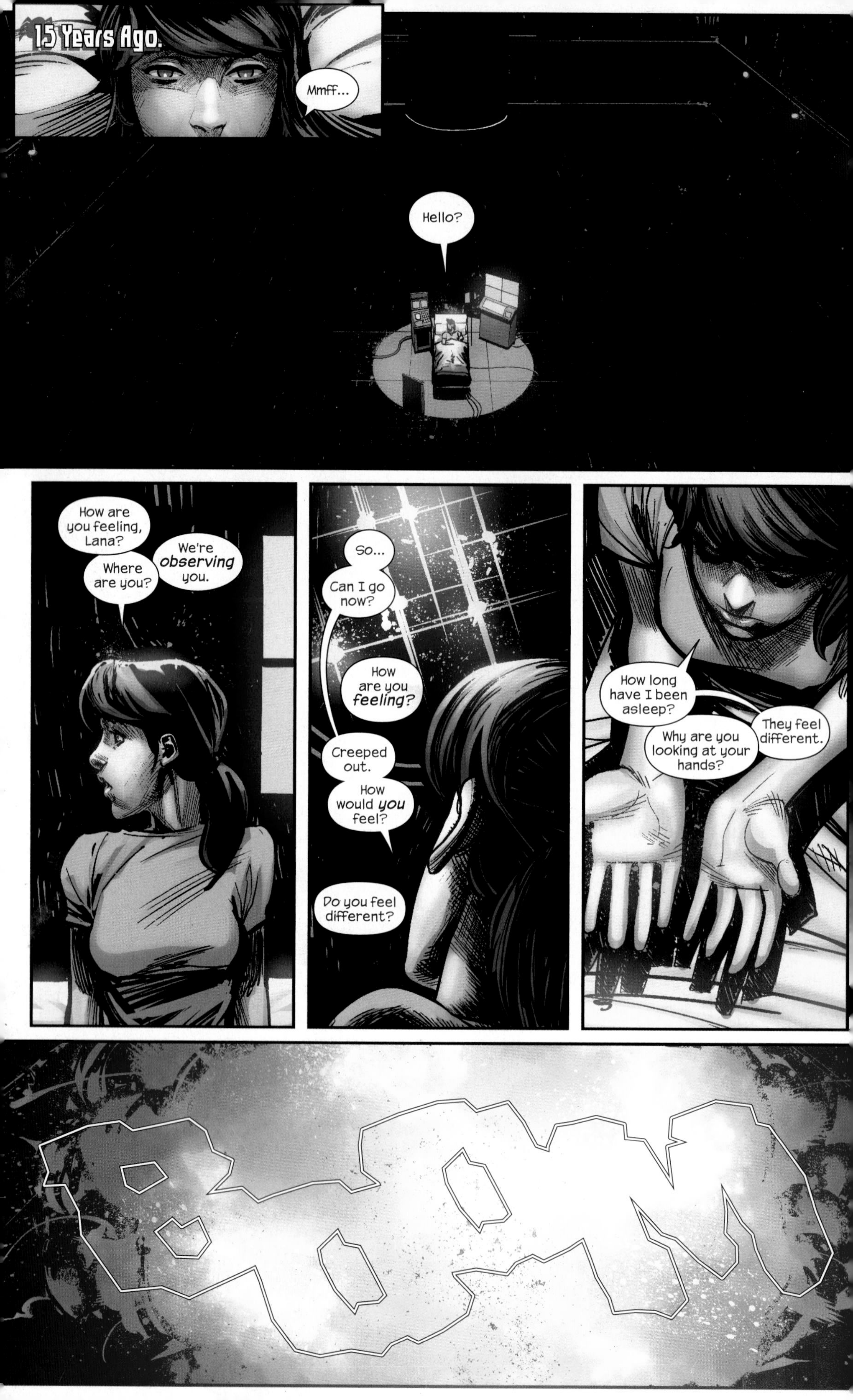
15 Years Ago.
Mmff...
Hello?
How are you feeling, Lana?
Where are you?
We're *observing* you.
So...
Can I go now?
How are you *feeling?*
Creeped out.
How would *you* feel?
Do you feel different?
How long have I been asleep?
Why are you looking at your hands?
They feel different.
BOOM

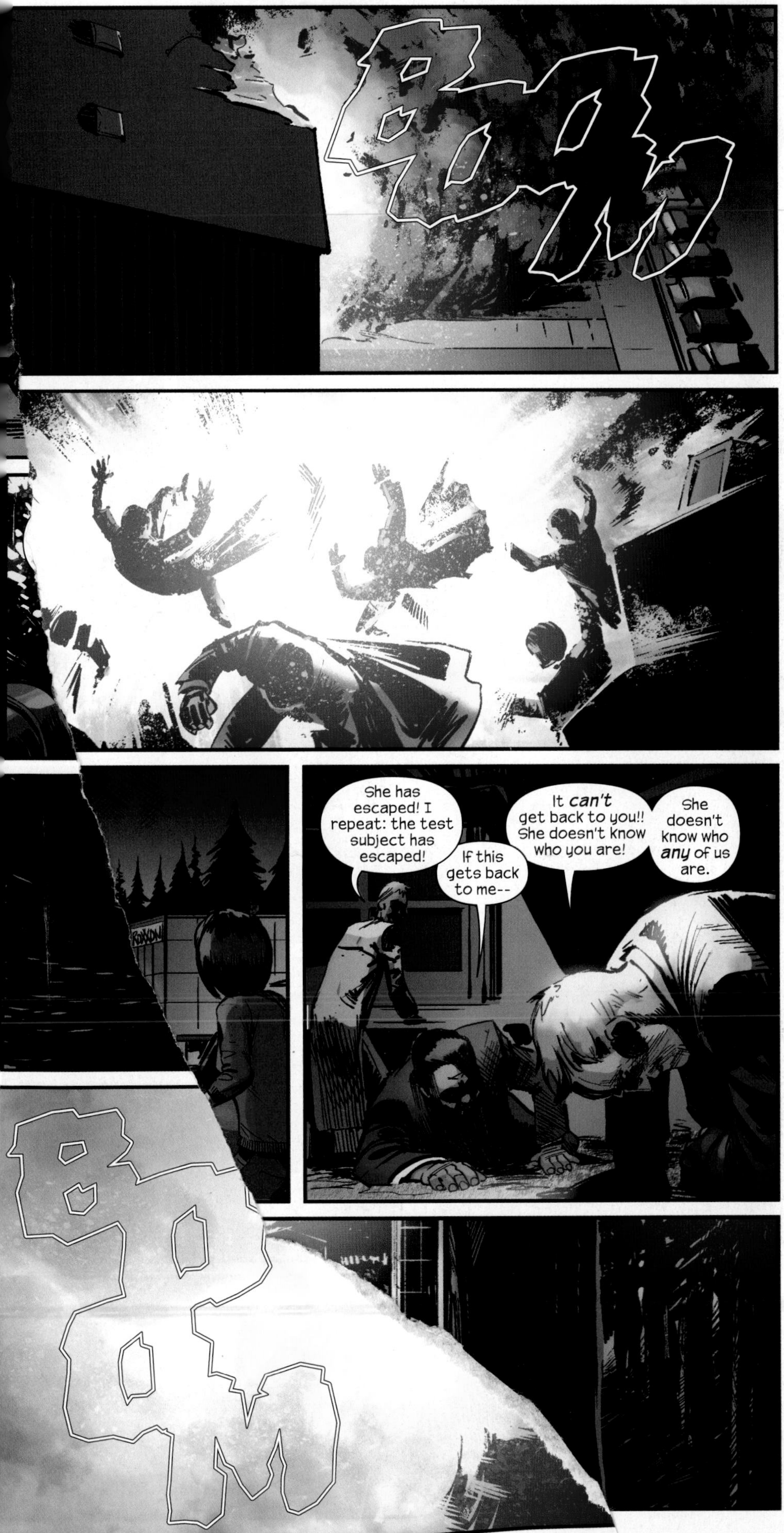
BOOM
She has escaped! I repeat: the test subject has escaped!
If this gets back to me--
It *can't* get back to you!! She doesn't know who you are!
She doesn't know who *any* of us are.
BOOM

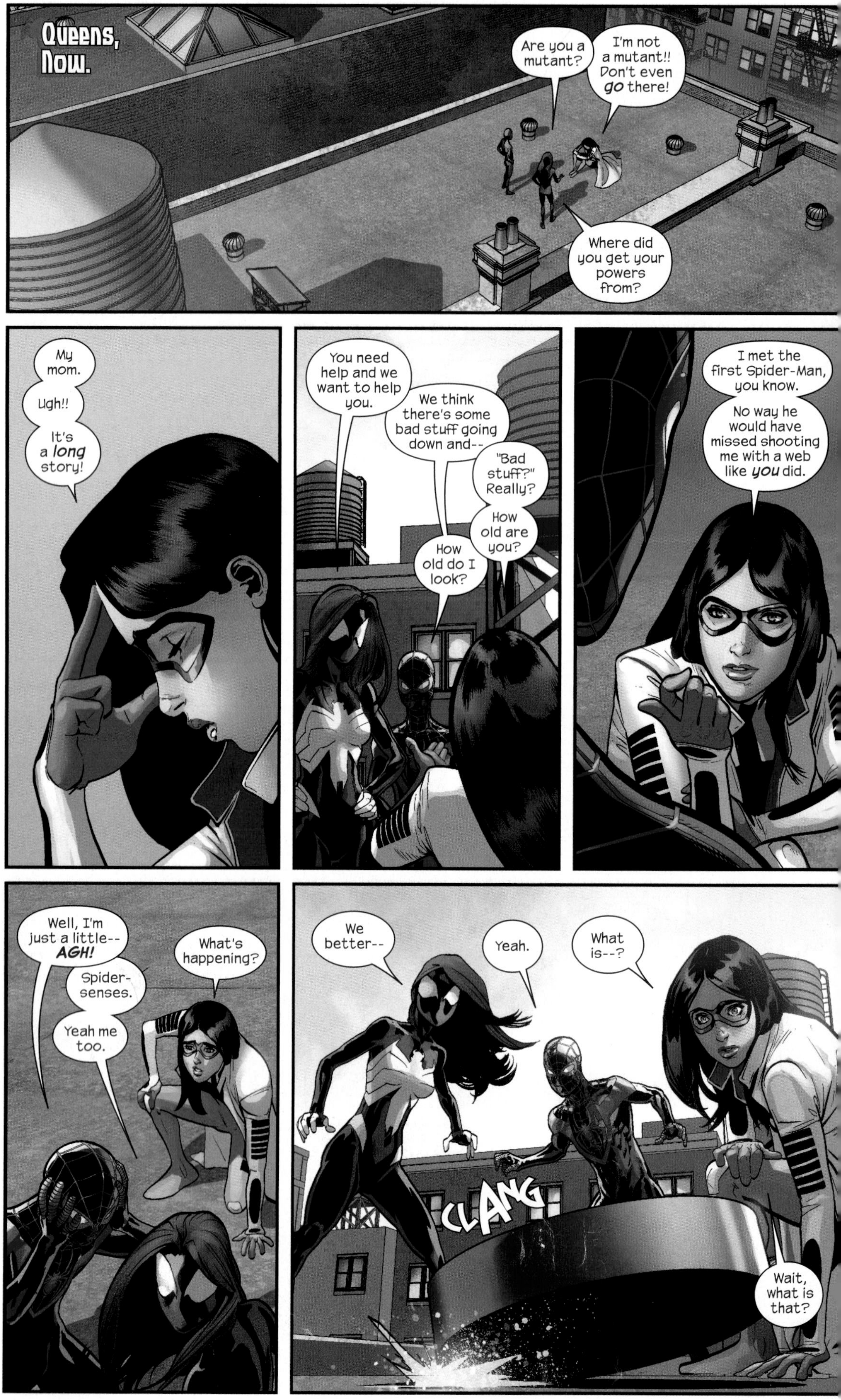
Queens, Now.
Are you a mutant?
I'm not a mutant!! Don't even go there!
Where did you get your powers from?
My mom.
Ugh!!
It's a long story!
You need help and we want to help you.
We think there's some bad stuff going down and--
"Bad stuff?" Really?
How old are you?
How old do I look?
I met the first Spider-Man, you know.
No way he would have missed shooting me with a web like you did.
Well, I'm just a little-- AGH!
What's happening?
Spider-senses.
Yeah me too.
We better--
Yeah.
What is--?
CLANG
Wait, what is that?

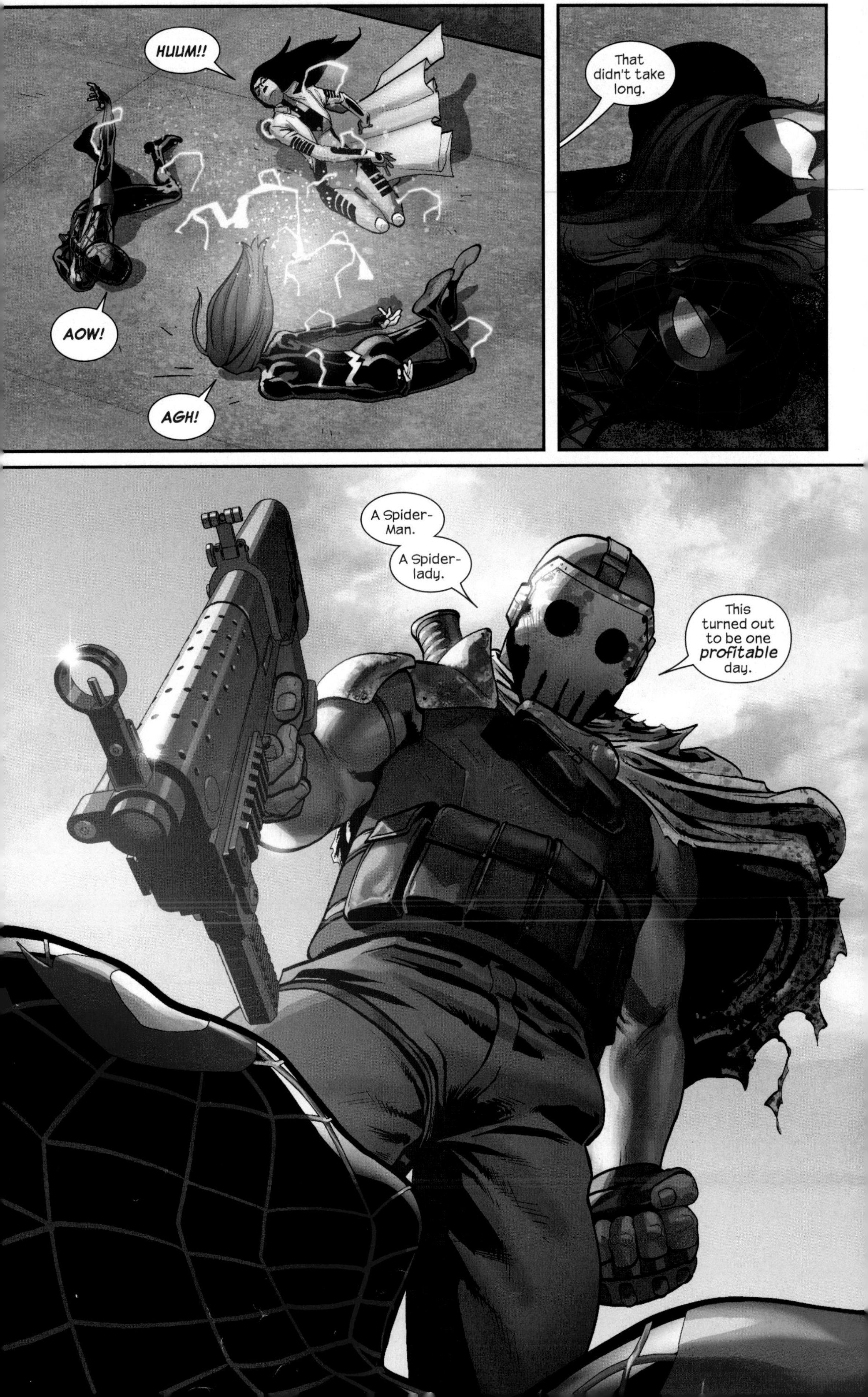
HUUM!!
AOW!
AGH!
That didn't take long.
A Spider-Man.
A Spider-lady.
This turned out to be one *profitable* day.

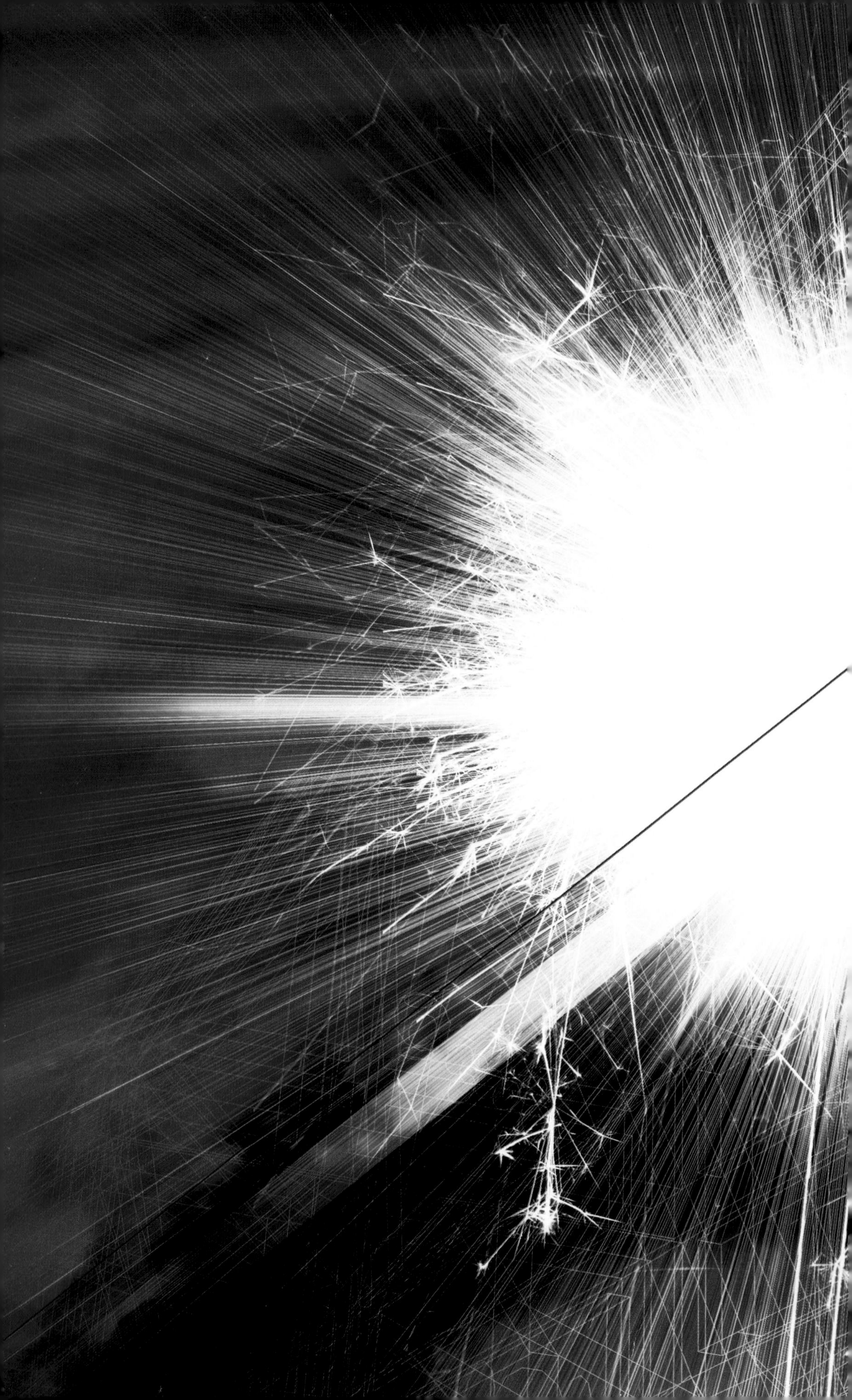

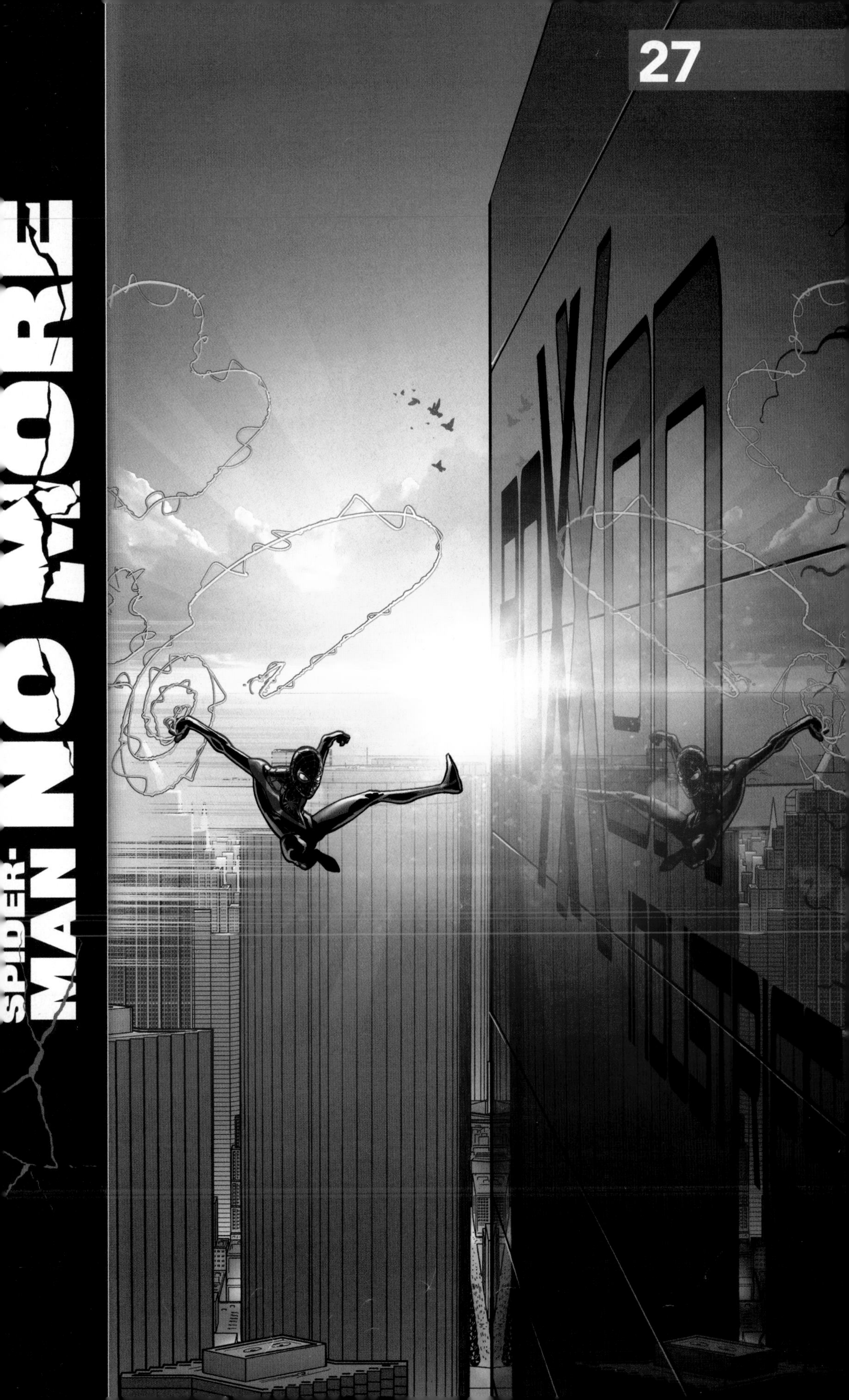
27
SPIDER-MAN NO MORE

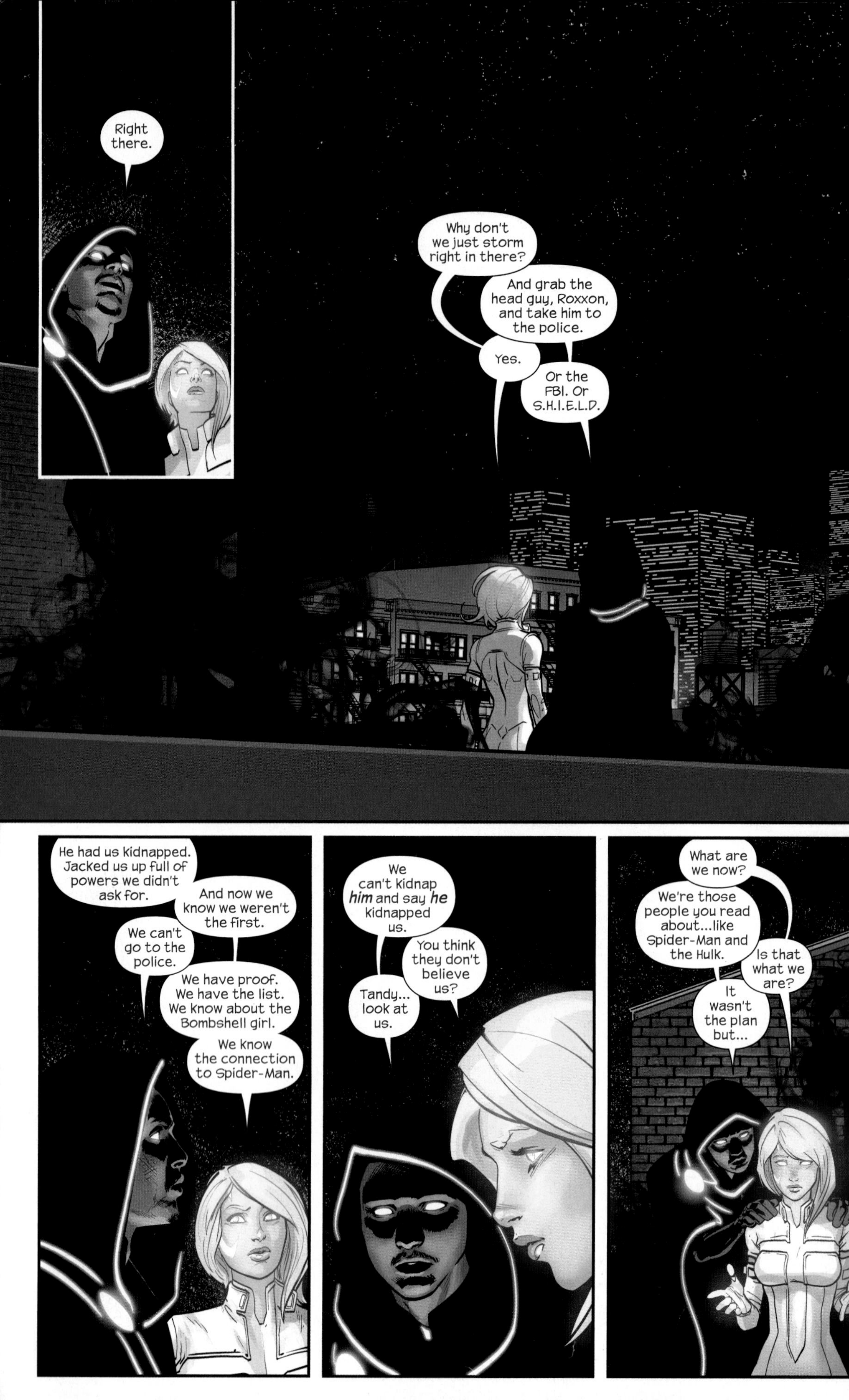
Right there.
Why don't we just storm right in there?
And grab the head guy, Roxxon, and take him to the police.
Yes.
Or the FBI. Or S.H.I.E.L.D.
He had us kidnapped. Jacked us up full of powers we didn't ask for.
And now we know we weren't the first.
We can't go to the police.
We have proof. We have the list. We know about the Bombshell girl.
We know the connection to Spider-Man.
We can't kidnap *him* and say *he* kidnapped us.
You think they don't believe us?
Tandy... look at us.
What are we now?
We're those people you read about...like Spider-Man and the Hulk.
Is that what we are?
It wasn't the plan but...

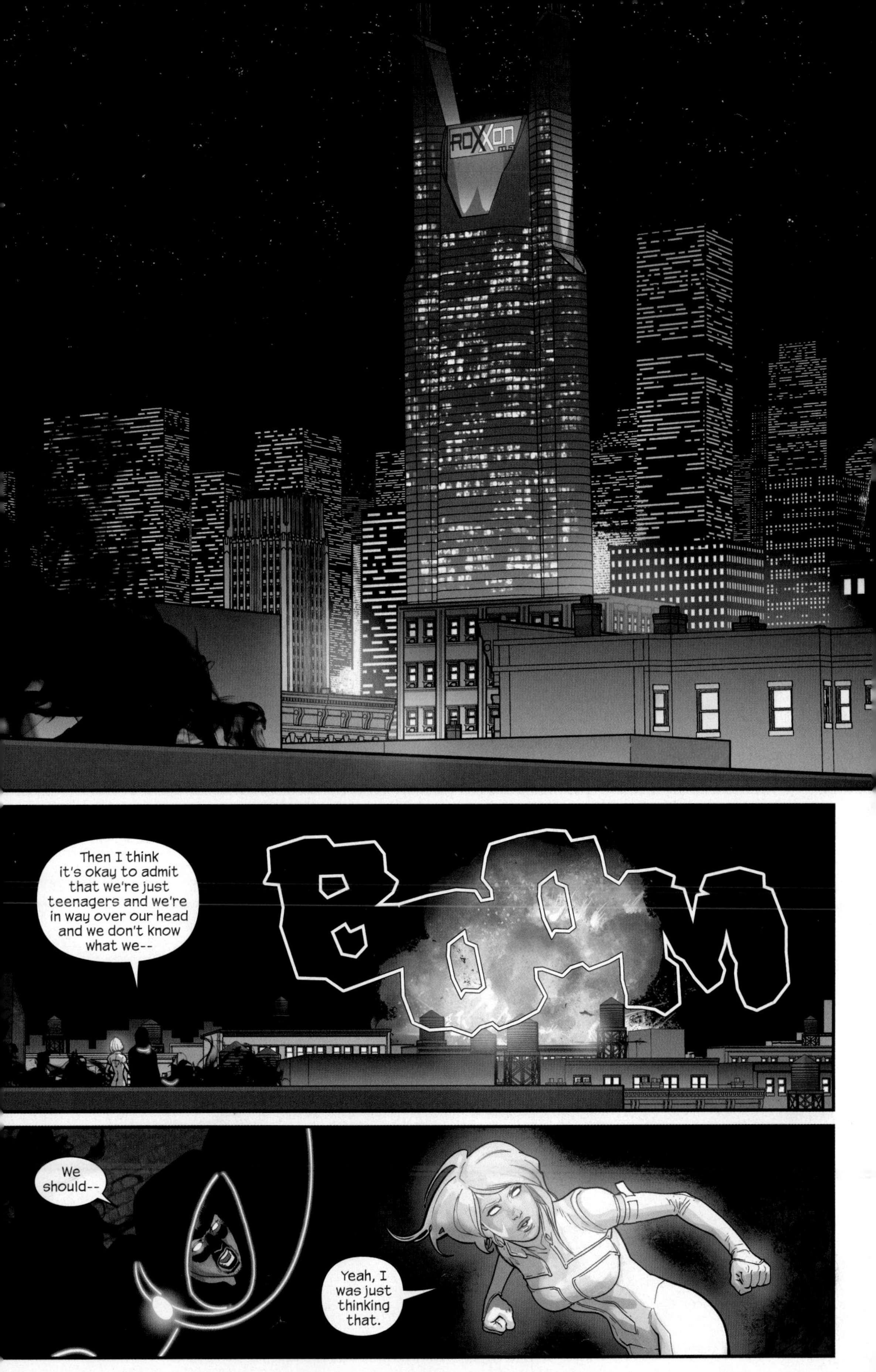
ROXXON
Then I think it's okay to admit that we're just teenagers and we're in way over our head and we don't know what we--
BOOM
We should--
Yeah, I was just thinking that.

...up being Spider-Man?

Oh yeah, stuff like this.

I don't know who this guy is or *how* he found us or *what* he wants or how he has us all *paralyzed*.

(Which feels very freaky weird, by the way.)

Agh!

Aow!

HUUM!

I can't even move my mouth to ask--wait!!

What is he doing?

The *new* Spider-Man.

I bet I could turn this intel into a retirement.

Oh no.

He's going for my mask.

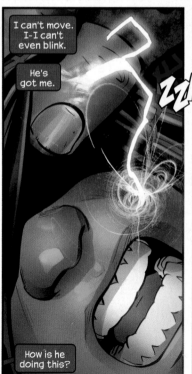

I can't move. I-I can't even blink.

He's got me.

ZZAAAATTT

How is he doing this?

Ah!

What *the hell*, kid?!

You booby-trapped or--

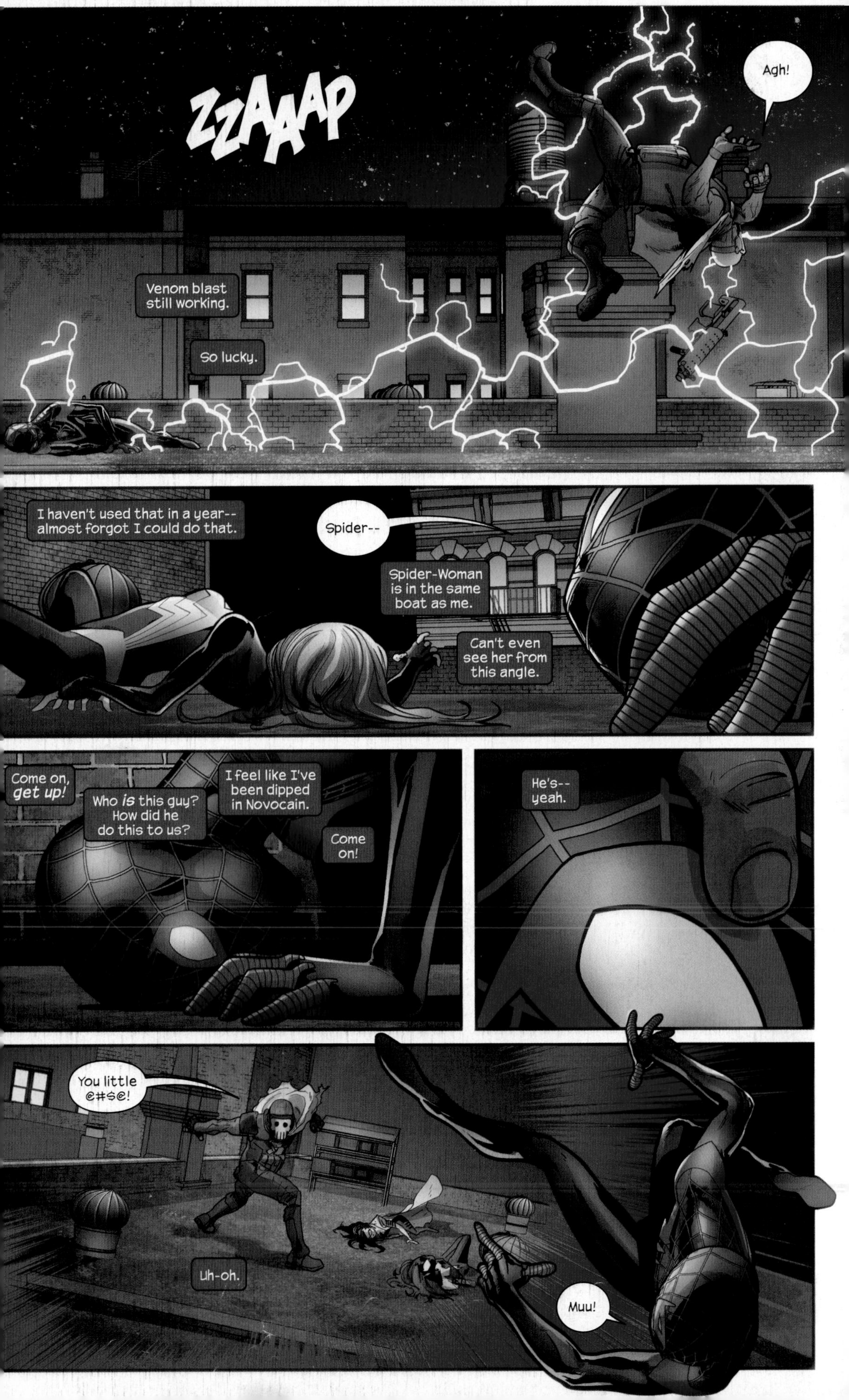

ZZAAAP
Agh!
Venom blast still working.
So lucky.
I haven't used that in a year-- almost forgot I could do that.
Spider--
Spider-Woman is in the same boat as me.
Can't even see her from this angle.
Come on, *get up!*
Who *is* this guy? How did he do this to us?
I feel like I've been dipped in Novocain.
Come on!
He's-- yeah.
You little @#$@!
Uh-oh.
Muu!

Sure, great, *NOW* my arms work!!
Aaggh!
And my vocal cords.
Guess I'm far enough away from whatever he was using to paralyze us.
Everything is starting to move again but I'm still webbing blind!
THWIP
SPACK
Oh god.
My legs don't work.
I can't feel my butt.
Shoulda learned my lesson from that thing with Wolverine in Kuwait.
This is going to hurt.
Never mess around with you powered types.
Bullet to the head and figure it out...
...Later.

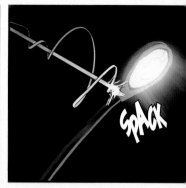

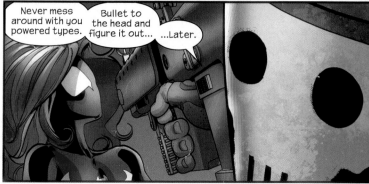

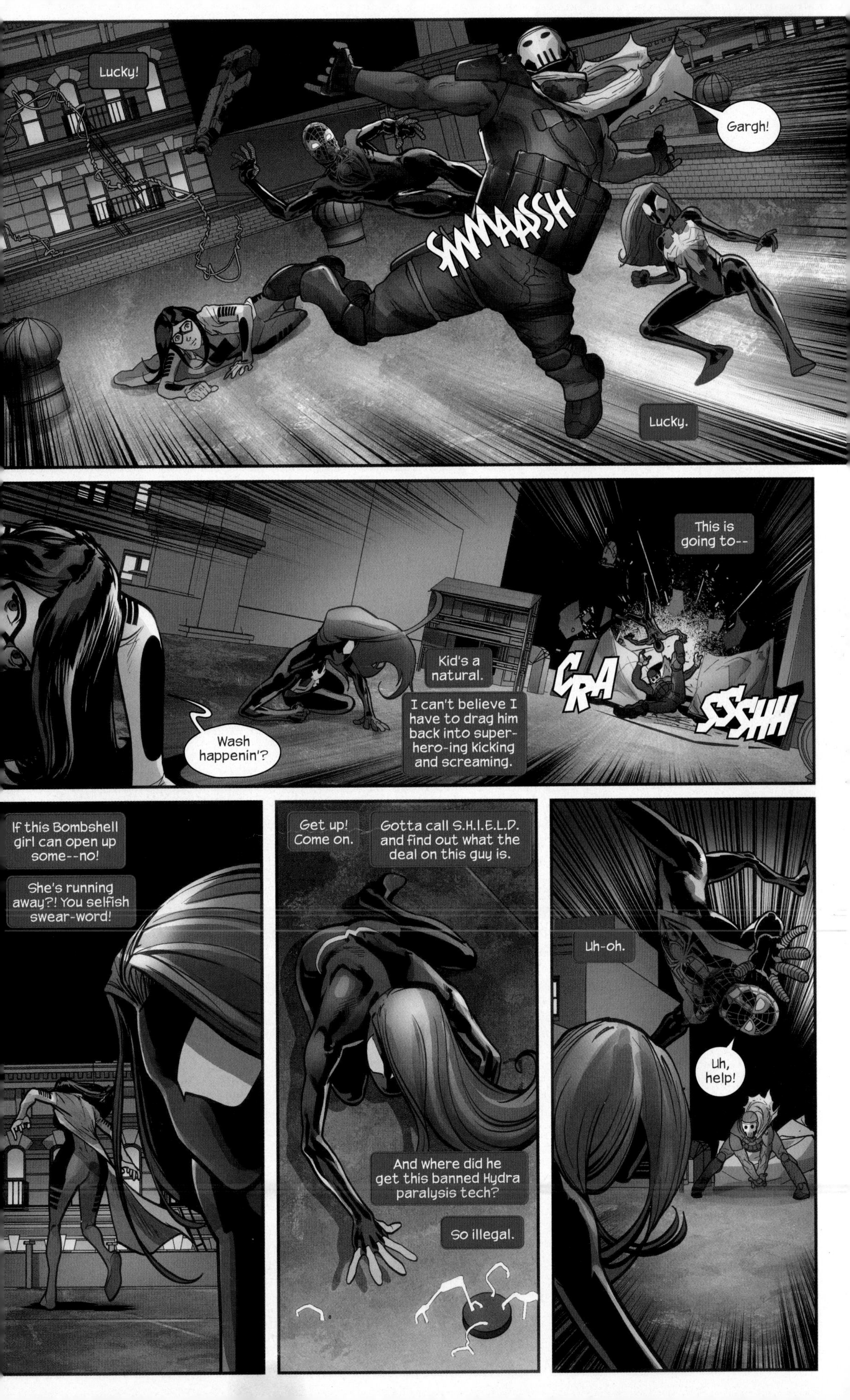
Lucky!
Gargh!
SMAASH
Lucky.
This is going to--
CRA
SSHH
Kid's a natural.
I can't believe I have to drag him back into super-hero-ing kicking and screaming.
Wash happenin'?
If this Bombshell girl can open up some--no!
She's running away?! You selfish swear-word!
Get up! Come on.
Gotta call S.H.I.E.L.D. and find out what the deal on this guy is.
And where did he get this banned Hydra paralysis tech?
So illegal.
Uh-oh.
Uh, help!

THWIP

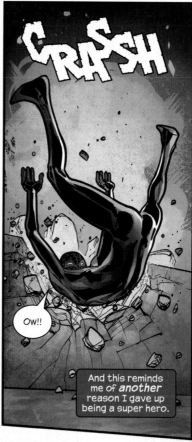

CRASSH

Ow!!

And this reminds me of *another* reason I gave up being a super hero.

S.H.I.E.L.D.? Wow.

Pfftt!

Ha!

Aaaaacome on!!

SHOOM SHOOM SHOOM

Guy's big and jacked. And fast.

Unnaturally.

As in he's either a mutant or—

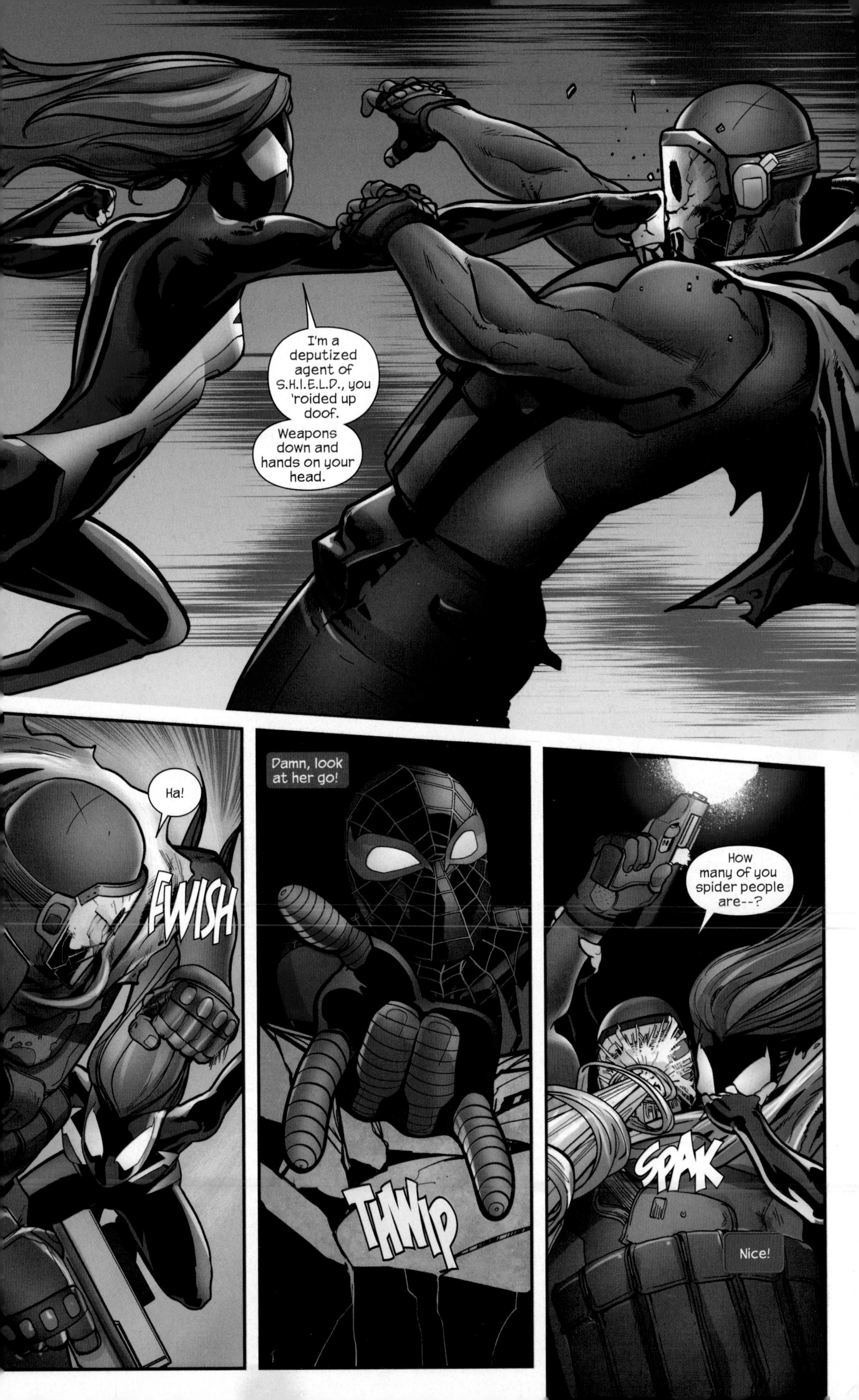
I'm a deputized agent of S.H.I.E.L.D., you 'roided up doof.
Weapons down and hands on your head.
Ha!
FWISH
Damn, look at her go!
THWIP
How many of you spider people are--?
SPAK
Nice!

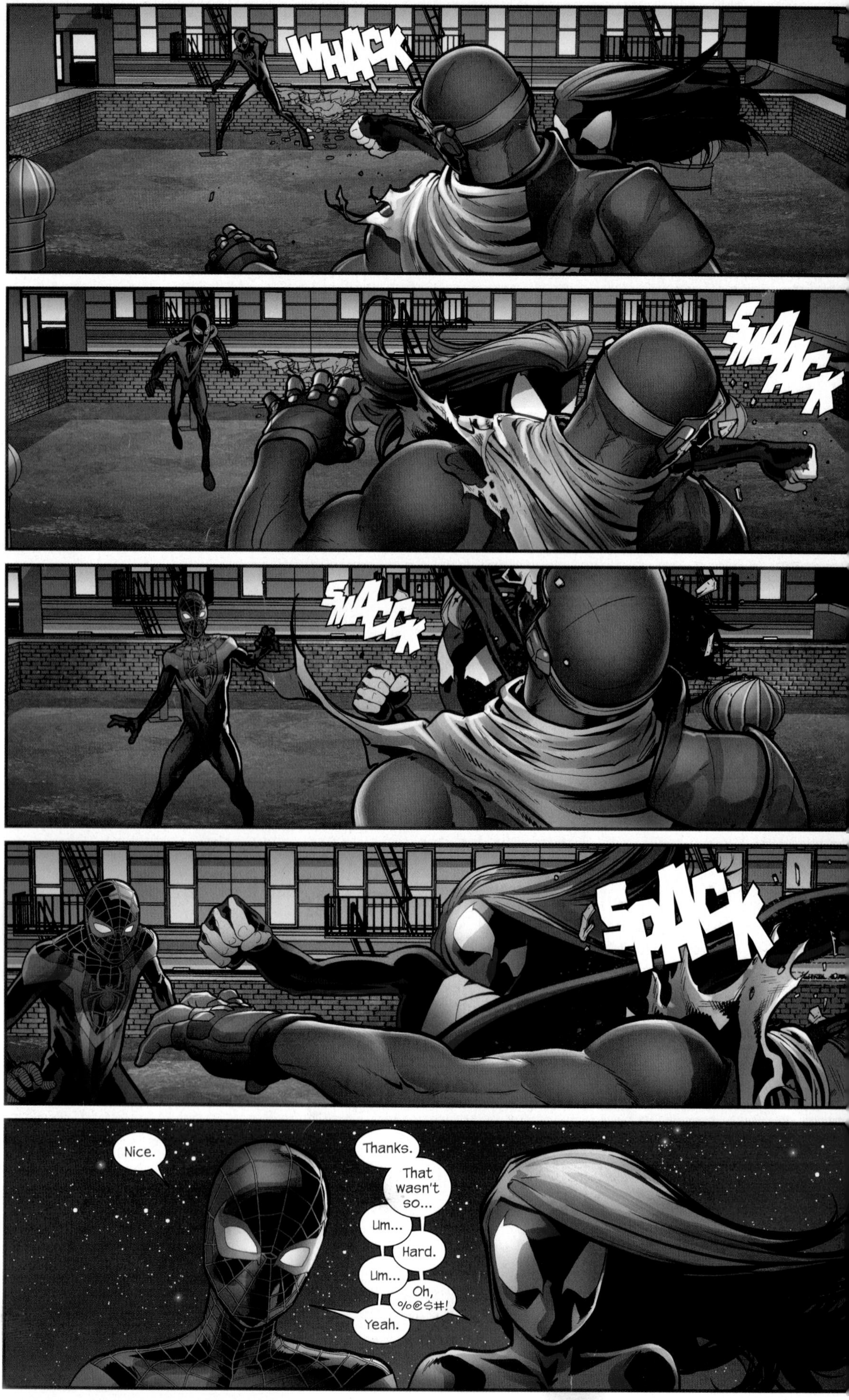
WHACK
SMAACK
SMACCK
SPACK
Nice.
Thanks.
That wasn't so...
Um...
Hard.
Um...
Oh, %@$#!
Yeah.

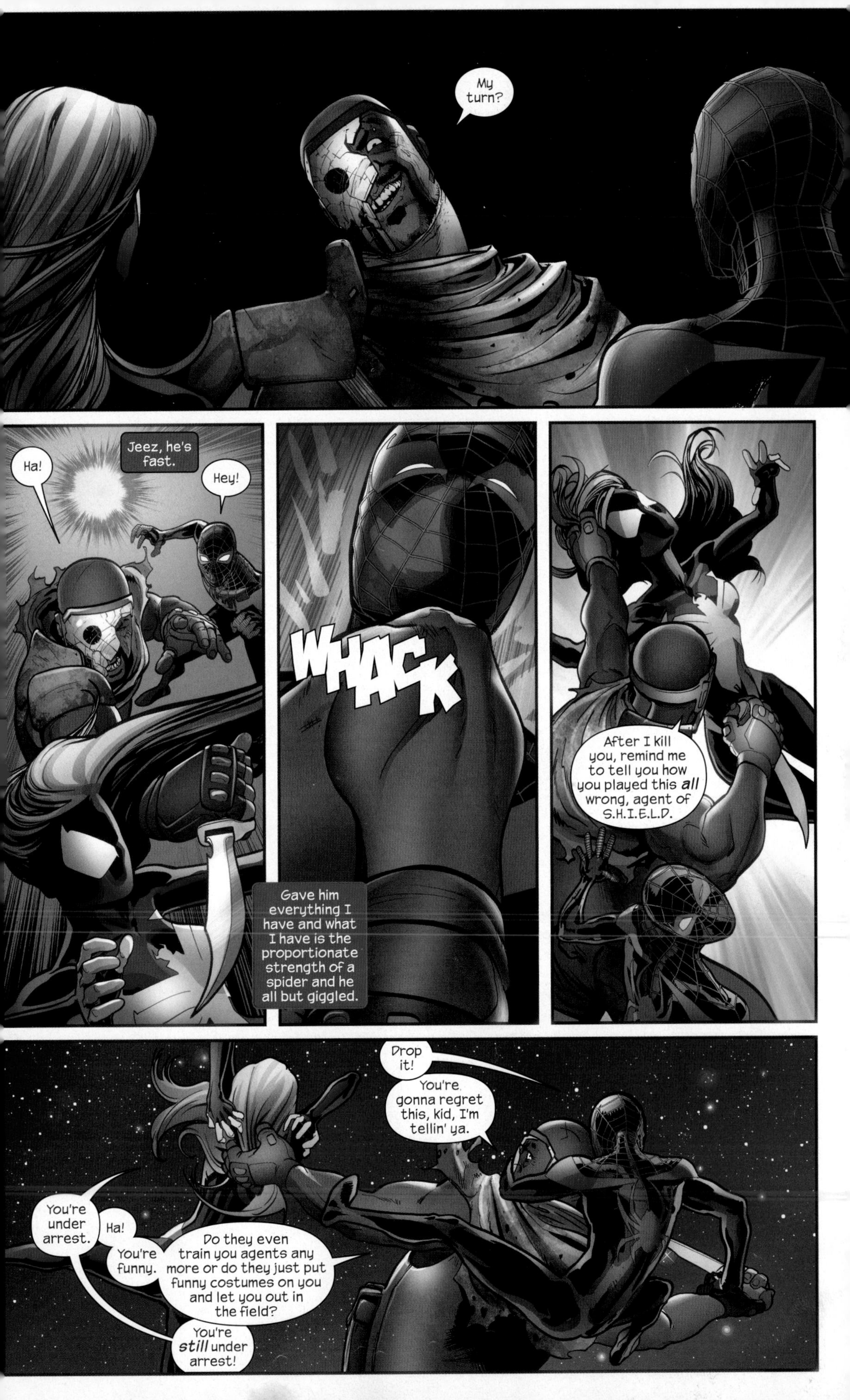
My turn?
Ha!
Jeez, he's fast.
Hey!
WHACK
Gave him everything I have and what I have is the proportionate strength of a spider and he all but giggled.
After I kill you, remind me to tell you how you played this *all* wrong, agent of S.H.I.E.L.D.
Drop it!
You're gonna regret this, kid, I'm tellin' ya.
You're under arrest.
Ha!
You're funny.
Do they even train you agents any more or do they just put funny costumes on you and let you out in the field?
You're *still* under arrest!

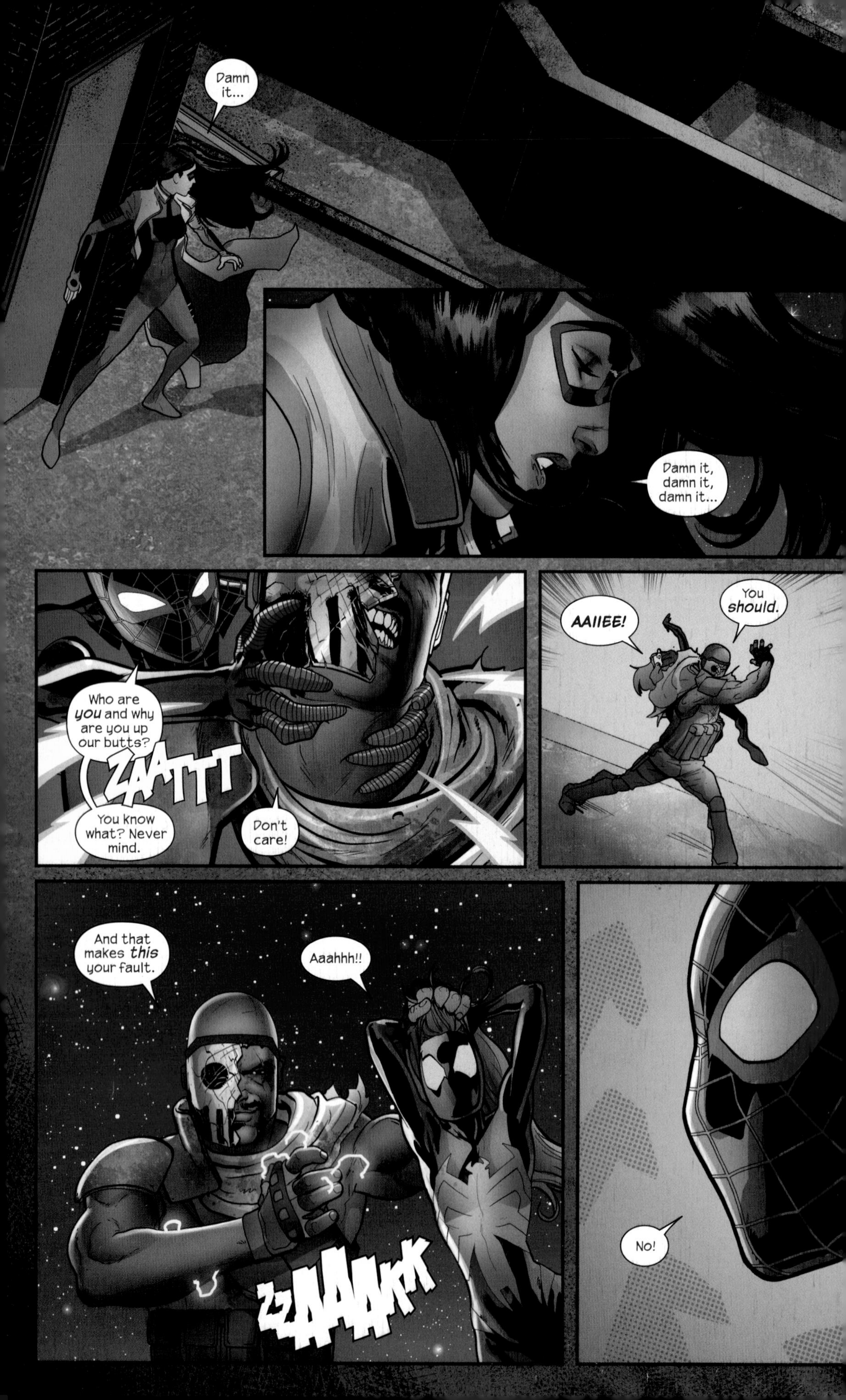

Damn it...
Damn it, damn it, damn it...
Who are *you* and why are you up our butts?
ZAATTT
You know what? Never mind.
Don't care!
AAIIEE!
You *should.*
And that makes *this* your fault.
Aaahhh!!
ZZAAAKK
No!

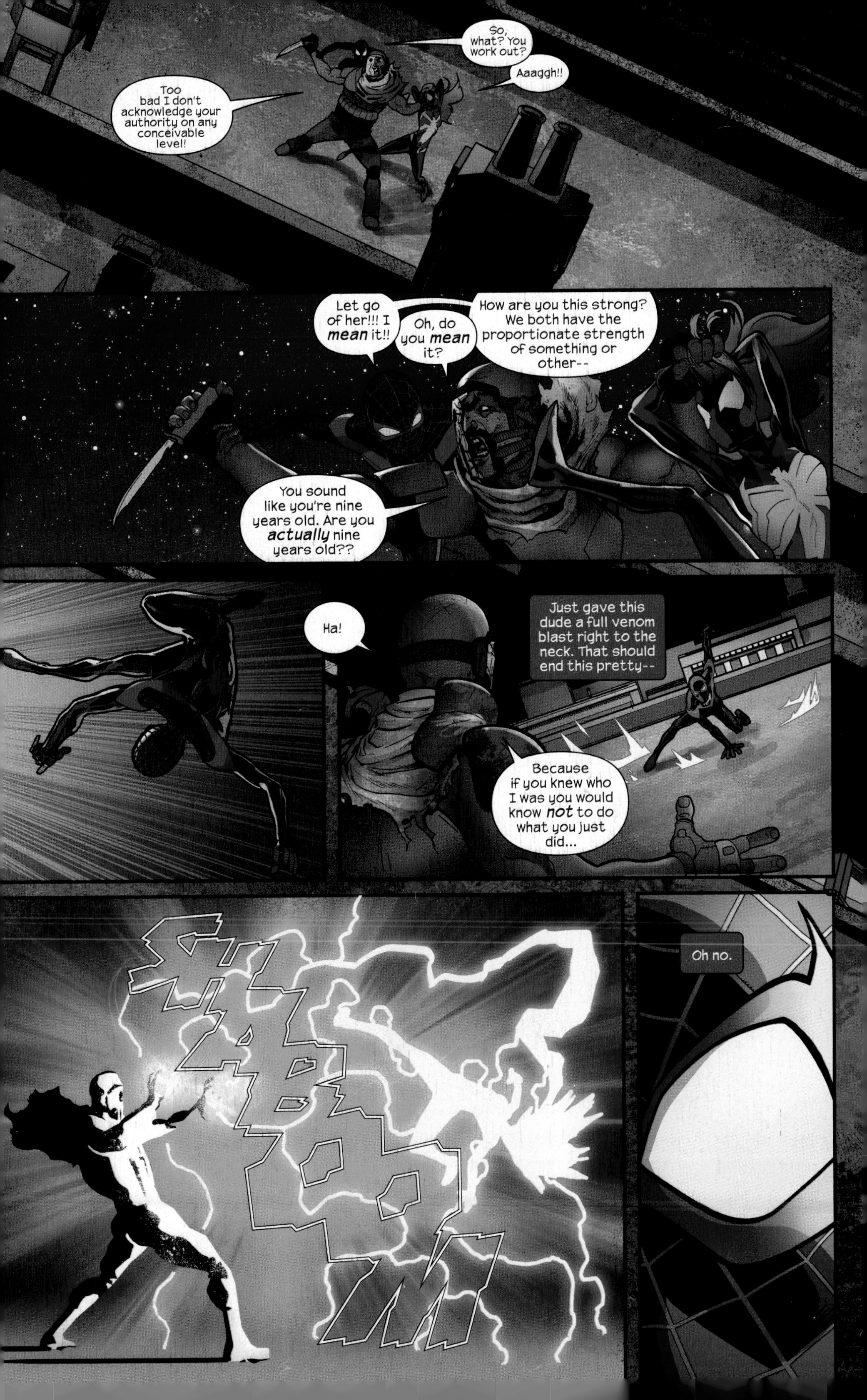
So, what? You work out?
Aaaggh!!
Too bad I don't acknowledge your authority on any conceivable level!
Let go of her!!! I *mean* it!!
Oh, do you *mean* it?
How are you this strong? We both have the proportionate strength of something or other--
You sound like you're nine years old. Are you *actually* nine years old??
Ha!
Just gave this dude a full venom blast right to the neck. That should end this pretty--
Because if you knew who I was you would know *not* to do what you just did...
Oh no.

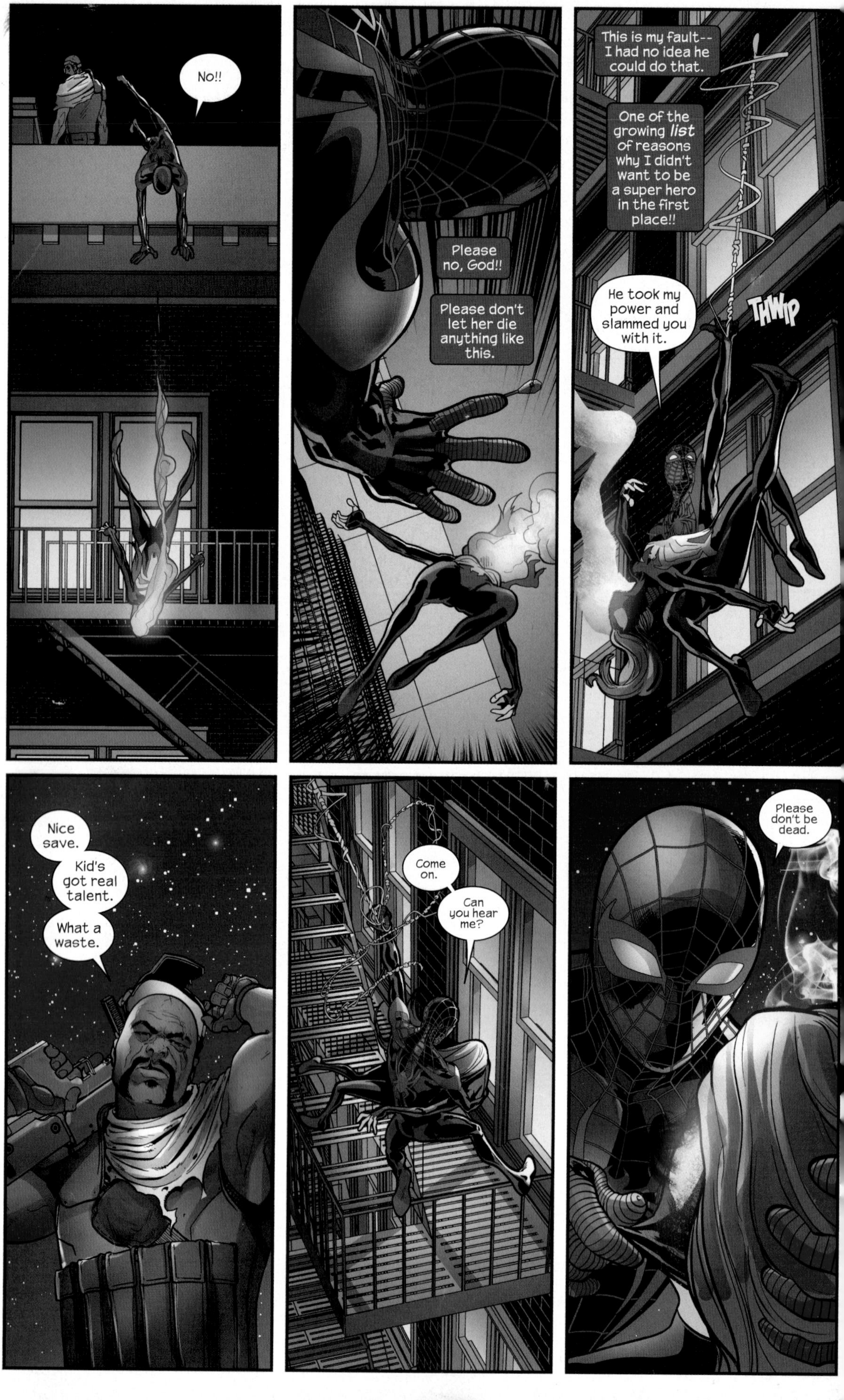
No!!
Please no, God!!
Please don't let her die anything like this.
This is my fault-- I had no idea he could do that.
One of the growing *list* of reasons why I didn't want to be a super hero in the first place!!
He took my power and slammed you with it.
THWIP
Nice save.
Kid's got real talent.
What a waste.
Come on.
Can you hear me?
Please don't be dead.

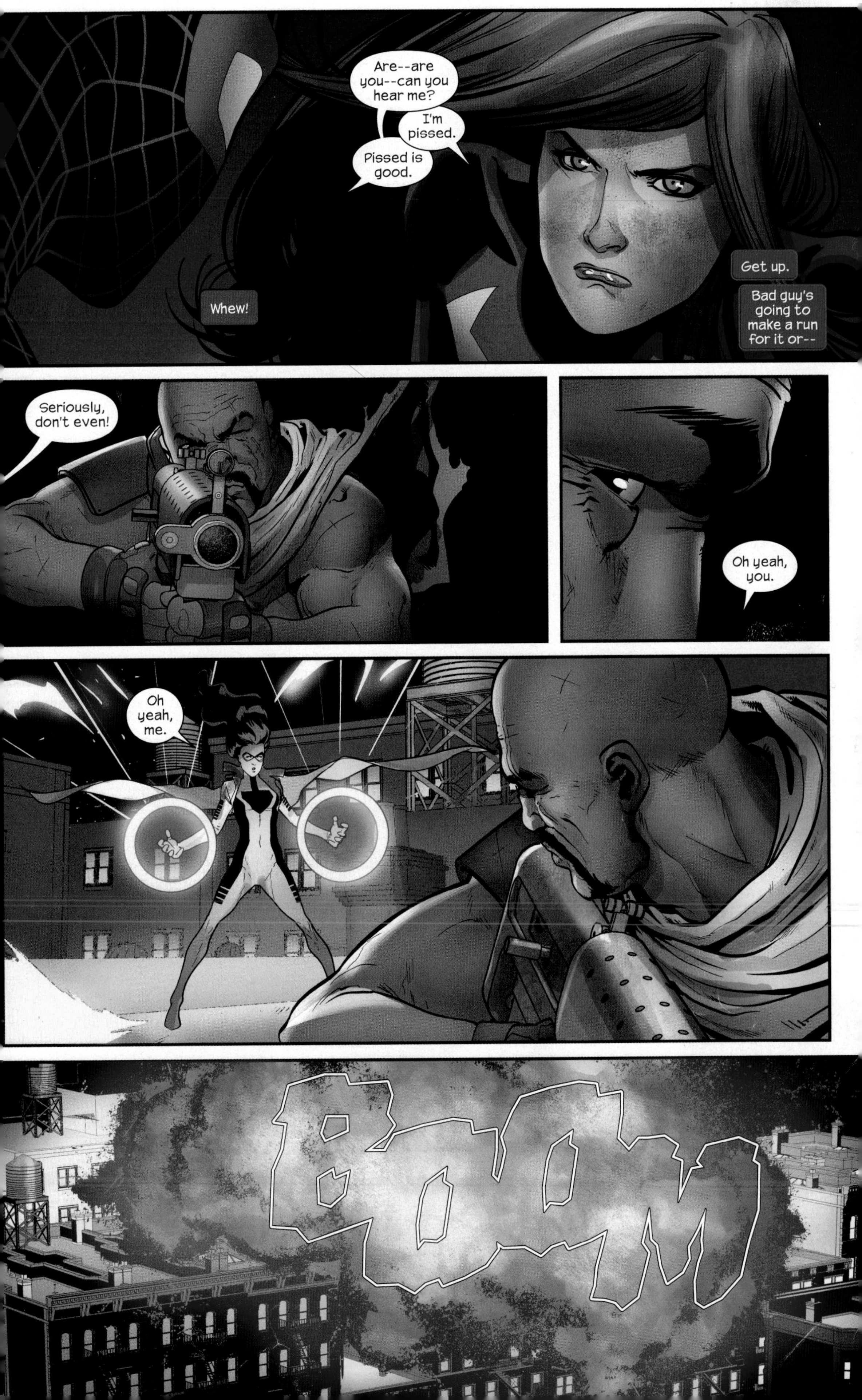

Are--are you--can you hear me?
I'm pissed.
Pissed is good.
Whew!
Get up.
Bad guy's going to make a run for it or--
Seriously, don't even!
Oh yeah, you.
Oh yeah, me.
BOOM

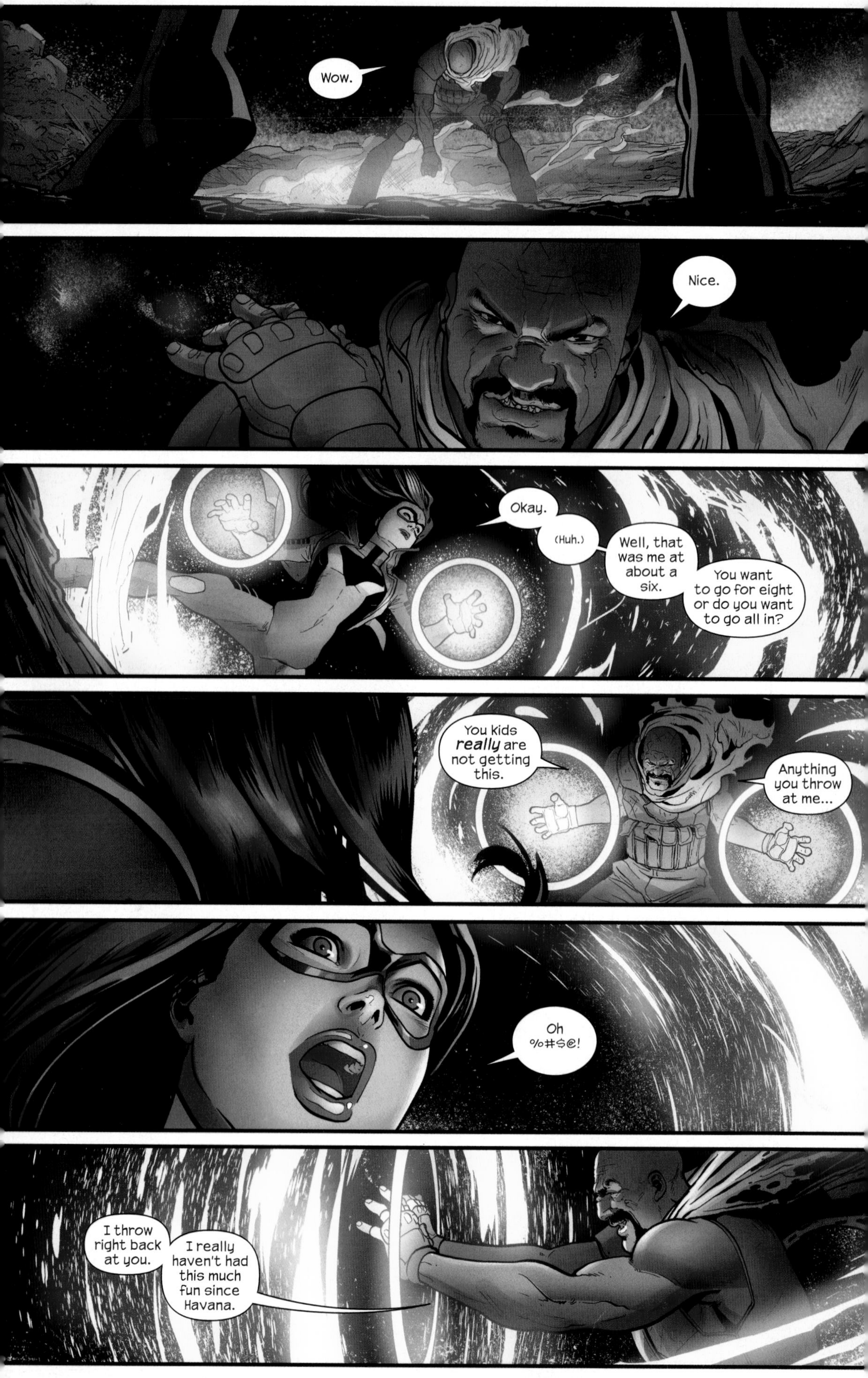

Wow.
Nice.
Okay.
(Huh.)
Well, that was me at about a six.
You want to go for eight or do you want to go all in?
You kids **really** are not getting this.
Anything you throw at me...
Oh %#$@!
I throw right back at you.
I really haven't had this much fun since Havana.

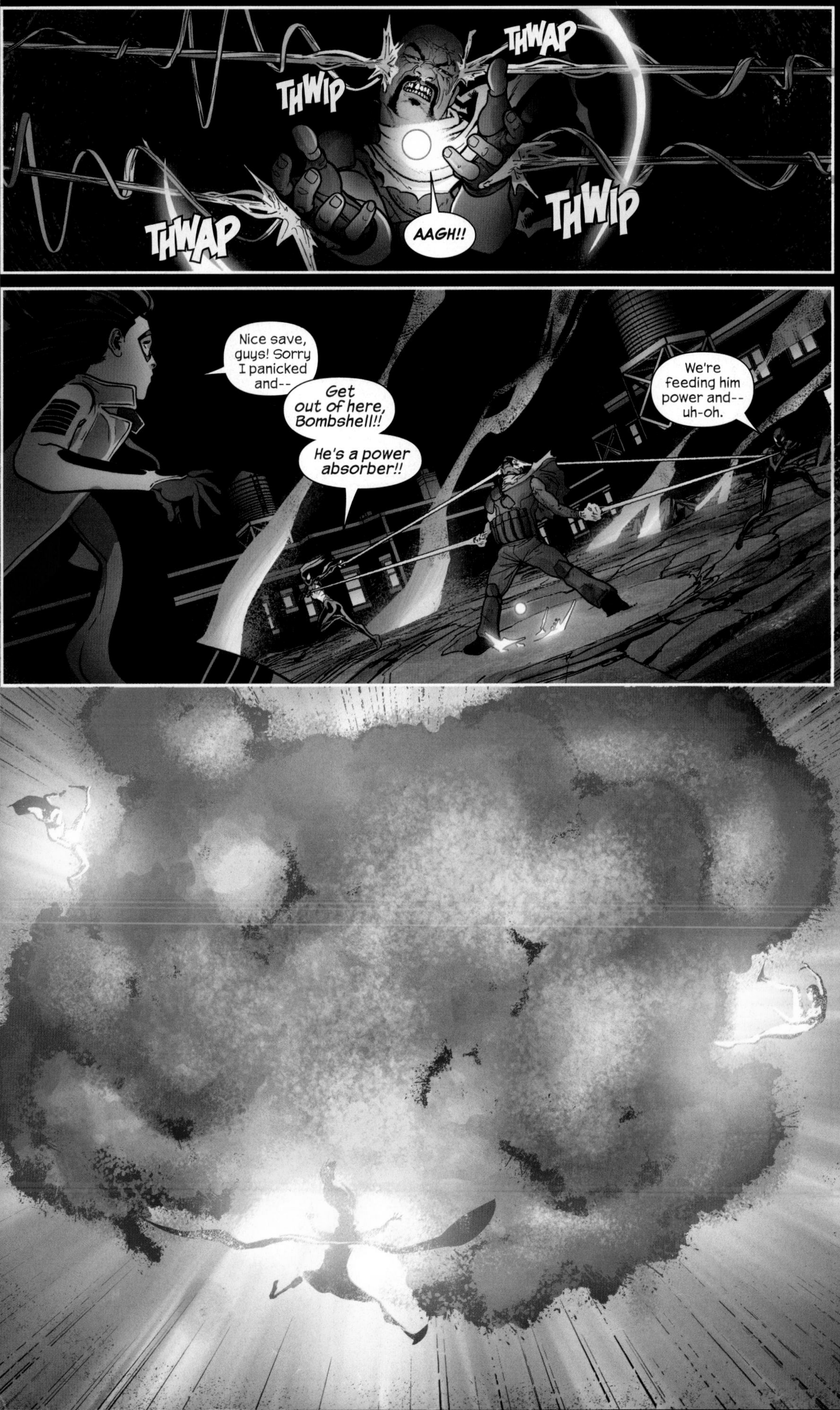
THWIP
THWAP
THWAP
AAGH!!
THWIP
Nice save, guys! Sorry I panicked and--
Get out of here, Bombshell!!
He's a power absorber!!
We're feeding him power and-- uh-oh.

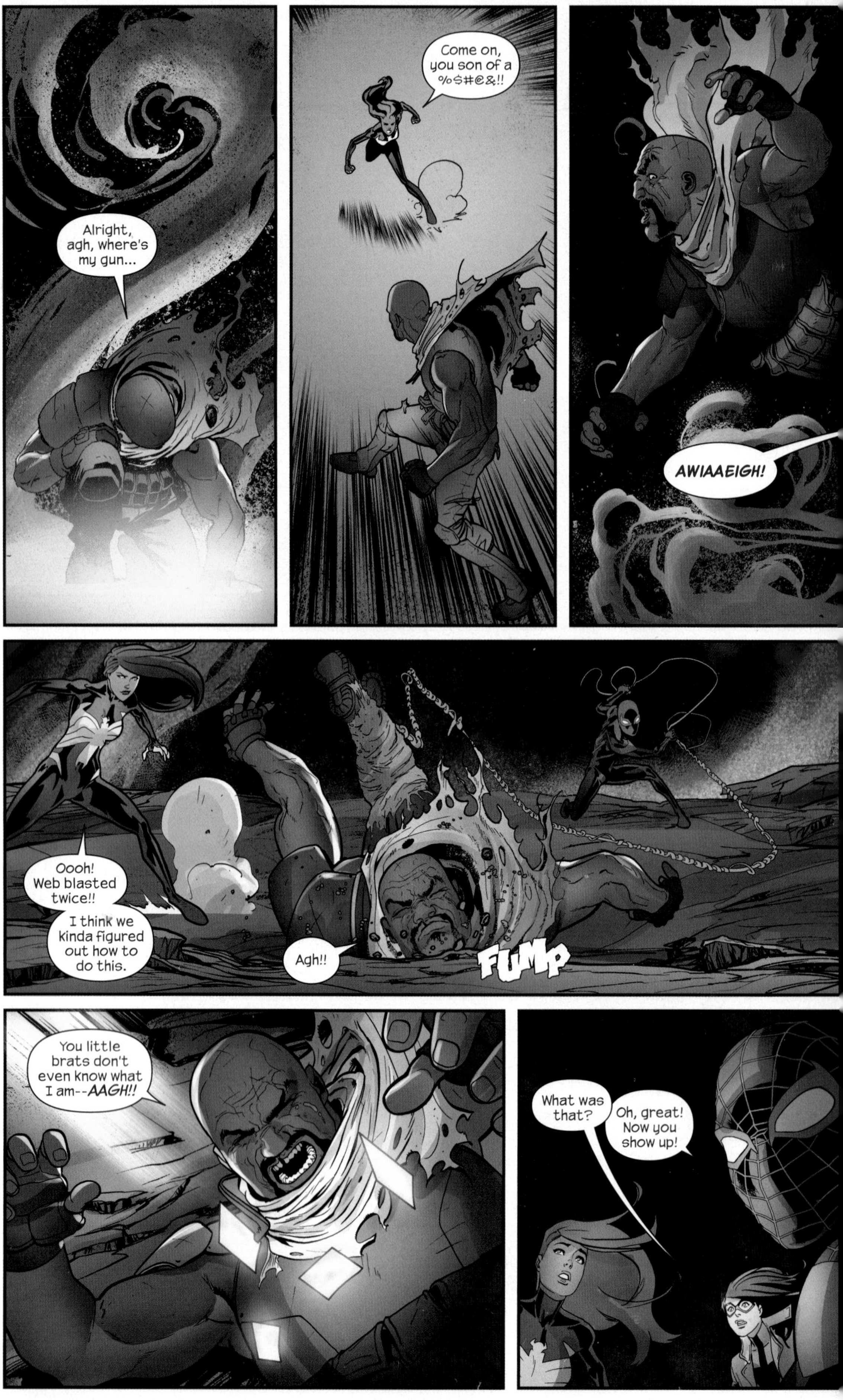
Alright, agh, where's my gun...
Come on, you son of a %$#@&!!
AWIAAEIGH!
Oooh! Web blasted twice!!
I think we kinda figured out how to do this.
Agh!!
FUMP
You little brats don't even know what I am--AAGH!!
What was that?
Oh, great! Now you show up!

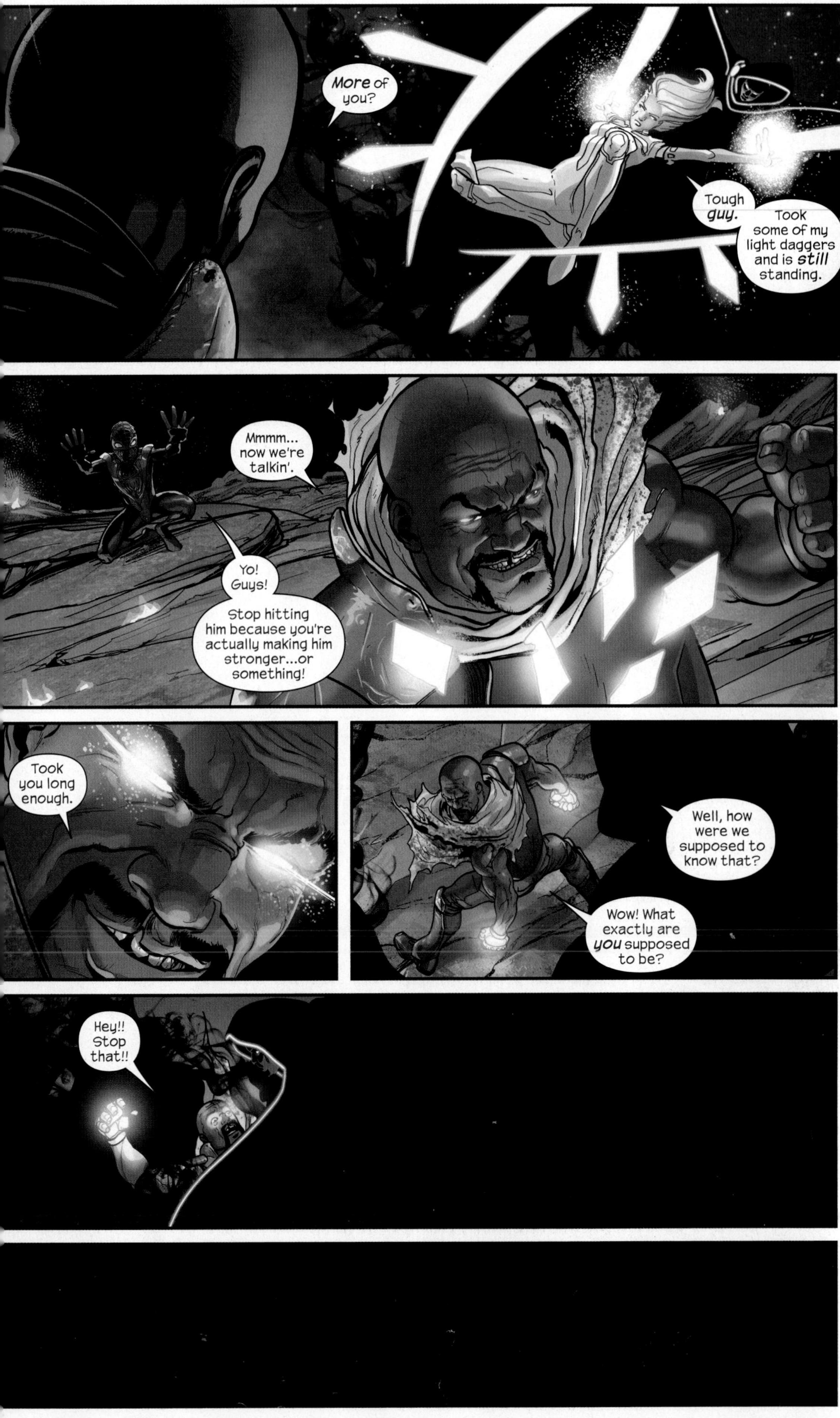
More of you?
Tough guy.
Took some of my light daggers and is still standing.
Mmmm... now we're talkin'.
Yo! Guys!
Stop hitting him because you're actually making him stronger...or something!
Took you long enough.
Well, how were we supposed to know that?
Wow! What exactly are you supposed to be?
Hey!! Stop that!!

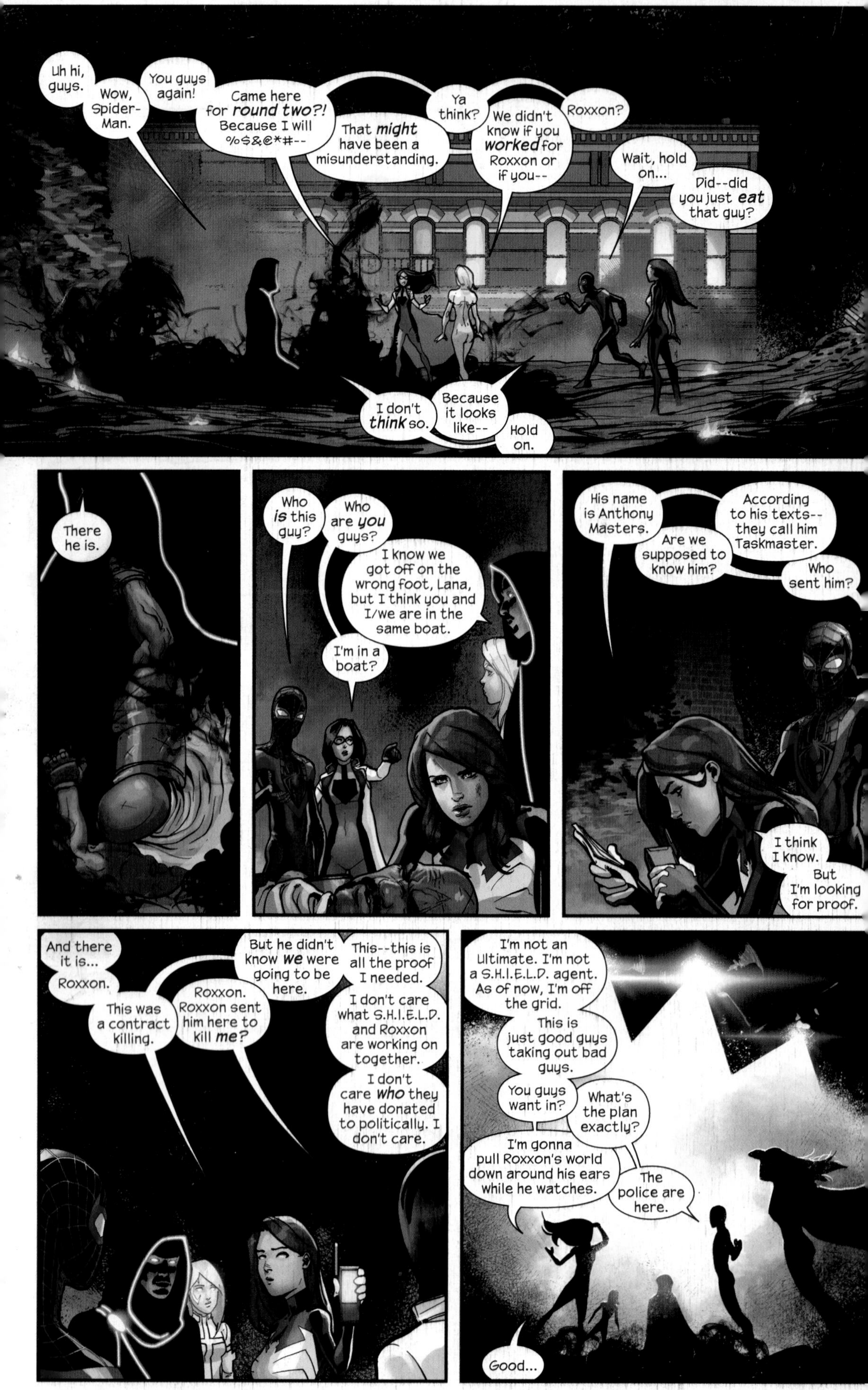
Uh hi, guys.
Wow, Spider-Man.
You guys again!
Came here for round two?! Because I will %$&@*#--
That might have been a misunderstanding.
Ya think?
We didn't know if you worked for Roxxon or if you--
Roxxon?
Wait, hold on...
Did--did you just eat that guy?
I don't think so.
Because it looks like--
Hold on.
There he is.
Who is this guy?
Who are you guys?
I know we got off on the wrong foot, Lana, but I think you and I/we are in the same boat.
I'm in a boat?
His name is Anthony Masters.
According to his texts--they call him Taskmaster.
Are we supposed to know him?
Who sent him?
I think I know.
But I'm looking for proof.
And there it is...
Roxxon.
This was a contract killing.
Roxxon. Roxxon sent him here to kill me?
But he didn't know we were going to be here.
This--this is all the proof I needed.
I don't care what S.H.I.E.L.D. and Roxxon are working on together.
I don't care who they have donated to politically. I don't care.
I'm not an Ultimate. I'm not a S.H.I.E.L.D. agent. As of now, I'm off the grid.
This is just good guys taking out bad guys.
You guys want in?
What's the plan exactly?
I'm gonna pull Roxxon's world down around his ears while he watches.
The police are here.
Good...

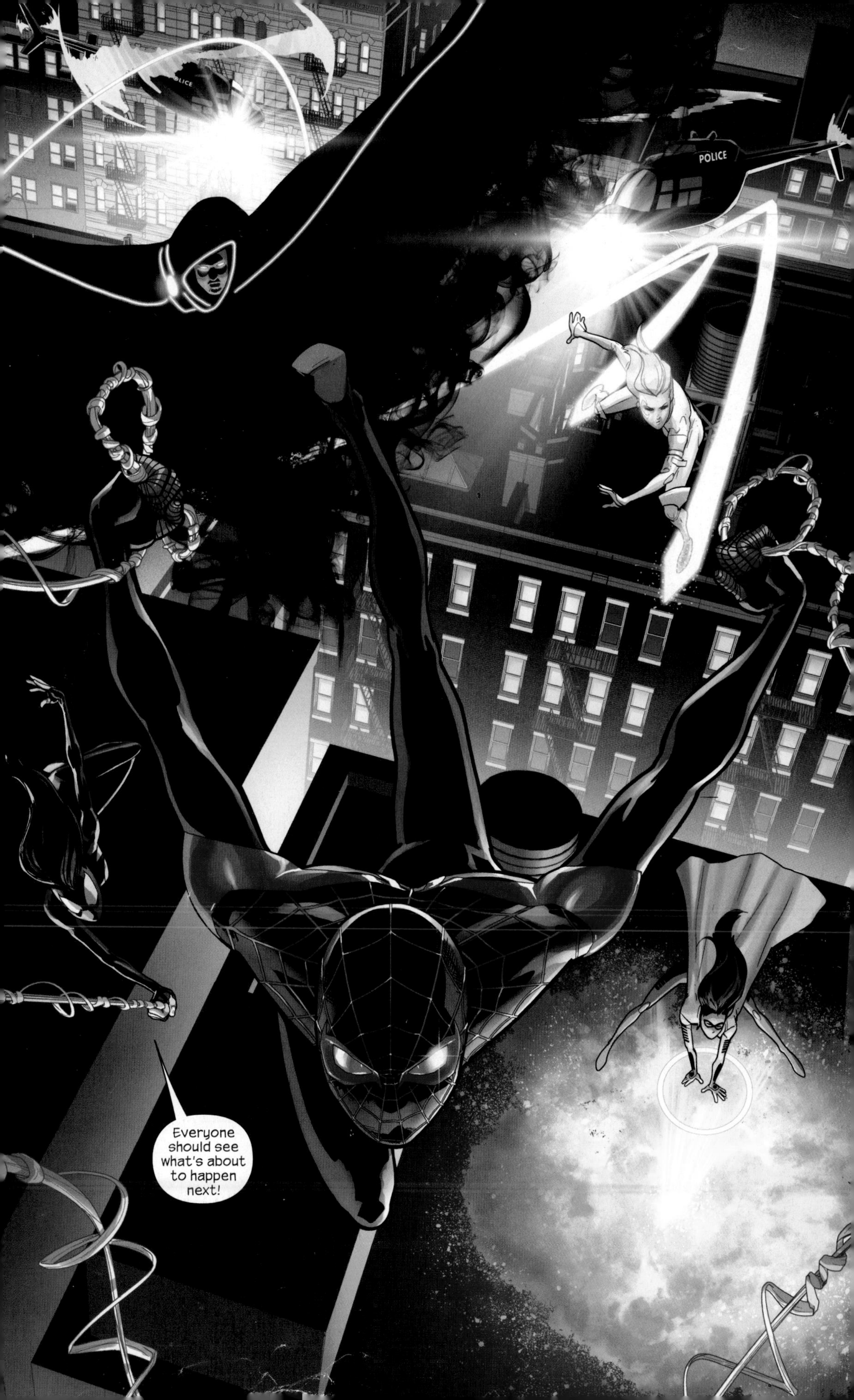
POLICE
POLICE
Everyone should see what's about to happen next!

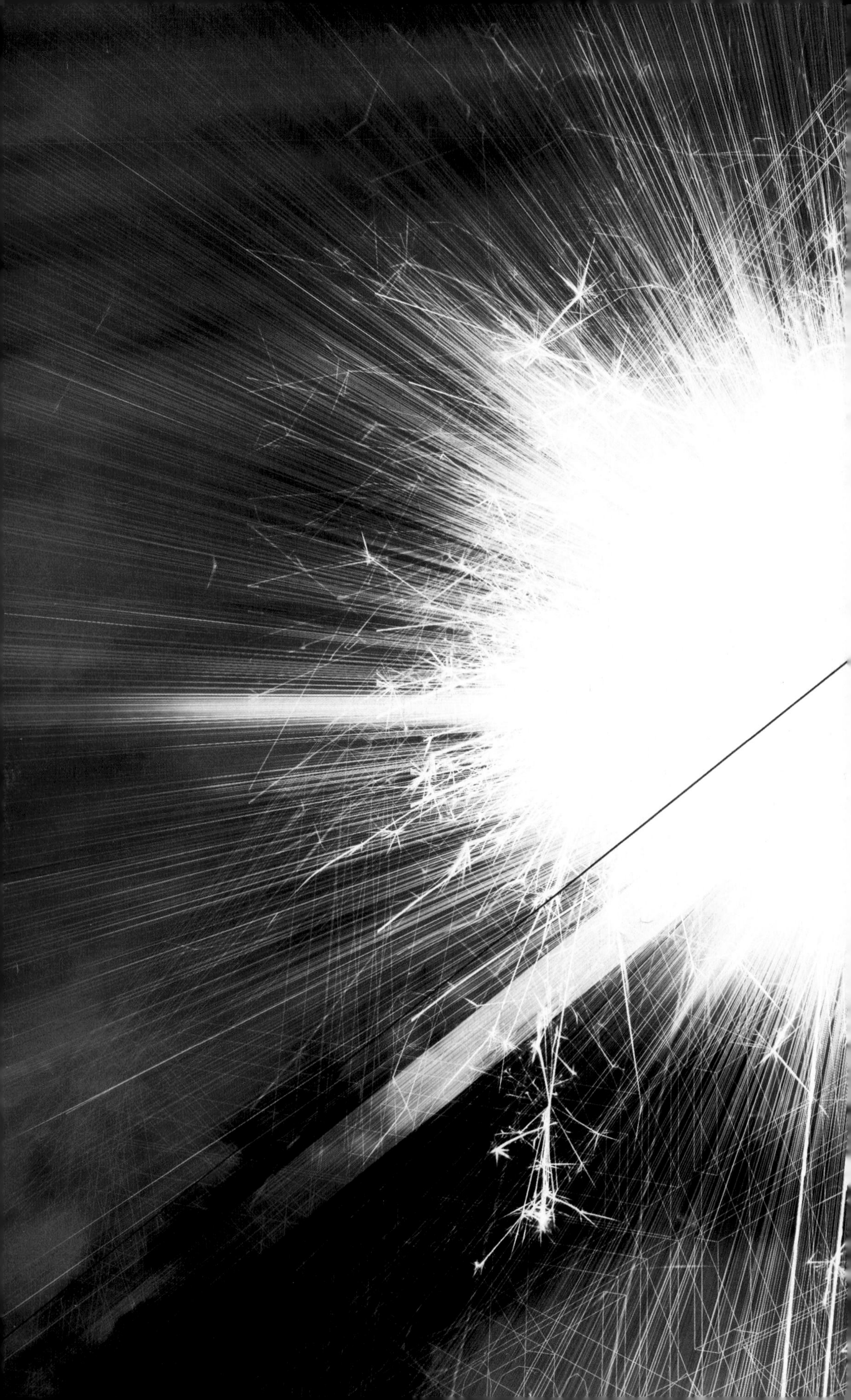

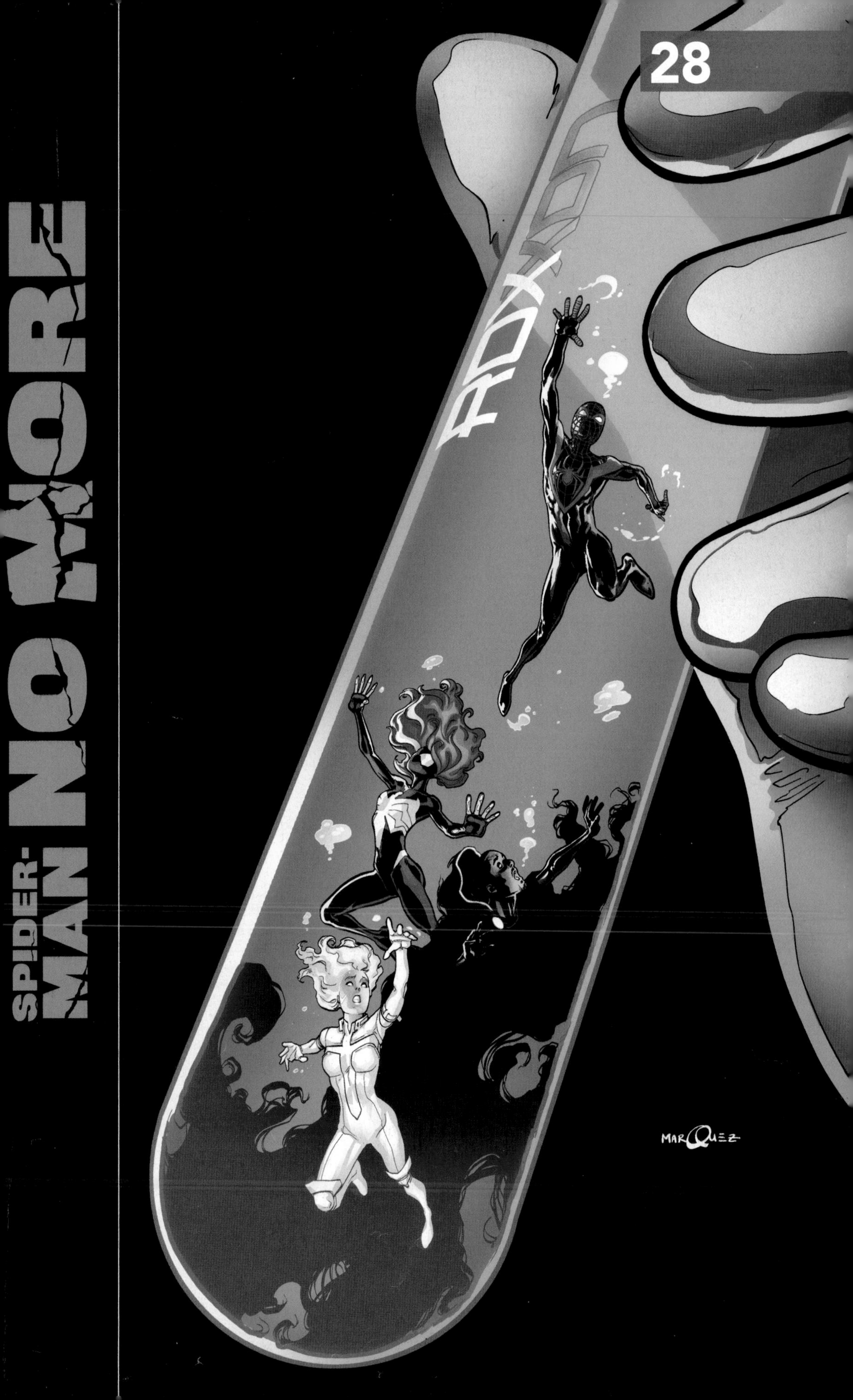
SPIDER-MAN NO MORE
28
MARQUEZ

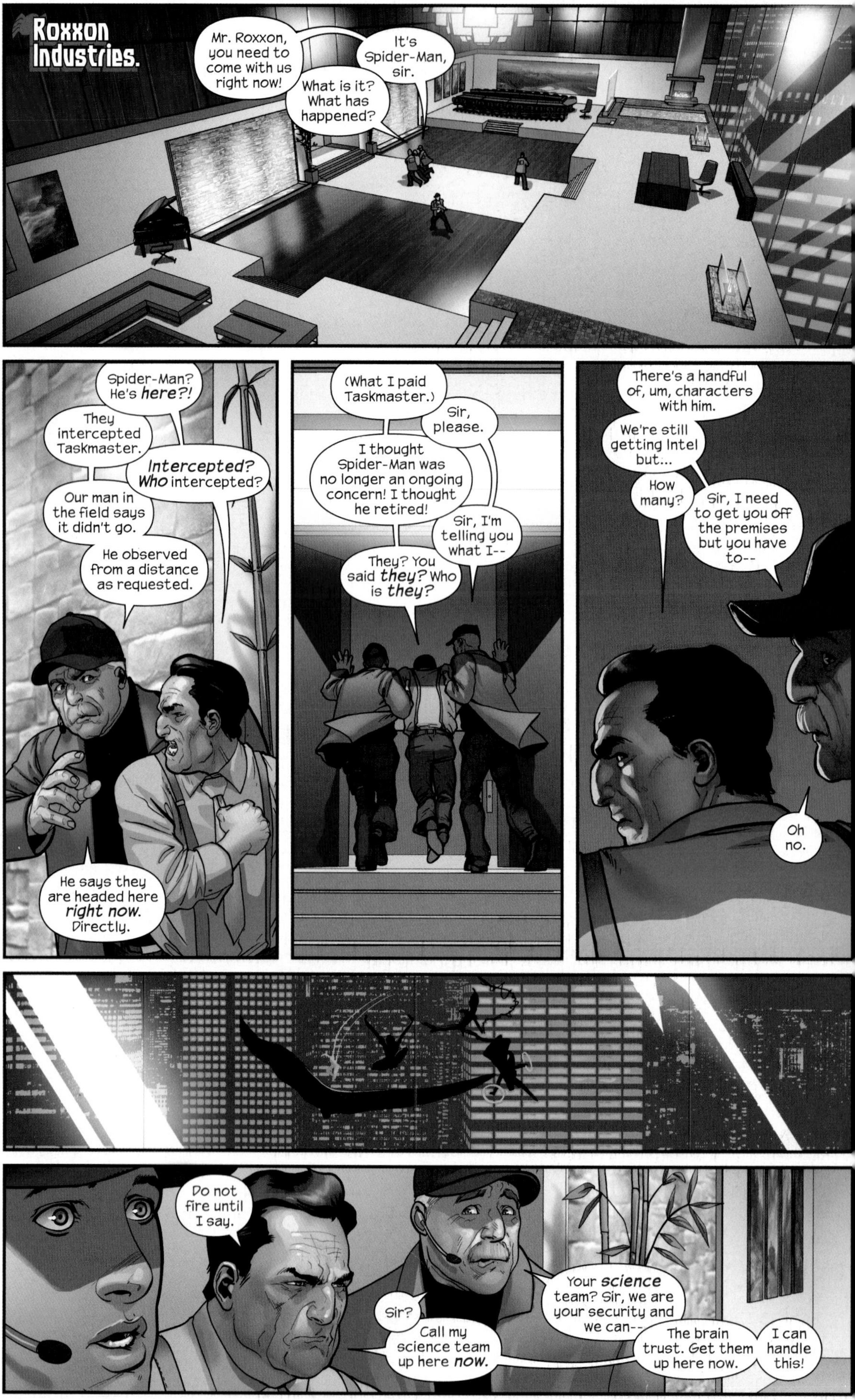
Roxxon Industries.
Mr. Roxxon, you need to come with us right now!
It's Spider-Man, sir.
What is it? What has happened?
Spider-Man? He's here?!
They intercepted Taskmaster.
Intercepted? Who intercepted?
Our man in the field says it didn't go.
He observed from a distance as requested.
He says they are headed here right now. Directly.
(What I paid Taskmaster.)
Sir, please.
I thought Spider-Man was no longer an ongoing concern! I thought he retired!
Sir, I'm telling you what I--
They? You said they? Who is they?
There's a handful of, um, characters with him.
We're still getting Intel but...
How many?
Sir, I need to get you off the premises but you have to--
Oh no.
Do not fire until I say.
Sir?
Call my science team up here now.
Your science team? Sir, we are your security and we can--
The brain trust. Get them up here now.
I can handle this!

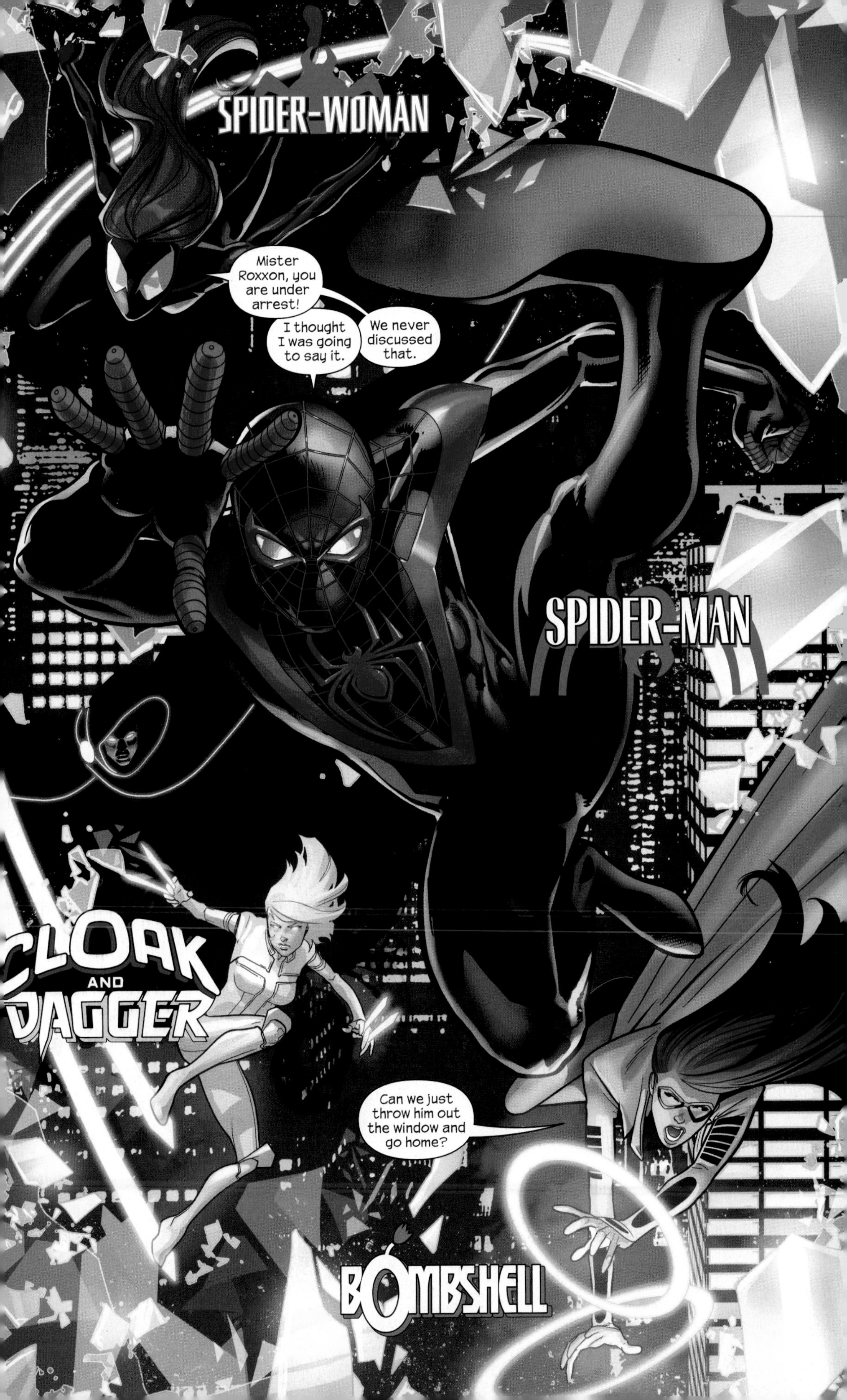
SPIDER-WOMAN
Mister Roxxon, you are under arrest!
I thought I was going to say it.
We never discussed that.
SPIDER-MAN
CLOAK AND DAGGER
Can we just throw him out the window and go home?
BOMBSHELL

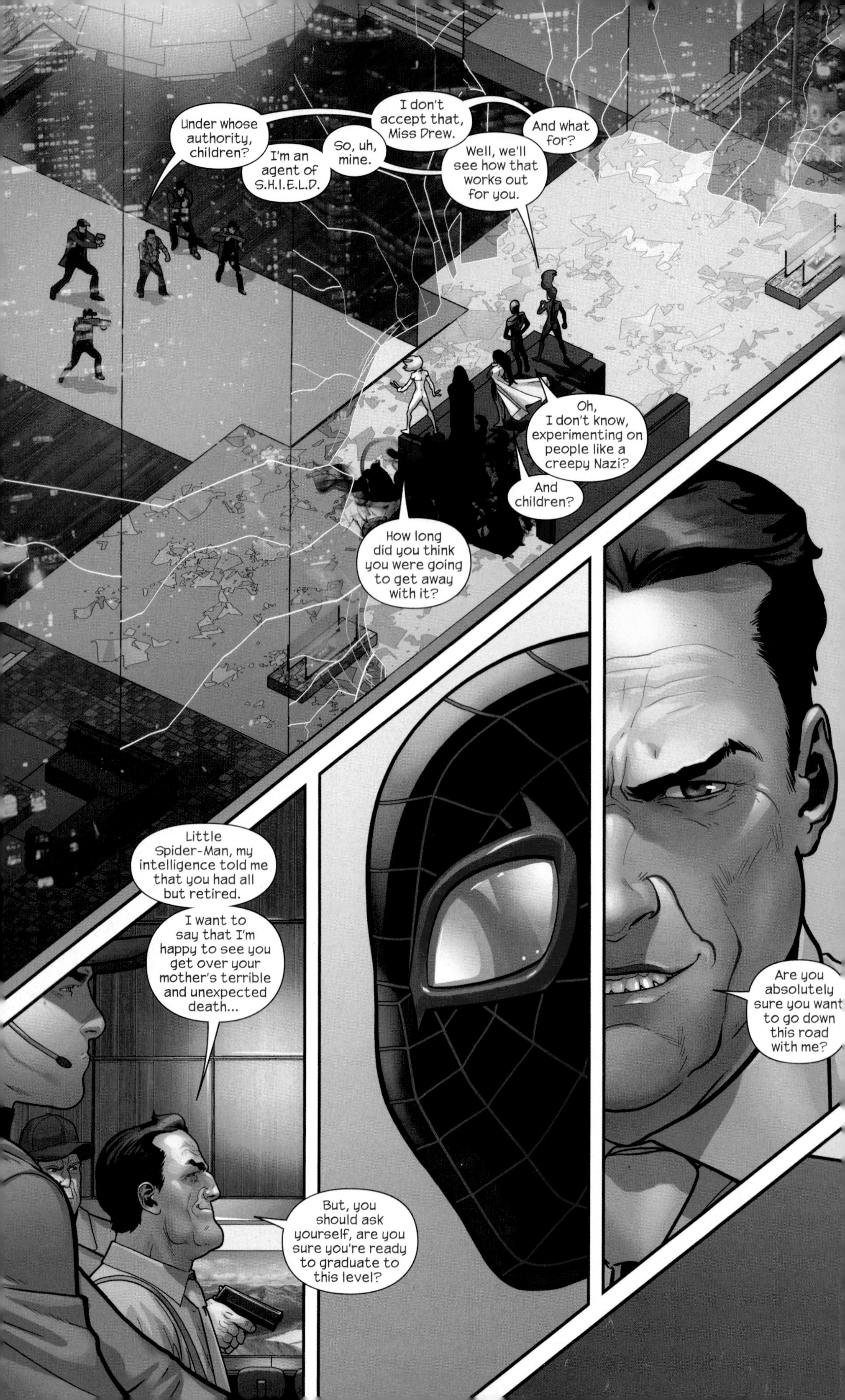
Under whose authority, children?
I'm an agent of S.H.I.E.L.D.
So, uh, mine.
I don't accept that, Miss Drew.
Well, we'll see how that works out for you.
And what for?
Oh, I don't know, experimenting on people like a creepy Nazi?
And children?
How long did you think you were going to get away with it?
Little Spider-Man, my intelligence told me that you had all but retired.
I want to say that I'm happy to see you get over your mother's terrible and unexpected death...
But, you should ask yourself, are you sure you're ready to graduate to this level?
Are you absolutely sure you want to go down this road with me?

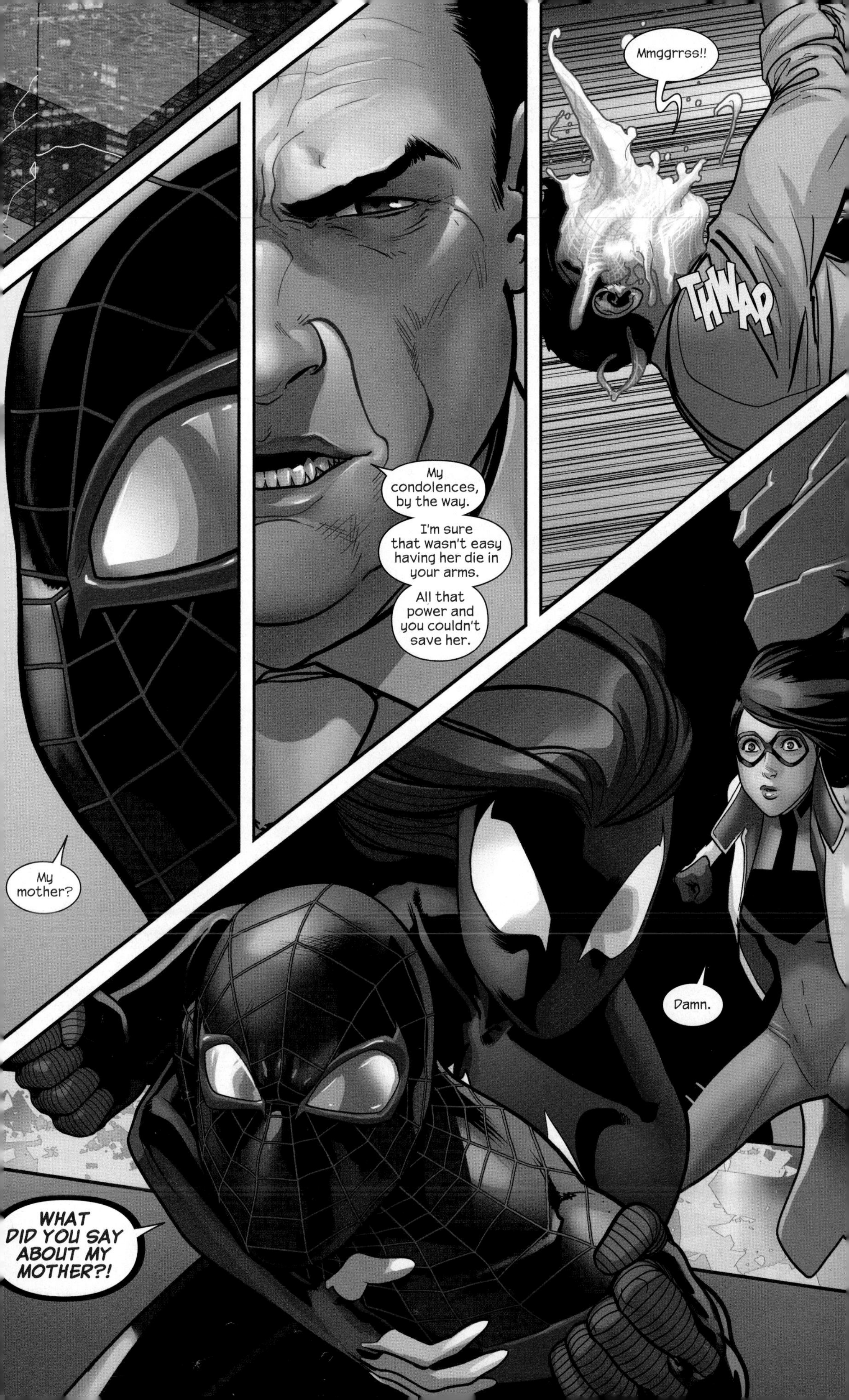

My condolences, by the way.
I'm sure that wasn't easy having her die in your arms.
All that power and you couldn't save her.
Mmggrrss!!
THWAP
My mother?
Damn.
WHAT DID YOU SAY ABOUT MY MOTHER?!

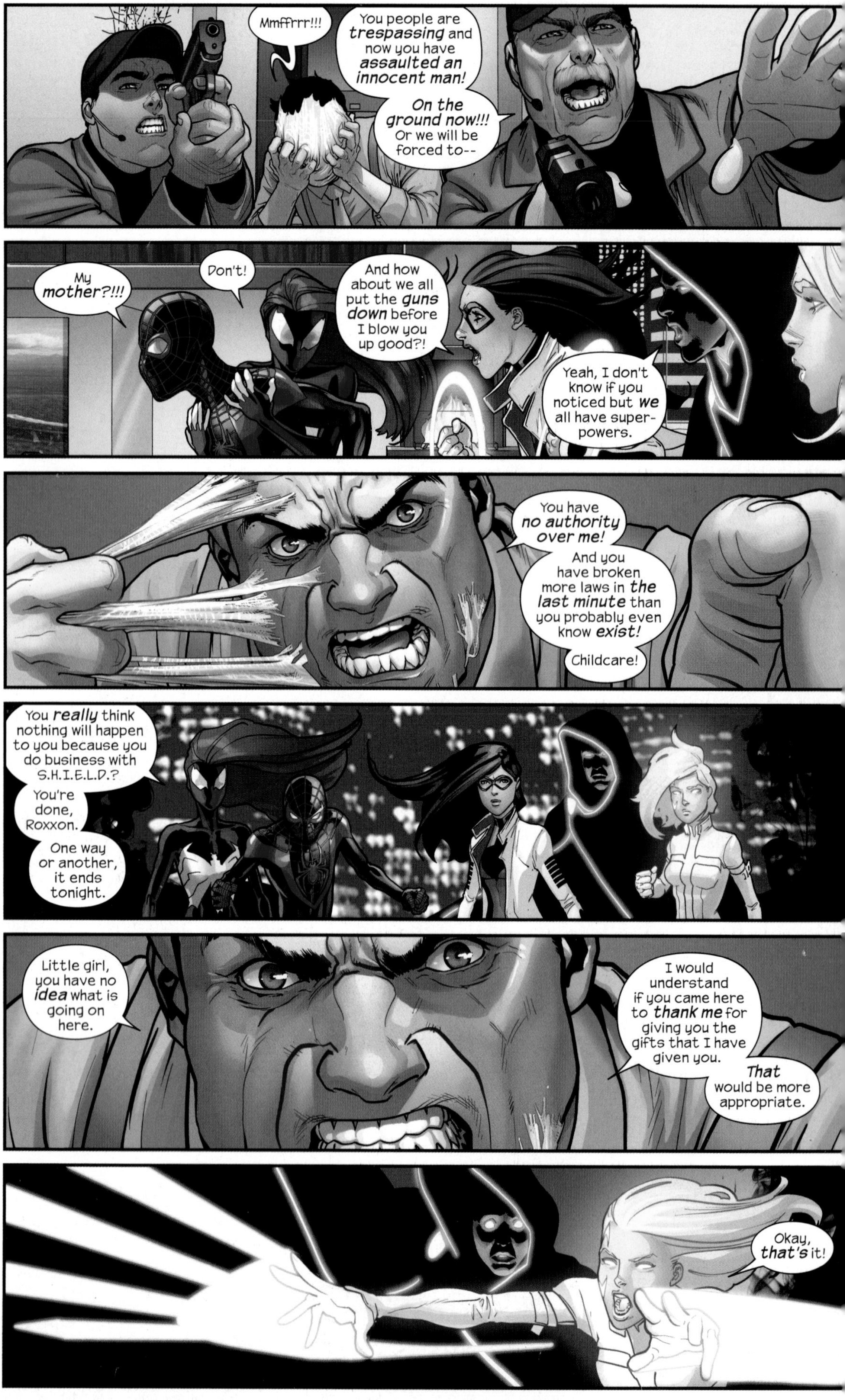

Mmffrrr!!!
You people are trespassing and now you have assaulted an innocent man!
On the ground now!!! Or we will be forced to--
My mother?!!!
Don't!
And how about we all put the guns down before I blow you up good?!
Yeah, I don't know if you noticed but we all have superpowers.
You have no authority over me!
And you have broken more laws in the last minute than you probably even know exist!
Childcare!
You really think nothing will happen to you because you do business with S.H.I.E.L.D.?
You're done, Roxxon.
One way or another, it ends tonight.
Little girl, you have no idea what is going on here.
I would understand if you came here to thank me for giving you the gifts that I have given you.
That would be more appropriate.
Okay, that's it!

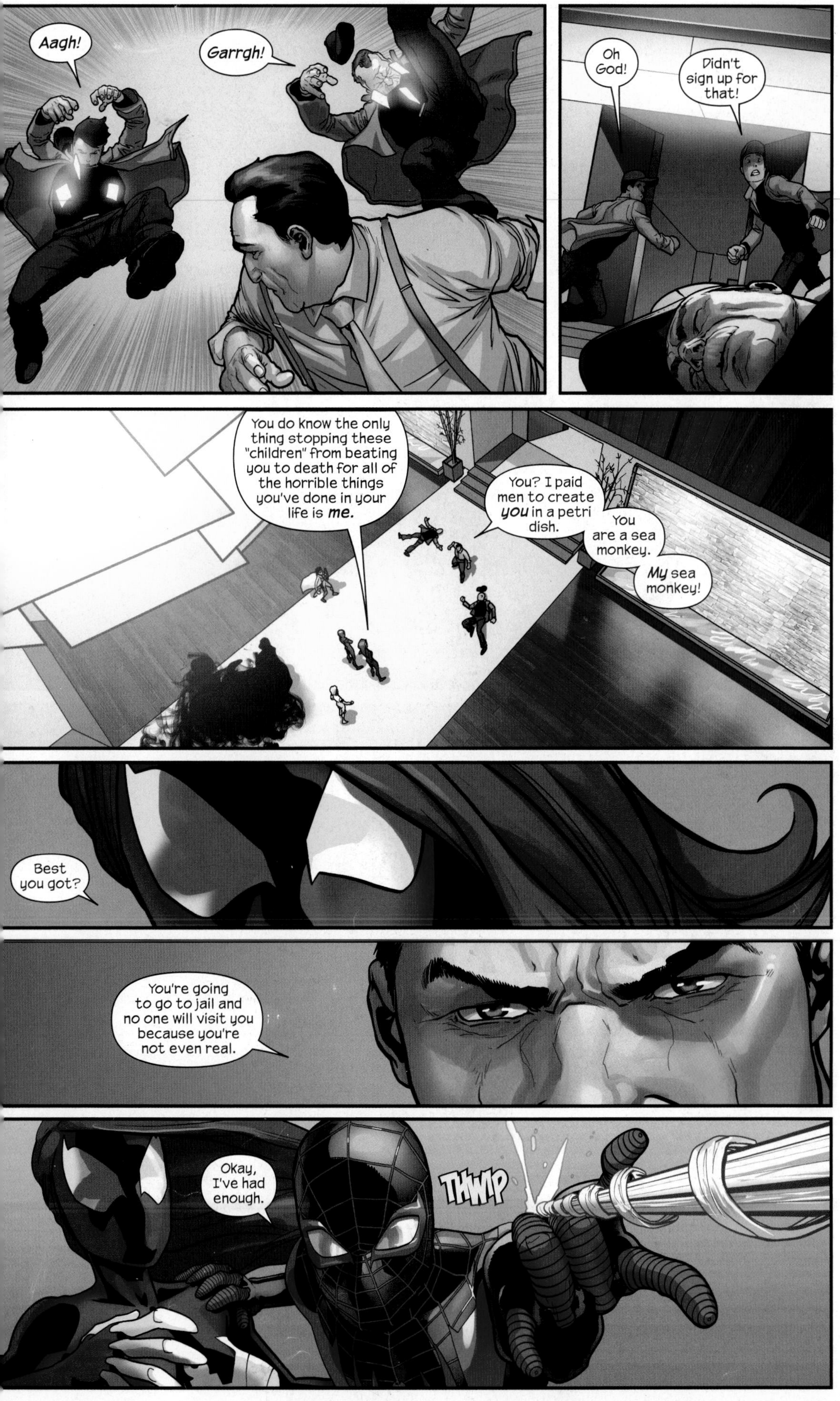
Aagh!
Garrgh!
Oh God!
Didn't sign up for that!
You do know the only thing stopping these "children" from beating you to death for all of the horrible things you've done in your life is *me.*
You? I paid men to create *you* in a petri dish.
You are a sea monkey.
My sea monkey!
Best you got?
You're going to go to jail and no one will visit you because you're not even real.
Okay, I've had enough.
THWIP

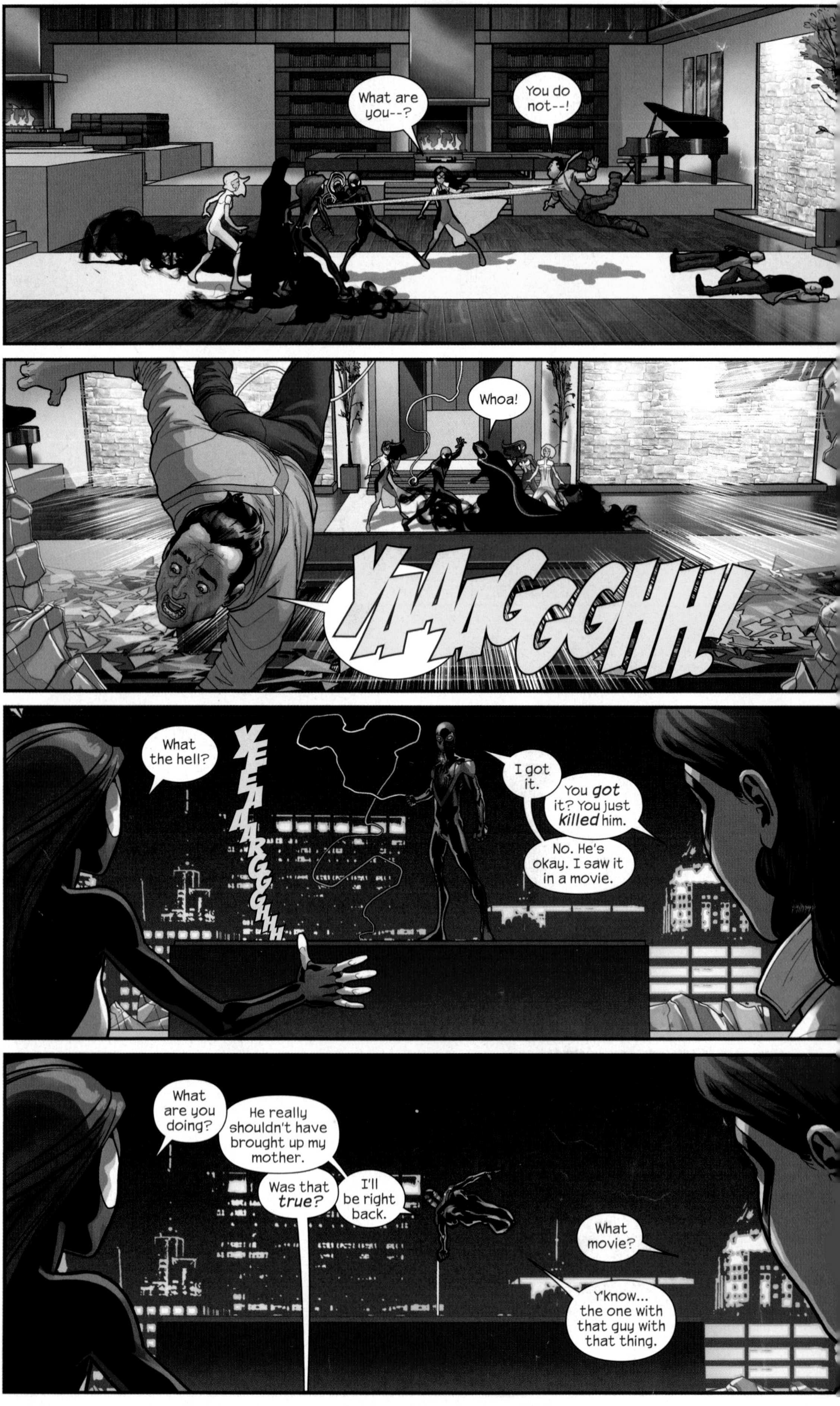
What are you--?
You do not--!
Whoa!
YAAAGGGHH!
What the hell?
YEAAARGGGHHH
I got it.
You got it? You just killed him.
No. He's okay. I saw it in a movie.
What are you doing?
He really shouldn't have brought up my mother.
Was that true?
I'll be right back.
What movie?
Y'know... the one with that guy with that thing.

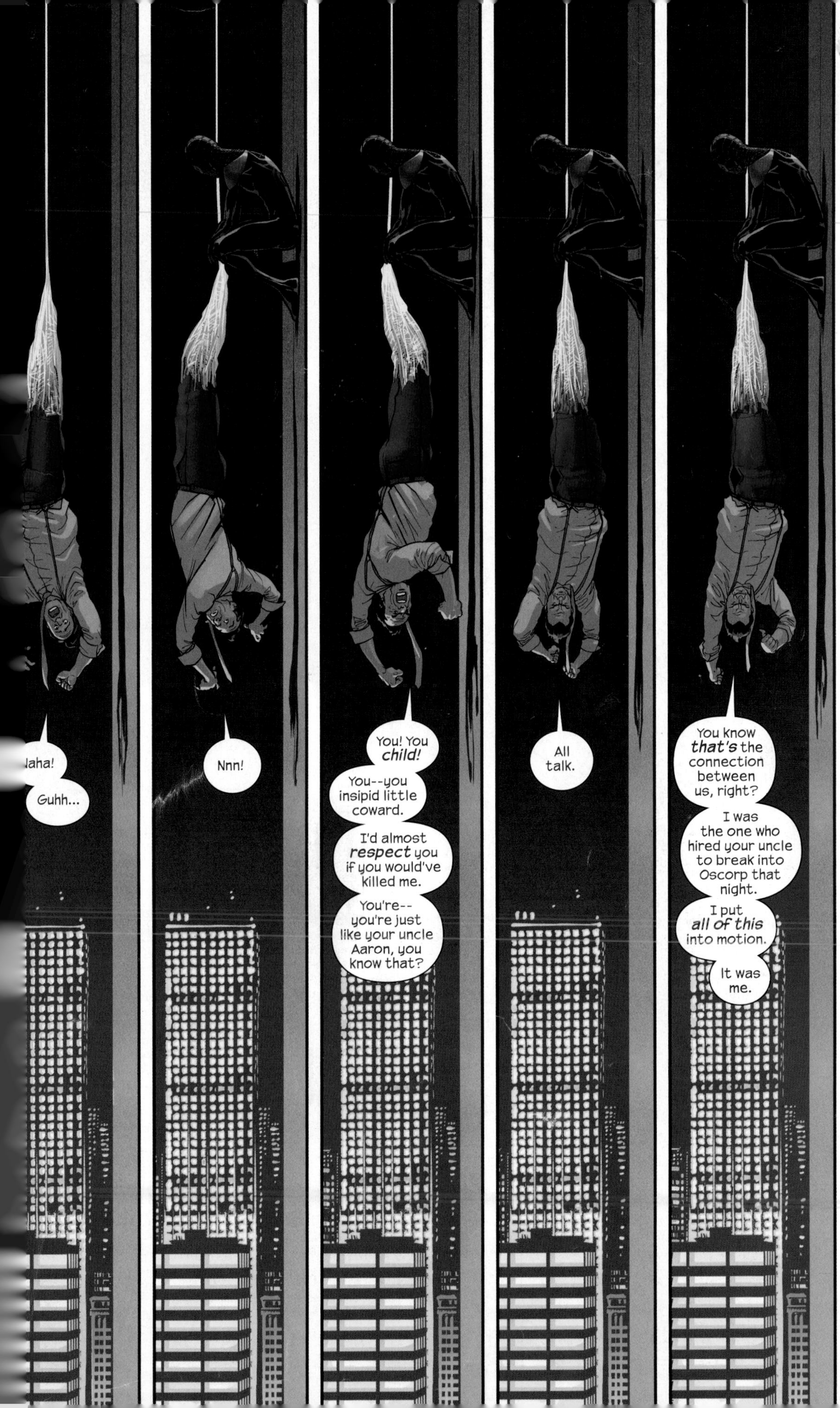
Guhh...
Nnn!
You! You *child!*
You--you insipid little coward.
I'd almost *respect* you if you would've killed me.
You're-- you're just like your uncle Aaron, you know that?
All talk.
You know *that's* the connection between us, right?
I was the one who hired your uncle to break into Oscorp that night.
I put *all of this* into motion.
It was me.

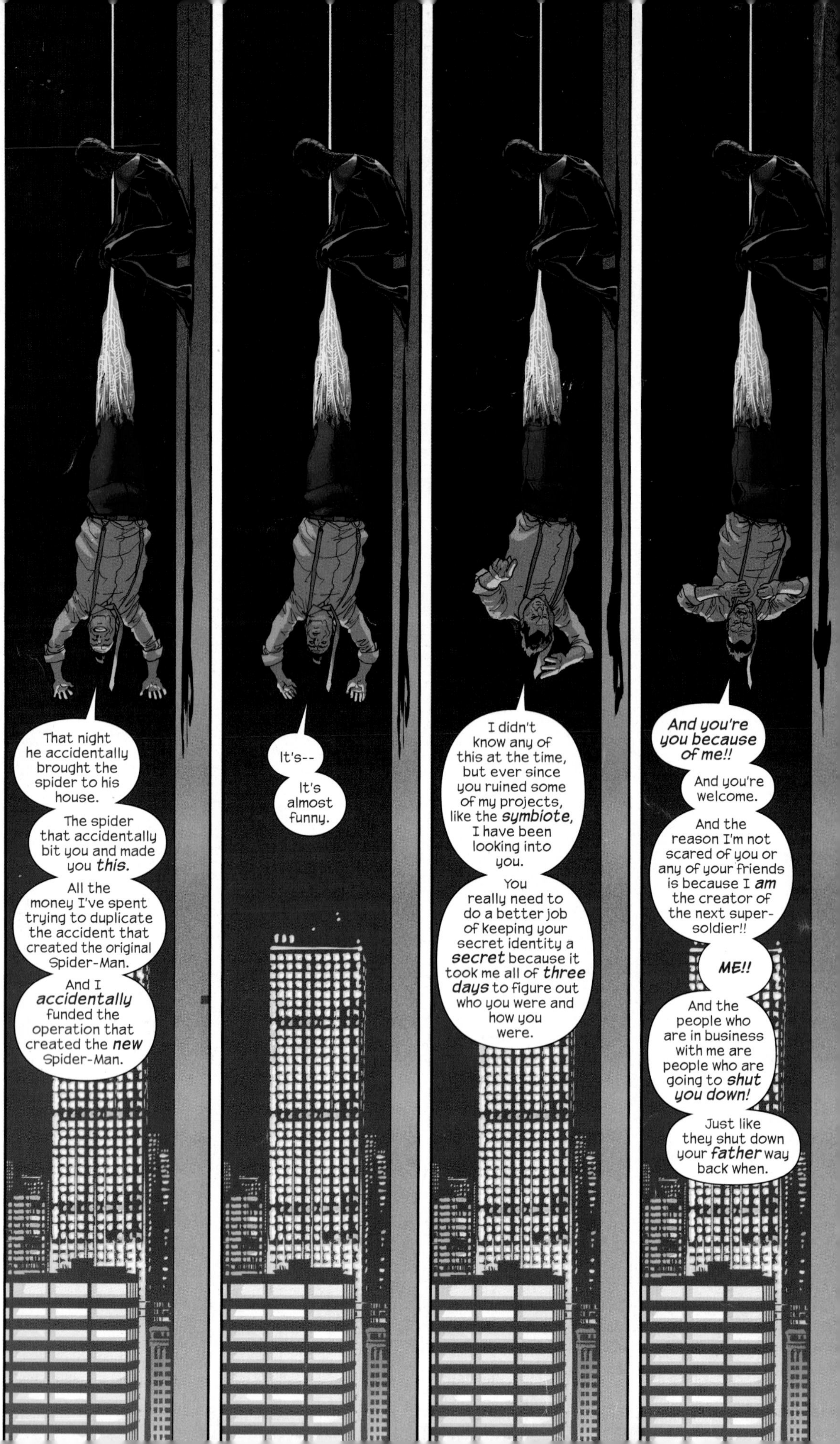
That night he accidentally brought the spider to his house.
The spider that accidentally bit you and made you *this.*
All the money I've spent trying to duplicate the accident that created the original Spider-Man.
And I *accidentally* funded the operation that created the *new* Spider-Man.
It's--
It's almost funny.
I didn't know any of this at the time, but ever since you ruined some of my projects, like the *symbiote*, I have been looking into you.
You really need to do a better job of keeping your secret identity a *secret* because it took me all of *three days* to figure out who you were and how you were.
And you're you because of me!!
And you're welcome.
And the reason I'm not scared of you or any of your friends is because I *am* the creator of the next super-soldier!!
ME!!
And the people who are in business with me are people who are going to *shut you down!*
Just like they shut down your *father* way back when.

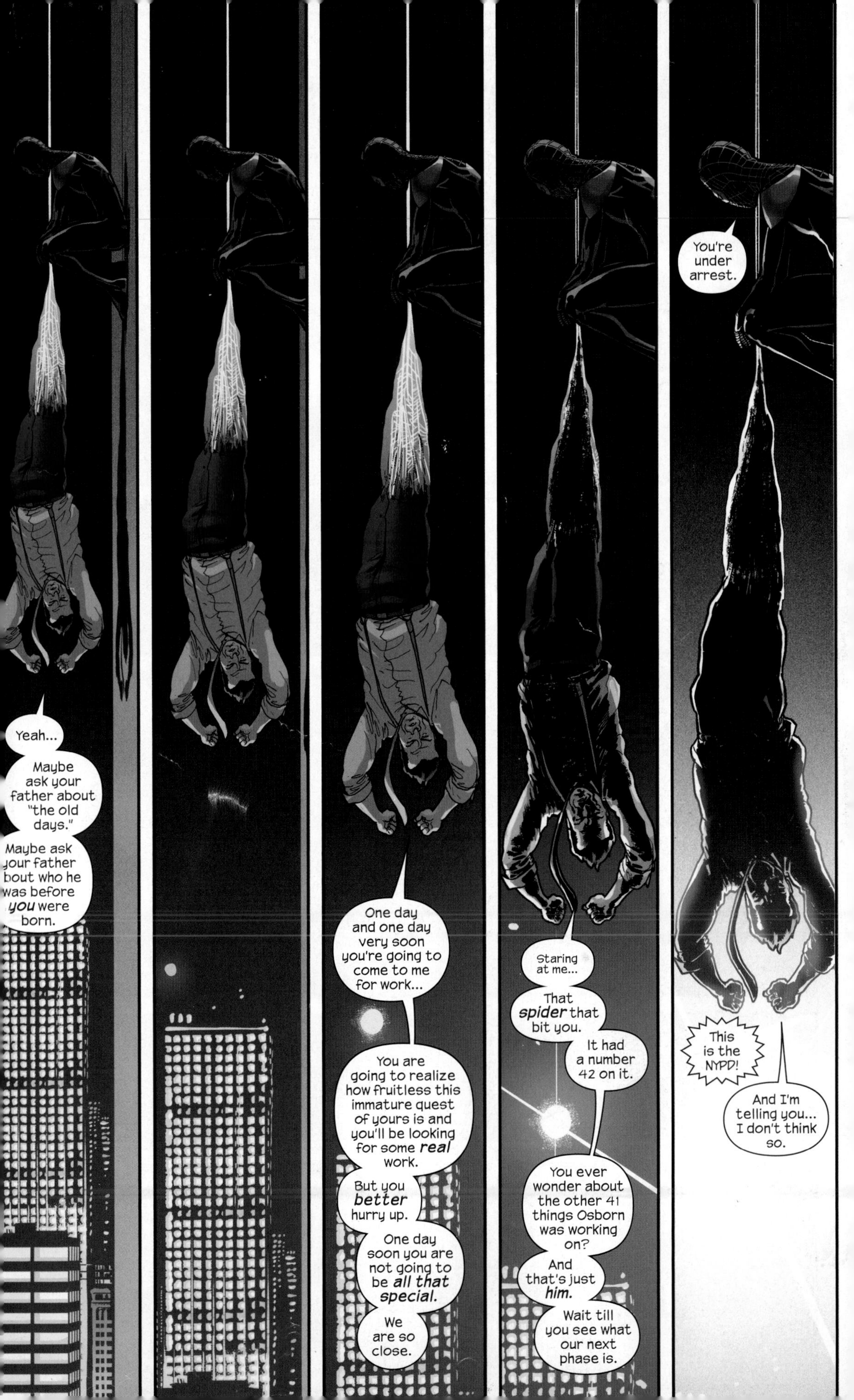
Yeah...
Maybe ask your father about "the old days."
Maybe ask your father bout who he was before *you* were born.
One day and one day very soon you're going to come to me for work...
You are going to realize how fruitless this immature quest of yours is and you'll be looking for some *real* work.
But you *better* hurry up.
One day soon you are not going to be *all that special.*
We are so close.
Staring at me...
That *spider* that bit you.
It had a number 42 on it.
You ever wonder about the other 41 things Osborn was working on?
And that's just *him.*
Wait till you see what our next phase is.
You're under arrest.
This is the NYPD!
And I'm telling you... I don't think so.

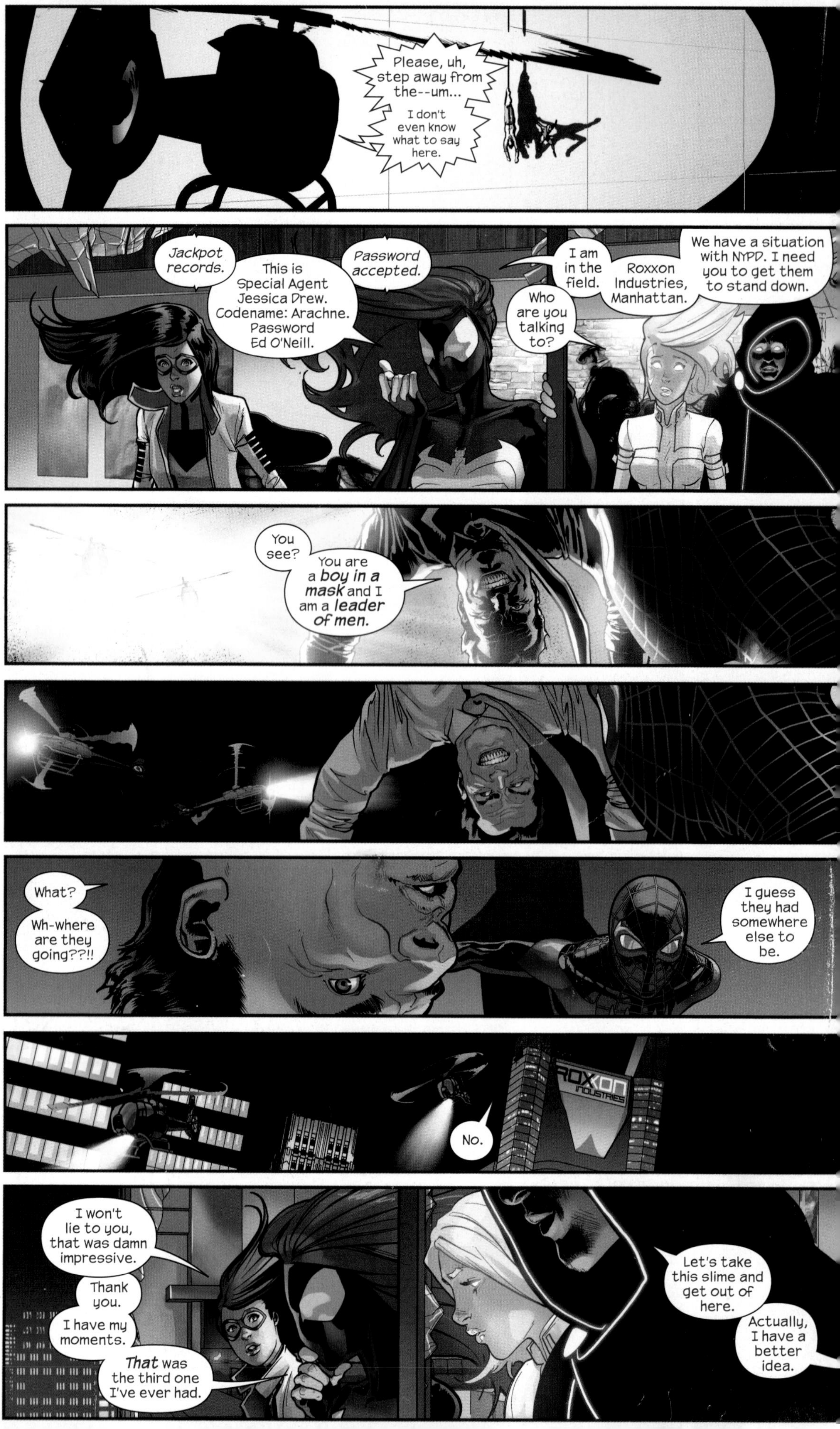

Please, uh, step away from the--um...
I don't even know what to say here.
Jackpot records.
This is Special Agent Jessica Drew. Codename: Arachne. Password Ed O'Neill.
Password accepted.
I am in the field.
Who are you talking to?
Roxxon Industries, Manhattan.
We have a situation with NYPD. I need you to get them to stand down.
You see?
You are a boy in a mask and I am a leader of men.
What?
Wh-where are they going??!!
I guess they had somewhere else to be.
No.
ROXXON INDUSTRIES
I won't lie to you, that was damn impressive.
Thank you.
I have my moments.
That was the third one I've ever had.
Let's take this slime and get out of here.
Actually, I have a better idea.

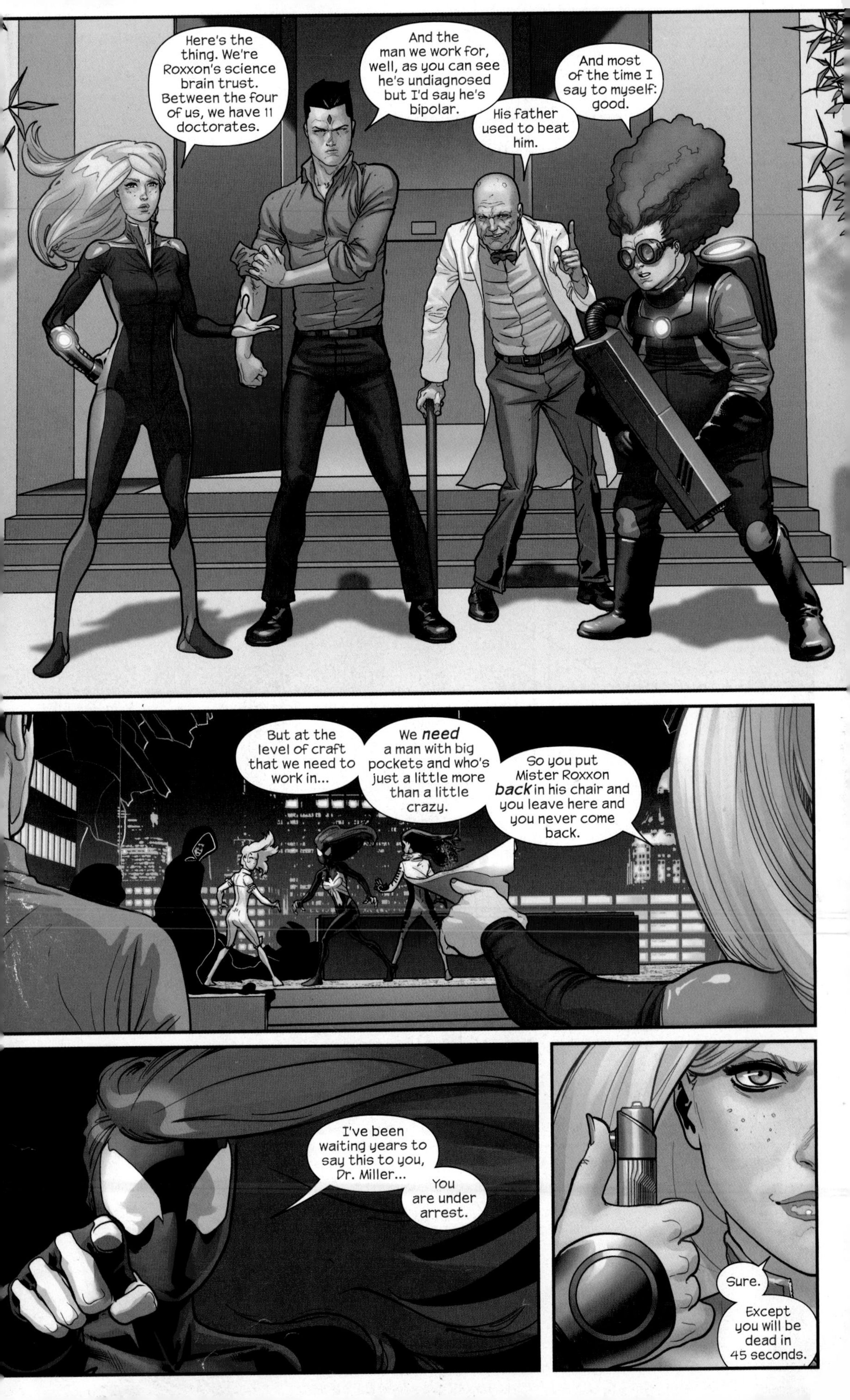
Here's the thing. We're Roxxon's science brain trust. Between the four of us, we have 11 doctorates.
And the man we work for, well, as you can see he's undiagnosed but I'd say he's bipolar.
His father used to beat him.
And most of the time I say to myself: good.
But at the level of craft that we need to work in...
We *need* a man with big pockets and who's just a little more than a little crazy.
So you put Mister Roxxon *back* in his chair and you leave here and you never come back.
I've been waiting years to say this to you, Dr. Miller...
You are under arrest.
Sure.
Except you will be dead in 45 seconds.

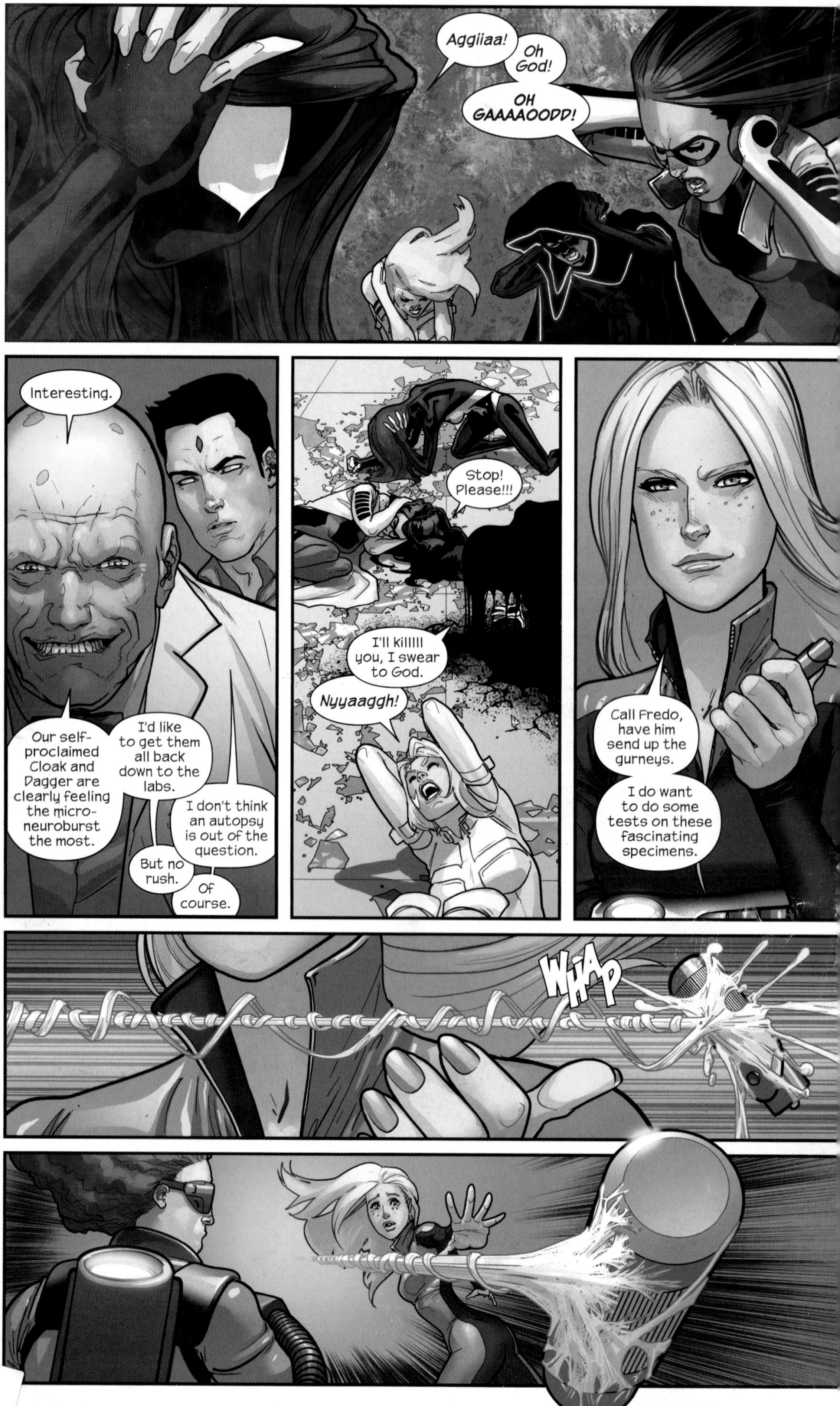
Aggiiaa!
Oh God!
OH GAAAAOODD!
Interesting.
Our self-proclaimed Cloak and Dagger are clearly feeling the micro-neuroburst the most.
I'd like to get them all back down to the labs.
But no rush.
I don't think an autopsy is out of the question.
Of course.
Stop! Please!!!
I'll killlll you, I swear to God.
Nyyaaggh!
Call Fredo, have him send up the gurneys.
I do want to do some tests on these fascinating specimens.
WHAP

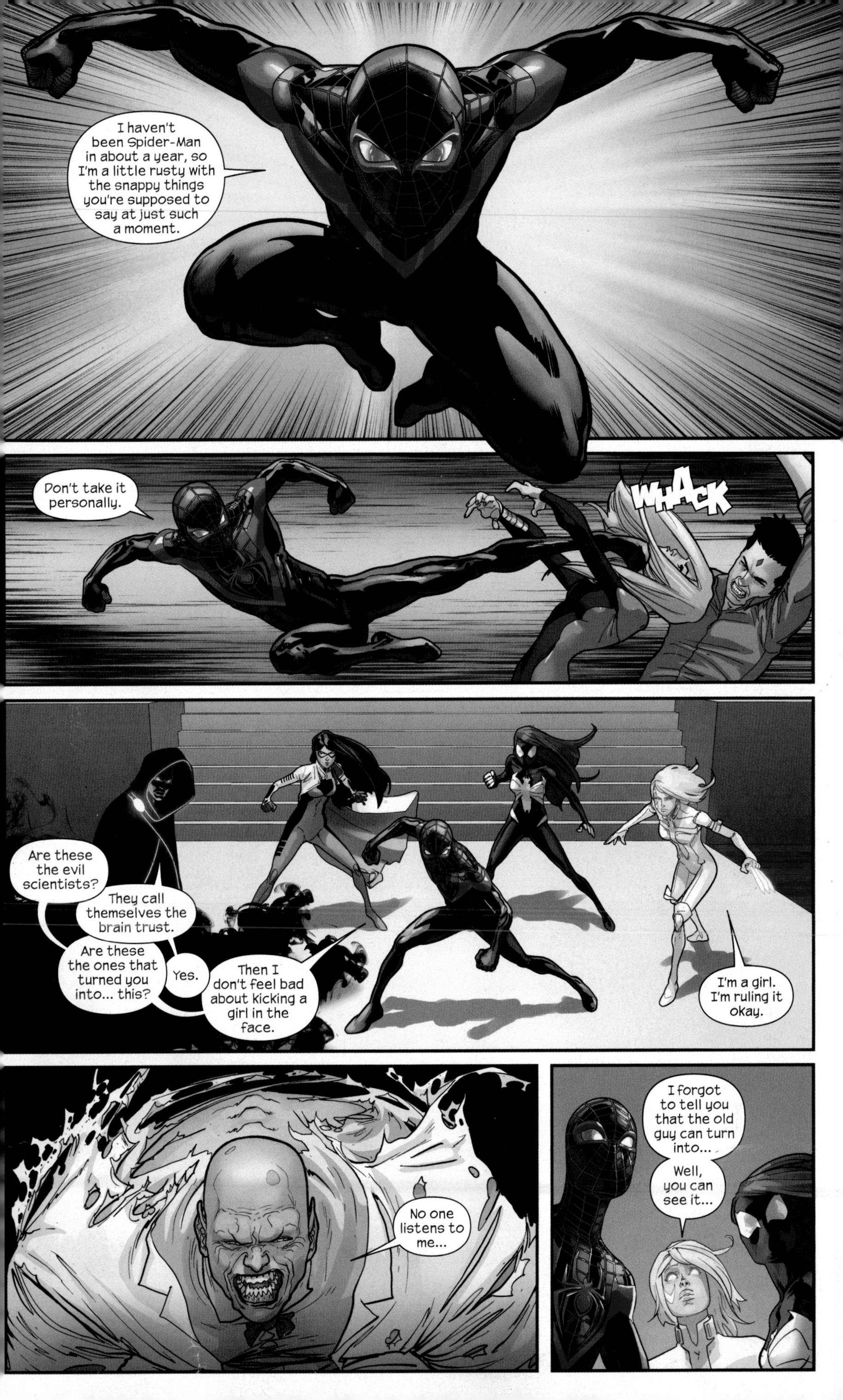
I haven't been Spider-Man in about a year, so I'm a little rusty with the snappy things you're supposed to say at just such a moment.
Don't take it personally.
WHACK
Are these the evil scientists?
They call themselves the brain trust.
Are these the ones that turned you into... this?
Yes.
Then I don't feel bad about kicking a girl in the face.
I'm a girl. I'm ruling it okay.
No one listens to me...
I forgot to tell you that the old guy can turn into...
Well, you can see it...

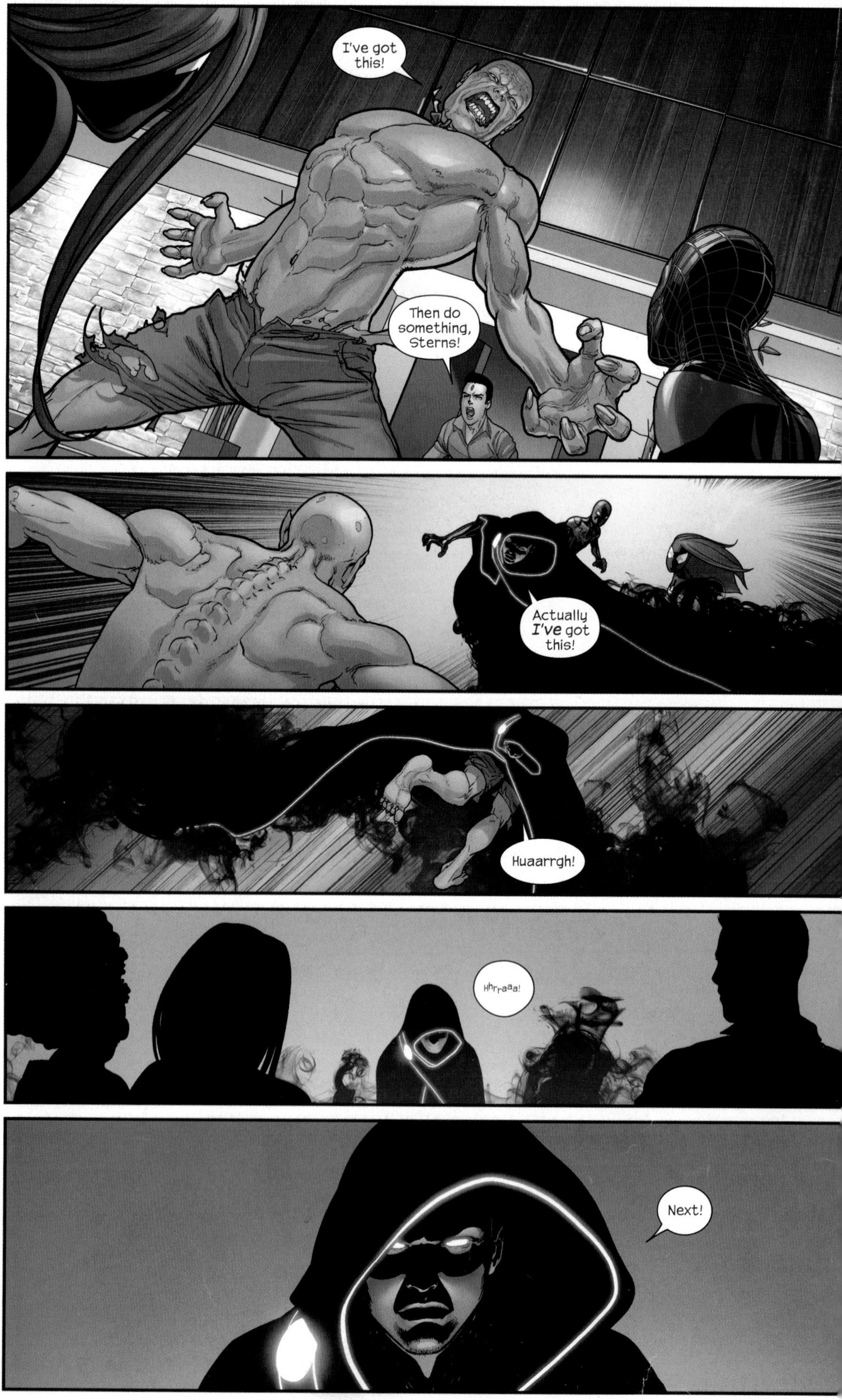
I've got this!
Then do something, Sterns!
Actually *I've* got this!
Huaarrgh!
Hhrraaa!
Next!

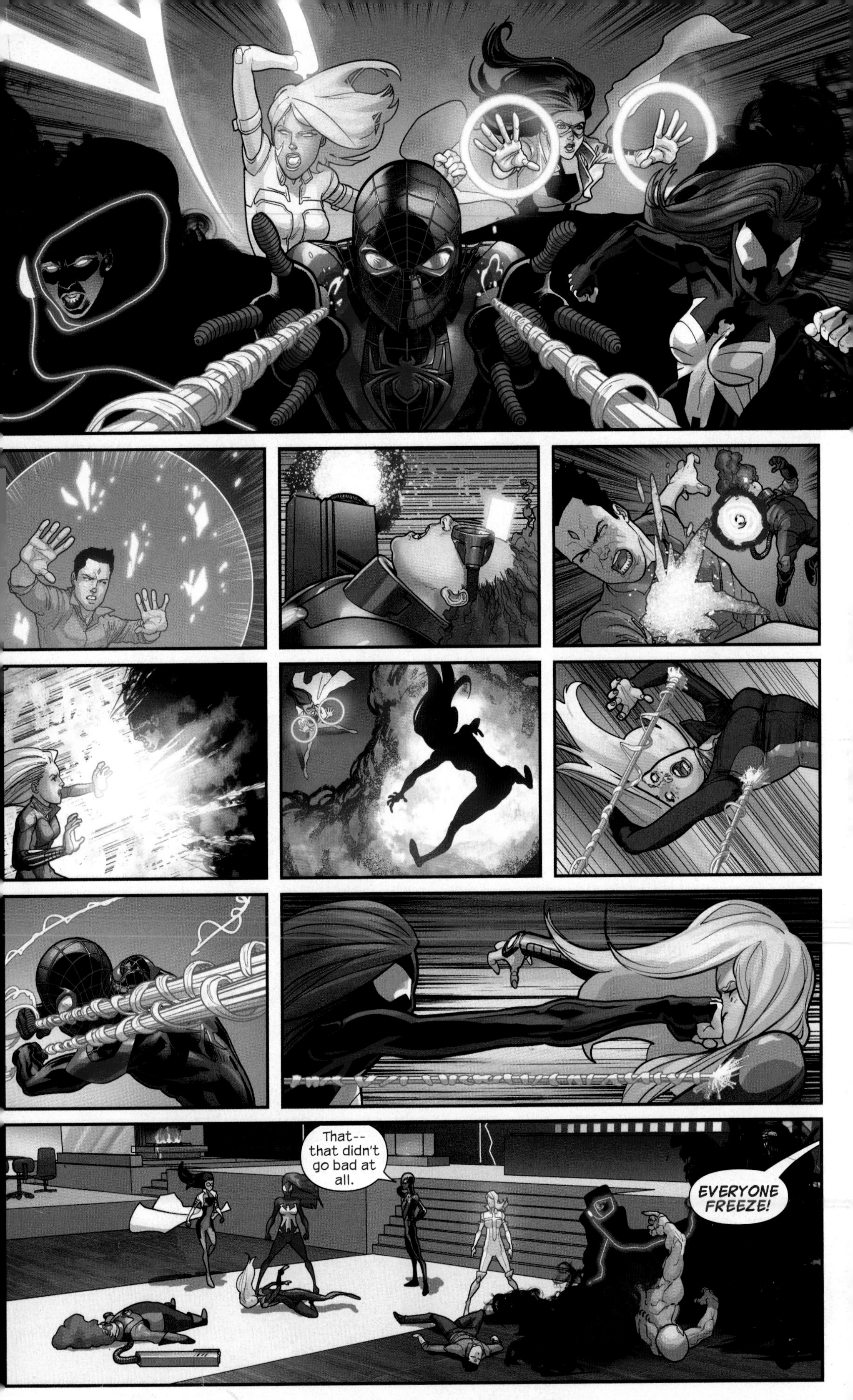
That--
that didn't
go bad at
all.
EVERYONE
FREEZE!

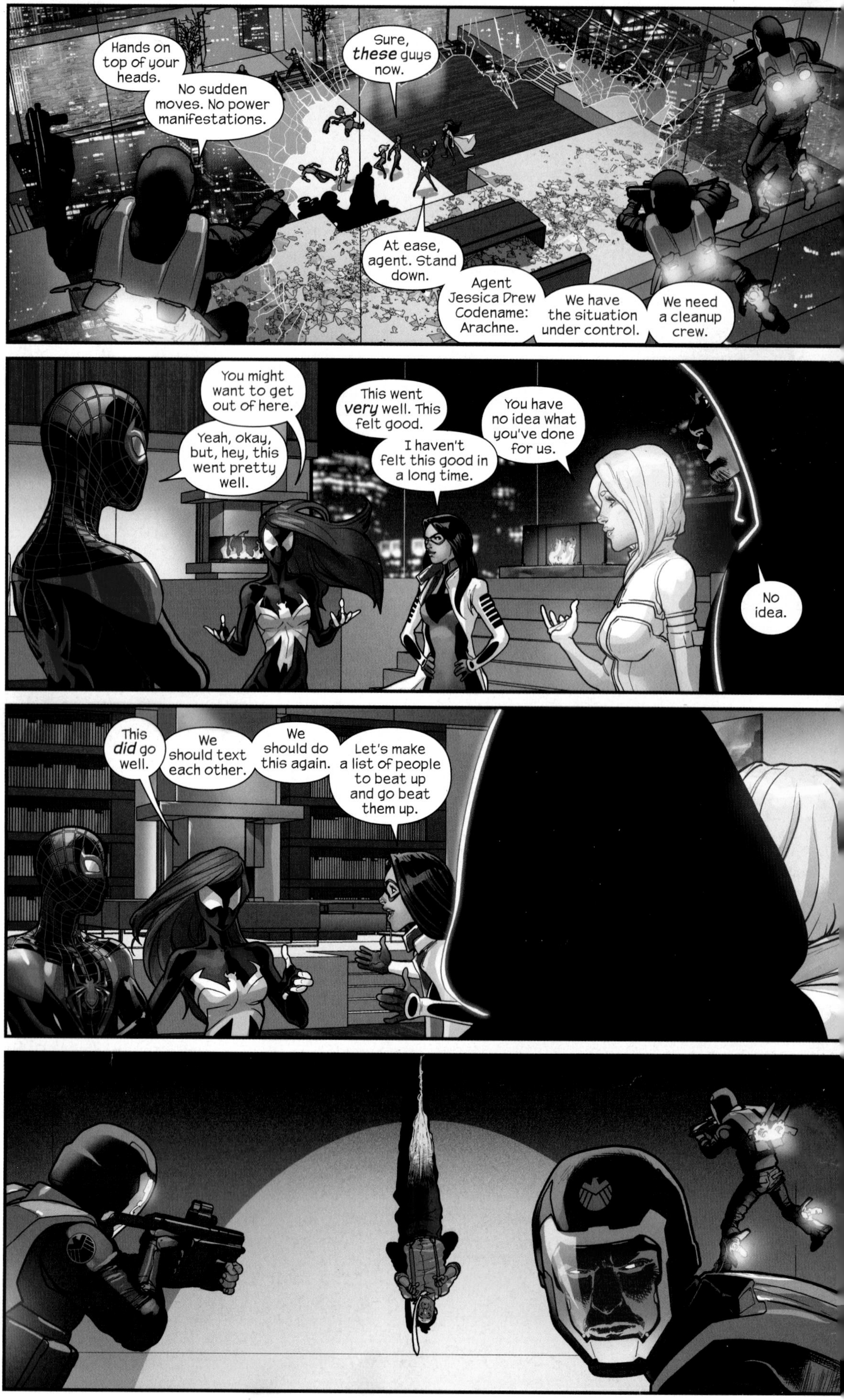

Hands on top of your heads.
No sudden moves. No power manifestations.
Sure, *these* guys now.
At ease, agent. Stand down.
Agent Jessica Drew Codename: Arachne.
We have the situation under control.
We need a cleanup crew.
You might want to get out of here.
Yeah, okay, but, hey, this went pretty well.
This went *very* well. This felt good.
I haven't felt this good in a long time.
You have no idea what you've done for us.
No idea.
This *did* go well.
We should text each other.
We should do this again.
Let's make a list of people to beat up and go beat them up.

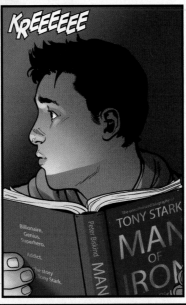

KREEEEEE

Billionaire.
Genius.
Superhero.

Addict.

The story
of Tony Stark.

Peter Biskind

The unauthorized biography of
TONY STARK
MAN
OF
IRON

Dude.

Sshh!

Dude,
are--are
you--

Ganke,
whisper.

Are you--
are you *back*?
Are you, you know,
him again?

Just
listen...

I'm sorry
I was being like
that and I'm sorry
I was making
you mad.

You were
right.

Thank you
for hanging in
there with me.

Just, you
know, thank
you.

For
everything.

Aw...
Dude.

Just tell
me you're back
for real.

Tell me
this is for
real.

I'm telling
you...you're
right, Ganke.

You
were totally
right.

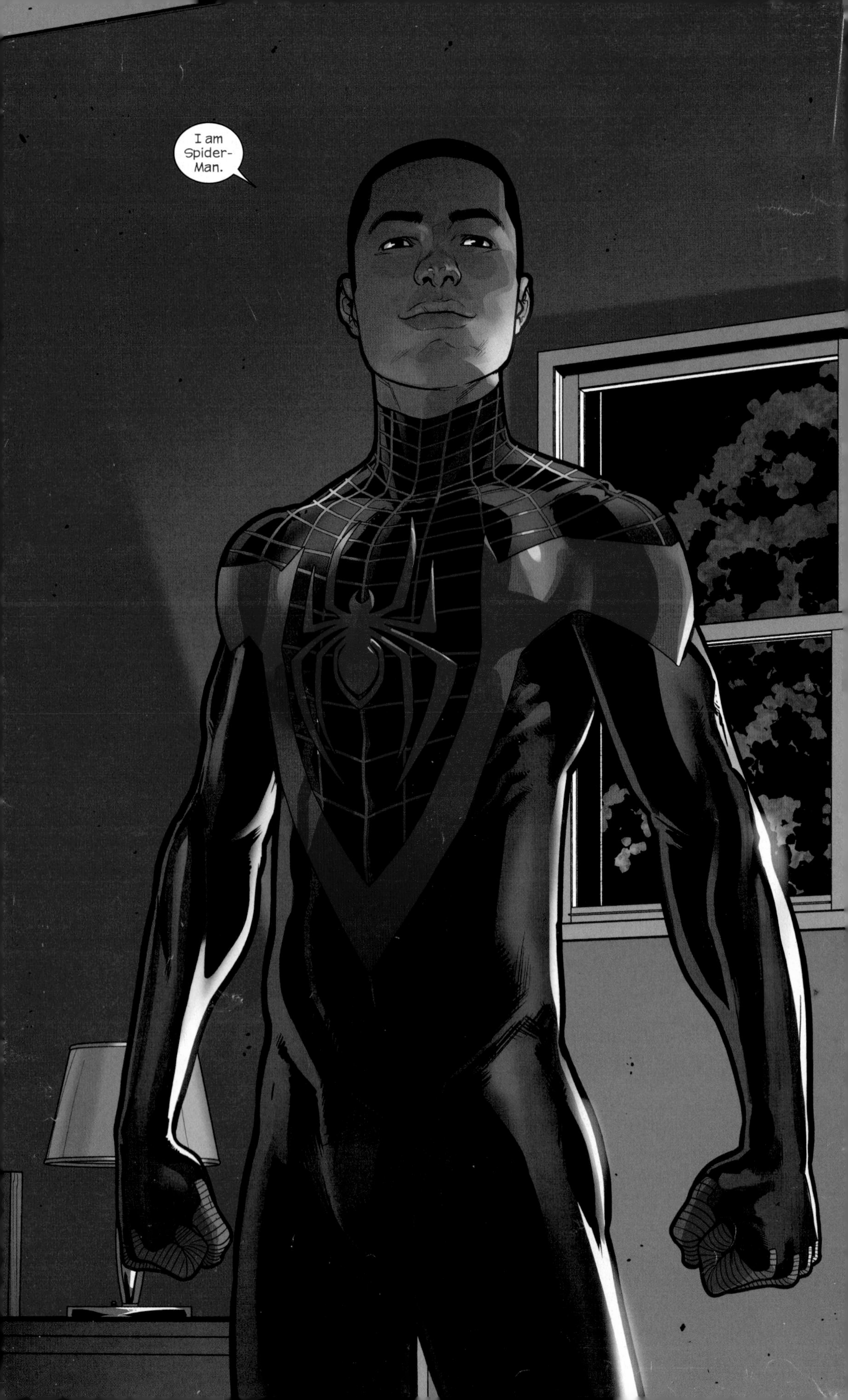
I am Spider-Man.

Dad?

"Maybe ask your father about 'the old days.'"

"Maybe ask your father about who he was before you were born."

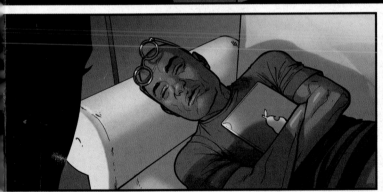

"So obviously I was a little surprised that you went on a little field trip to Roxxon Industries without even a 'by your leave.'"

"What do you have to say for yourself?"

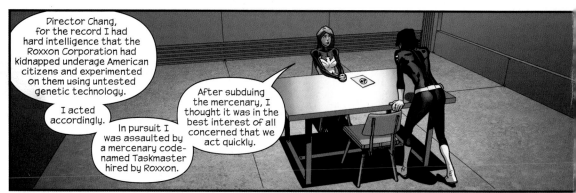

Director Chang, for the record I had hard intelligence that the Roxxon Corporation had kidnapped underage American citizens and experimented on them using untested genetic technology.

I acted accordingly.

In pursuit I was assaulted by a mercenary code-named Taskmaster hired by Roxxon.

After subduing the mercenary, I thought it was in the best interest of all concerned that we act quickly.

I am willing to testify to all of this under oath so that the Roxxon Corporation is put down for good once and for all.

You did all that, did you?

Do you know that we do business with the Roxxon Corporation? That we have standing military contracts?

That is above my pay grade, ma'am.

I'm sure that if you knew Roxxon was kidnapping children and experimenting on them you would cease all business.

And who were these children you had deputized for your operation?

So very glad you asked.

I think we have something here...

I think we have the beginnings of something very special.

The End
Next: Cataclysm!